TROUBLE IN MIND

Bernard O'Mahoney is the bestselling author of *Essex Boys*, *Essex Boys: The New Generation*, *Bonded by Blood*, *Fog on the Tyne* and numerous other acclaimed true-crime titles.

TROUBLE IN MIND

AN AUTOBIOGRAPHY

BERNARD O'MAHONEY

MAINSTREAM
PUBLISHING

EDINBURGH AND LONDON

First published in Great Britain in 2011 by
MAINSTREAM PUBLISHING COMPANY
(EDINBURGH) LTD
7 Albany Street
Edinburgh EH1 3UG

ISBN 9781845967789

A catalogue record for this book is available
from the British Library

Printed in Great Britain by
CPI Mackays, Chatham ME5 8TD

1 3 5 7 9 10 8 6 4 2

ACKNOWLEDGEMENTS

I would like to dedicate this book to my mother, who died in my arms on 20 January 2010. I love you, Mum. Until we meet again, may you rest in peace.

I would also like to remember my brother-in-law Elric Tierney, who died suddenly on 16 July 2010, aged 33. A life spent in the fast lane – better to burn out than to rust.

Those who have passed leave us all legacies from which I hope my children – Adrian, Vinney, Karis, Paddy, Daine, Lydia – and others will learn.

Thank you to my brothers, Jerry and Michael.

Last, but by no means least, I would like to thank my wife, Roshea, for the strength she has shown throughout the many difficult challenges that life has presented us with.

May your God, whatever, whoever he, she or it may be, be good to you.

CONTENTS

INTRODUCTION

FOR what you are about to read may the Lord make me truly thankful. I say that because, looking back on my life to date, I have to concede that I am fortunate to still be amongst the living. War on the streets of Ulster, civil war on the streets of South Africa and gang wars on the streets of Essex: you name it and – excluding Morris dancing – I've probably experienced it. My beautiful late mother is the person I have to thank for helping me survive the madness in which I have found myself immersed. Not only did she give me the gift of life, she taught me by example how to overcome any hardship, to survive brutality and, more importantly, to get back on my feet after being knocked down.

Extreme violence has been a prominent feature of my existence ever since my birth. My father's psychotic abuse physically hardened me, but it left me with a seething hatred for those who tried to control me. Physical ability combined with mental instability is a dangerous mix.

I careered through my formative years venting my inner anger on all that I encountered. This brought me to the attention of the police and, henceforth, my future appeared to be mapped out. When my tyrannical father eventually left home, I followed suit. I believed I was giving my mother the peace and quiet she deserved: a new start, a new beginning. I knew that it was what we both needed.

But it's fair to say my new start failed miserably. However, I followed my mother's example and never gave up trying to better myself and my situation. I joined the army; I started a 'new life' in London, following a prison sentence; I attempted another 'new start' in South Africa, and another re-birth followed in Essex. It, too, failed when three friends were murdered. My umpteenth attempt at finding tranquillity ended when my 26-year-old wife died suddenly after just 19 weeks of marriage.

Thirty-five years after walking out of my mother's front door, I am embarking upon yet another 'new life'. I have re-married and have once more walked away from all the elements that I have blamed for previous failures. I sincerely hope that this time I will succeed – despite my failures, I have never doubted that one day I will eventually achieve my goal.

A positive attitude to overcoming the hurdles that we all face in life is one that my mother instilled in me by example and one that has helped me to survive the numerous extraordinary events detailed in this book.

Sitting comfortably? You won't be for long.

1

BEWARE THE IDES OF MARCH

BEWARE the Ides of March, they say; only bad things happen on that day. My mother didn't know 15 March had ancient links with impending danger, although she did know something was up when I started kicking my way out of her womb as she did her shopping. The year was 1960 and the place was Dunstable in Bedfordshire. My mother collapsed in the street with the first contractions, then picked herself up and staggered home to our council maisonette. She sent my four-year-old brother out to summon help, but he went to play in the garden instead. So, as always, she just got on with it. Apparently – it's not one of my memories – I made my way out easy enough and emerged onto the front-room floor. My mother broke the umbilical cord with her hands and I started screaming. Perhaps I knew what was coming; perhaps I had picked up in the womb that I was about to move into the domestic equivalent of what the army call a 'hostile environment'.

My mother came from Sligo town in Ireland, one of thirteen children raised in a four-bedroom council house. I was her third child; there were two boys before me, Jerry and Paul. I was christened Patrick Bernard, taking the first name from my father and the second from my uncle. As soon as I could exercise a choice in the matter, I stopped using my father's name. He came from Dungarvan in County Waterford but never told me anything about his background; in fact, he never told me anything about anything, there was no such thing as a normal conversation in our home. Over the years, I have pieced together fragments of his story and, although I'll never forgive the bastard, I have come to understand why he became such a bitter and twisted individual.

Things started going wrong for him at birth. He was born illegitimate at a time when – and in a place where – illegitimacy stamped you with the mark of the beast. Hate the sin but love the sinner, Christians sometimes say, but at that time in Catholic Ireland I think they must have hated the sinner and the product of the sin. His childhood experiences killed any decency within him and convinced him that only by suppressing any normal human emotion could he hope to survive. That was what life had taught him and it was the only lesson he wanted to pass on to his children. He hated to see us showing emotion. Even as infants he expected us to behave like grown men – or rather like the man he had grown into: cold, hard and ruthless. But still those first few years in Dunstable were relatively happy, at least compared to what came later. My mother had quite fond memories of those times: going for walks on the downs, visiting nearby Whipsnade Zoo and getting money regularly from my father, who worked on the production line at the nearby Vauxhall car factory. However, for reasons known only to my father, when I was four, he decided he wanted to move to Bilbrook, near Wolverhampton. Almost as soon as we arrived things changed for the worse. My father, who always drank, began to drink to excess. He also became extremely violent towards all of us, my mother especially. He would come home barely able to stand, spitting obscenities at my mother before beating her senseless and slouching off to bed. Memories of my mother screaming as she was beaten still haunt me. She would be screaming for him to stop and we children would be screaming with fear. Other nights, even without much drink taken, he would turn off the television and sit there slandering her family, humiliating her, degrading her, even questioning the point of her existence. His most decent act would be to send us to bed. I would lie awake in the darkness, listening to her sobbing downstairs, pleading with him to stop. As I got older, I would sometimes overcome my fear and shout out, 'Leave her alone, you bastard.' Then he would come running up the stairs to beat me with whichever weapon he had picked up en route.

My father had his increasingly heavy drink habit to finance and so the money he gave my mother for our upkeep gradually became less until some weeks there would be nothing at all. I hid in the front room with her when the creditors came knocking, which was often. My mother took on three jobs to feed us, cleaning in the very early morning, working on a factory production line during the day and cleaning again at night. Sometimes my father would even manage to take the little she earned off her.

I grew very close to my mother and only felt secure when she was near. For this reason, one of the most traumatic days in my life was my first day at school. I remember the pain and sadness I felt as I left her at the cast-iron railings of St Peter and St Paul's in the centre of Wolverhampton. She was crying and I was crying. She told me to hang on to the toy red petrol tanker she had given me. The next thing I remember is standing in a queue with the other boys. An older boy grabbed hold of my toy and said toys were not allowed. He tried to pull it from me; I pulled it back. A struggle developed and the other boys started shouting, 'Fight! Fight!' A nun swooped down and separated us. She asked my name.

'Bernard O'Mahoney,' I said.

She said I had to call her 'sister' whenever I spoke to her.

'You're going to be trouble, aren't you, O'Mahoney?'

I said yes.

She screamed, 'Yes, what?'

I said, 'Yes, I am going to be trouble.'

She put her hands on my shoulders and shook me. 'What did I just tell you? You must call me sister! You must always call me sister! Do you understand?'

I can still remember the smells that day, especially at lunchtime. I did not like liver – I hated the stench of it and never ate it at home – so, of course, my first school meal just had to be liver. Its smell had contaminated everything on the plate, so I sat at the dinner table hardly able to touch anything. Another nun spotted me. She came over and lectured me about the world's starving children, then force-fed me through my tears. Finally, I swallowed the last revolting mouthful, and ran to the toilet and vomited everything up. When the final bell went that day, I was a ball of emotion. I couldn't wait to get out of that hellish place. I ran to the gates, where my mother was waiting, and hurled myself into her arms. As we travelled home on the bus, I felt secure once again. I prayed for the bus to keep on going and going, away from the school and my bastard father.

When I was six, my father had another notion to move, this time to Codsall, a small village on the outskirts of Wolverhampton. He had found us a three-bedroom terraced house there that backed onto the main railway line. At night I felt as if the house was going to fall in on us as coal trains thundered past at the end of the garden.

In 1967, my youngest brother, Michael, was born prematurely and went into intensive care. Following the birth, my mother became extremely ill and had to stay in hospital. Michael grew stronger, but my mother grew weaker. One night, at my mother's insistence, my father took us to see her in hospital. She waved and smiled at us from behind a glass screen, but she looked so ill. I was terrified that she would never come home. My father showed concern for neither my mother nor his sons, including the newborn baby – he would not let anything interfere with his drinking. At one point, we did not see him for three days. There was no money and no food in the house. We survived on school dinners. Our local GP even called on my father and appealed to him to take better care of us, but my father ignored him. In the end, my mother was so worried about us that she discharged herself from hospital.

As I grew older, I didn't try to hide my hatred for my father. I forced myself to endure his violence stoically; I didn't want him to know that he was hurting me. His dislike for me seemed to grow in response to my defiance. His physical violence only ended up hardening me, but his verbal abuse had a far more disturbing effect. He would grip me by the throat or hair and shout obscenities in my face while prodding or punching me in the head or body. His favourite insult to me was a reference to the circumstances of my birth.

'You were born in the gutter,' he would say, 'and you'll die in the gutter.'

One Mother's Day, I brought home a card I'd made at school. My mum put it on the sill above the kitchen sink. I was still sitting at the table eating my dinner when my father staggered home, stinking of drink. He saw the card and picked it up. 'Is this what your little pet got you, is it? Mother's little fucking pet.' My mother asked him to stop, but that only made him worse. He turned to her and said, 'Shall I give you something for Mother's Day, shall I?' He picked up a plate off the draining board and went to smash it over her head. She raised her arm to protect herself and the plate broke across it, cutting it wide open. She spent the rest of Mother's Day in casualty getting her arm stitched.

Another evening he came home and complained his dinner wasn't freshly cooked, just heated up. Presumably he expected my mother to guess what time he'd crawl back from the pub. He threw the dinner and the plate against the wall, grabbed my mother by the hair and started punching her. She was bleeding from the nose and mouth, but he kept punching her until she collapsed on the floor. He stood over her as she lay there, his hands and shirt smeared with her blood.

My mother raised her head slightly, coughed up some blood and asked me to get her some water. My father said he'd get it. He walked out of the room and I helped my mother sit up. He came back holding a mug of water. 'Here, Anna. You wanted fucking water – take it.' And with that he dashed the mug into her face.

I used to go to school in the mornings like a bomb waiting to explode. I loathed the other children's happiness. *Daddy did this for me, Daddy did that for me.* I needed to shut them up. I used to fight them with a ferocity fuelled by my hatred of their normality and happiness.

Even at that young age I was developing a fearsome reputation for violence. I must have spent more time in front of the headmaster than I did in lessons. When those in authority were standing shouting at me, I would take myself to another place in my mind, reliving a favourite film or a great football moment. My seemingly cold and detached manner would infuriate them more and I would usually end up being physically shaken out of my daydreams – or, in the case of my father, punched out of them. He preferred to employ his fists than talk, regardless of how trivial the matter might have been.

I remember, just before I went to secondary school, my father showed me how to do up a tie. He made me stand still with my hands by my side. This meant I could only see his hands, not what he was doing with the knot. He then undid the tie and told me to try. I got it wrong. He grabbed the tie around my neck and began pulling me about with it, slapping me round the head, saying I was 'fucking stupid'.

Finally, I could take no more. 'I wish you were fucking dead,' I shouted at him, then punched him on the side of the head. I then ran out of the room and up the stairs. He caught me halfway up and laid into me with a vicious fury. I ended up at the foot of the stairs, curled into a ball to protect myself from his kicks, which were aimed at the small of my back. I thought he was going to kill me. My mother was screaming at him to stop.

Suddenly, I felt a sharp pain and my legs went numb. 'I can't feel my legs!' I shouted. 'I can't feel my legs!' Only then did he stop. He tried to get me onto my feet, but I kept collapsing. My mother ran out to call an ambulance. As I lay on the floor, waiting for assistance, my father knelt down beside me. He pulled my head up by my hair and said, 'Say you were playing and you fell down the stairs on your own or I'll fuckin' kill ye.' And that's what I told anyone who asked.

Fortunately, nothing was broken, but the discs in my spine had been damaged, so that even today it causes me pain.

I started going to Codsall Comprehensive, a school of around 1,200 pupils. I'd have fights with other boys almost every day of the week. If I came home with a black eye or another mark on me, my father would beat me and offer me the only bit of fatherly advice he ever gave any of us: 'Don't let people get away with hitting you. If they're bigger than you, hit them with something.' We all started following his advice.

My brother Paul got into a fight in a pub car park with a gang from another part of town. He ran at them with two screwdrivers, one in each hand. He stabbed three people before being beaten to a mess. He served two years in borstal.

The eldest, Jerry, took on a group of men in a pub. He'd armed himself with a large pair of mechanic's spanners and started clubbing all round him. The police arrived and he clubbed one of them, too, before being overpowered. He'd given one of the men a fractured skull; a policeman had a shattered knee. Jerry was sent to prison.

All of us, under my father's tutoring, had developed a capacity for extreme and awful violence. It set us apart – and set us against the world, especially the world of authority. I hardly needed to consult a fortune teller to know where I was heading.

* * *

The cause of my first criminal conviction was laughable. I had developed a passion for Manchester United and most Saturdays I would travel around the country to watch them play. One Saturday I was with my friend, Mickey, on a train going to Bristol. We stopped at one station where there was a small group of Manchester City supporters on the opposite platform. They started jeering and shouting insults and we responded in kind. Nobody took it seriously; it was all quite light-hearted, just kids engaging in a bit of banter. There was certainly not going to be a fight, if only because our train was about to move off.

Once the train got going, two middle-aged men in suits who had been sitting opposite us stood up and announced that they were British Transport Police. They said we were under arrest for using obscene language in a public place. They made Mickey and me stand in the corridor; they stood on either side of us, guarding the dangerous felons. They took us to Bristol police station, where a fat-faced desk sergeant formally charged us with using the F-word and gave us a date to appear at Bristol Magistrates Court. Then the sergeant – his fat face bloated further with glee – told us he was not going to release us until after the match had started. Presumably unaware of the irony, he said, 'Don't think you little fuckers can come to Bristol and cause fucking trouble.'

To top everything, my father, the man who from the cradle had taught me all the bad language I knew, had to accompany me to court. My mother had an appointment at the hospital that day. On the train journey, he made three brief points: one, he had lost a day's work because of me; two, I was an ungrateful little bastard; and three, I would fucking pay for it. I stood in that court feeling bewildered, confused and angry. The magistrate gave me a lecture about bad language and fined me £5. This was my first experience of the justice system – and it seemed no more justifiable than my father's.

On the journey back, I was slapped in the face and punched repeatedly in the head by my father. He told me that I would pay for the fine and the expenses he had incurred that day from the money I earned from my two jobs – doing a paper round and helping the milkman.

As I was one of only a few pupils with a criminal conviction at school, whenever anything punishable happened I was rounded up as the usual suspect. Admittedly, I did get up to a lot of mischief, but I also found myself blamed for things I hadn't done. After the window of the school coach was smashed, I was unjustly fined for the offence. I had to pay the fine over three months in weekly instalments. The money came from a part-time job I had recently started, killing turkeys at a local farm. At first I did various menial jobs there, but the boss soon promoted me to chief executioner – no other boy had the stomach for such grisly work. I had to put the squawking creatures head first into a cone-shaped metal bucket, trapping their necks between two metal bars; I would then simultaneously squeeze and pull down the bars, breaking their necks and killing them instantly. I think it's what they call a humane method. The birds would kick and scratch at the bucket as they fought for their lives, struggling with such force that the bars and my hands would shake. I used to close my eyes and imagine I was squeezing the life out of whoever had upset me that day, usually my father or one of my teachers. I despised the teachers at my school and I despised their justice, just as I despised the woman who'd slide back the hatch at the school office and take my hard-earned money.

For the first six weeks, she said the same thing: 'Oh, you ought to be putting this in the bank, O'Mahoney. Maybe next time you'll think before you act. Do you want a receipt?' I hated the bitch. One night I crept into the school grounds and hurled a crate of empty milk bottles through the headmaster's window. Then I sprayed blue paint over the school coach. I wasn't caught. For the next eight weeks, as I handed over my money, I used to smirk at the woman and ask, 'Have they caught anyone yet?'

My second criminal conviction was for an even more laughable offence. At the farm where I worked, I found a broken wristwatch on the floor in the yard. It was useless – one hand was missing – so I assumed someone had thrown it away. I took it home with me that evening to give to my brother Paul to tinker with, then I changed and went to play football at the nearby sports hall. Midway through the game, a policeman burst into the hall, marched up to me and announced that I was under arrest. I found out later that Paul had been outside a shop with his friends when the policeman had walked by and told them it was time to move on. Paul had said something cheeky like 'No, it's about eight o'clock, actually.' All the boys had laughed, and the policeman had asked if he was trying to be funny. He said he wasn't; it was just that his watch only had one hand. He showed it to the policeman, who asked him why he was bothering to wear something so useless. Paul explained that I had found it at work and given it to him to fix. The policeman asked where I was and Paul had told him. Hence his dramatic arrival at the sports hall.

I was completely embarrassed and bewildered when he put my arm behind my back and frogmarched me to his van in front of my friends. I sat in the front seat beside him.

As we were driving towards the police station, he kept asking me where I had got the watch. I told him the truth, but he kept saying that I was a liar and slapping me in the mouth with his glove. I was frightened, I didn't know what I had done to justify such treatment, so I leant over and grabbed the steering wheel, forcing him to slam on the brakes. The van skidded and struck the kerb before stopping.

He hit me a few times, and I shouted at him that I wasn't going to the police station without my mother and eventually he relented. My mother was picked up and we were taken to the police station, where

I was charged with 'theft by finding'. A magistrate later fined me £35 and gave me a lecture on morality.

To my adolescent mind, it seemed the forces of law and order could hound a boy for petty irrelevancies but couldn't intervene to prevent a man battering his wife and children half to death. Rage and resentment stewed inside me. School was a farce, the law was a farce, 'normal' life was a farce. But I wasn't going to take their shit for long. I planned to hit back.

No one ever seemed to question why I was so angry and unruly. People could only see this aggressive, couldn't-care-less delinquent. I was just 'bad', as far as those in authority were concerned, and I had to be punished. No one witnessed the physical and mental torture I endured at my father's hands. They didn't see me as the confused and frightened child I knew myself to be. I wish I could have broken and poured everything out to someone, but instead I continued to act out my bad-boy role because at least that way I could get a bit of adoration and recognition, which is what I craved. When my violence reached 'unacceptable levels', I was ordered to stand outside the headmaster's office at playtimes and I had to leave the school premises at lunchtimes. The teachers thought they were humiliating me, but some of my fellow pupils admired my anarchic spirit. The special treatment I received, and my reputation for violence, gained me what I thought was the respect of my peers; in fact, it was only deference based on fear, but I liked it. It made me feel powerful – an enjoyable sensation for someone who'd felt powerless for so long. I soaked up the attention of my minions. In my mind, I felt I was beginning to win the fight against those who tried to impose their authority on me. I thought I'd become a 'somebody' – a status they'd said I'd never achieve. In reality, I was systematically destroying myself and my future.

At home, throughout my early teens, I'd harm myself, gouging my stomach with a craft knife or broken glass. I still bear the scars of this self-mutilation. I didn't want to feel I was being hurt by my father and when I realised I was I hated my weakness and wanted to harm myself. Emotion and pain were for weak people. I'd learnt that from my tormentor.

At the end of the summer term of 1976, I left school without any qualifications. Aged 16, I had little fear of anything or anyone, and even less respect. Only my father continued to have the power – physical and psychological – to turn me into a frightened little boy. But that wasn't going to last much longer. He must have noticed what he'd turned his sons into – and he must have guessed the day of vengeance was on its way. In fact, it came in August 1976.

My father arrived home drunk as usual, and started beating my mother in the kitchen. My brother Paul and I were in the front room. We heard the familiar sounds. Paul looked at me, and I looked at him, and we both just got up and ran to my mother's aid.

'Leave her alone, you fucking bastard!' Paul shouted at my father. He lurched towards Paul and punched him. Paul snapped: he grabbed my father by his hair with one hand and with the other began punching him in the face with an unstoppable ferocity. I stood and watched as Paul went berserk, punching and kicking until my father lay on the floor, his face a bloody mess. Everything went quiet. The only sound was of Paul breathing heavily from his exertion. I suppose we all expected my father to get to his feet and inflict violent punishment on us for this outrage, but he stayed on the floor. He didn't move for a little while, but when he did, he averted his eyes from our gaze before slowly pulling himself up and onto his feet. Paul was ready for more, and I was ready to help him, but we could both see something had changed. The fight had gone out of my father. He didn't say anything. He just slouched off to bed. As he walked past me, I spat at him. He didn't respond. His face gave nothing away, but he had the air of a tyrant who knew his time had come. He left the house the next day – and never came back.

From the age of 15, I had been involved with a girl named Carole Lett. We had been in the same year at school and had somehow ended up together. I say somehow because Carole and I were chalk and cheese. Pretty, prim and proper, Carole would not have been able to sleep if she had forgotten to do her homework, whereas to most of the teachers I was the devil incarnate. They do say opposites attract, and attracted to one another we most certainly were. So much so, in fact, that in December 1977 Carole gave birth to our son Adrian.

Joy soon turned into anguish when Carole's parents understandably banished me from their home and their daughter's life. I could have fought harder to see my son – in fact, I know I should have – but sadly I didn't. I accepted their decision and in doing so I believe I let my son down. My absence did not prevent Carole from raising a decent and talented young man. At the age of ten, Adrian was signed by Arsenal Football Club and went on to play for Aston Villa, West Bromwich Albion, Wolverhampton Wanderers, Hereford and Bournemouth. I am pleased to say that in his teens Adrian and I did become acquainted and he is now as much a part of my life as any other member of my family. When Adrian's football career ended, he went on to serve in the Royal Navy before forging a career in the prison service.

By the age of 18, I too was destined to become an integral part of HM Prison Service. I had made 13 separate court appearances, during which I'd been convicted of more than 20 offences. I'd received almost every one of the legal system's alternatives to incarceration. By the end of 1978, I was subject to a supervision order for street robbery, I was carrying out 240 hours' community service for going equipped for theft and I was on bail for assault, theft, threatening behaviour and possessing an offensive weapon. I should have left it at that, really, but I became part of a criminal conspiracy to steal a blue-velvet jacket with huge lapels, like those worn by Marc Bolan. I think I intended to wear it.

Bad taste isn't a criminal offence. Theft is.

Store detectives caught me with the shoplifted jacket in my hand. Incarceration now seemed inevitable – unless I could think of a dodge. And that's how I ended up in the army. I signed up at a recruitment office in Wolverhampton town centre, although I had no intention of ever joining the ranks. My plan had been to wave my recruitment papers at the fearsome Robert Smythe, a stipendiary magistrate who'd already said he intended to impose a term of imprisonment. I hoped he'd let me off with a suspended sentence, then I'd 'resign' from the army.

At my hearing, Smythe looked at my army papers suspiciously. I said I'd always wanted to become a soldier. 'You might just be saying that,' Smythe said. He told me he intended to give me a total of six months' imprisonment but was prepared to defer sentencing for a little while. If I wasn't in the army on the day he set aside, then I'd be sent to jail. However, if I was a soldier by that date, he'd suspend the sentence for two years.

The army seemed the least unsatisfactory alternative, although my friends laughed hysterically at the idea of me as a soldier. They didn't think I'd last five minutes in an environment where I had to take orders.

I was sent to start my seven weeks of basic training with the Royal Armoured Corps in the Yorkshire garrison town of Catterick. A childhood of verbal and physical abuse had prepared me well for the training regime. Indeed, some days I used to feel my childhood was being repeated as pantomime farce. Unlike most of my fellow recruits, I found a lot of the extreme behaviour hilarious. None of the instructors ever talked normally. They barked, shouted or screamed every instruction and would often supplement their words with punches, slaps or kicks, perhaps afraid you hadn't heard them. The training left me physically exhausted all the time. One of the instructors' favourite games – usually played at 3 a.m. – was called 'Changing Parades'. They'd order us to change into a bizarre combination of clothing, which had to be worn in the stipulated order. Then they'd shout, 'Go! Go! Go!' and we'd have to run back upstairs to change, before running back down as fast as we could. The first three downstairs would be allowed back to bed; the others had to change into another combination, invariably involving a gas mask.

One recruit lived in fear of Changing Parades because he always ended up last in bed. Nicknamed Rommel because he spent his time sitting alone reading war comics or books about Hitler's elite troops, the Waffen SS, he was slightly built with short, dark hair parted to the side, just like his hero. He sometimes wore glasses, too. He didn't mix well and rarely spoke, but he knew everything you might possibly want to know about panzer divisions, especially the soldiers' clothing and weaponry. He wanted to join the Royal Tank Regiment because their tank crews wore black overalls like his SS panzer heroes; members of other tank regiments wore green. He also listened to tapes of the 'Speak German in a Fortnight' variety. We used to take the mickey out of him and sometimes he'd play up to us, goose-stepping up and down the room with his right arm outstretched in a Nazi salute. Though clearly army barmy, his enthusiasm didn't translate into efficiency, however, which was why he feared Changing Parades.

One night as we frantically changed and he was cursing that he was going to be last again, I suggested he jump out of the window to get downstairs quickly. As we were at least 20 feet up on the third floor I thought he'd take my suggestion as the joke I meant it to be. But in his desperation it must have seemed like a good idea, because the next second he was clambering out the window. The image that remains in my mind is of him looking back at me, eyes flickering madly, as he launched himself into the air. I heard a crunch and a piercing 'Argh!' and I ran to look out. Rommel was writhing on the ground.

'What are you doing, you silly cunt?' the instructors were standing over him shouting. Fortunately, he didn't break any bones. Unfortunately, he could hardly walk – and they made him crawl back upstairs to continue the game. Most recruits, especially those from normal, loving backgrounds, couldn't overcome the shock of army life. They cracked under the bombardment of abuse. At night, people would be talking about running away – or even suicide. Around two-thirds of the recruits in my intake didn't finish the course. It seemed to me that the whole selection process was designed to weed out normal people. Only the disturbed or desperate survived.

The shock of constant exercise can do strange things to your body, so I wasn't too worried when I noticed a swelling on one of my testicles. At a routine army medical I mentioned it to the doctor, who sent me for tests at the Duchess of Kent military hospital in Catterick. I was reluctant to go, mainly because I didn't want to lose any training days; if you missed too many, you faced being 'back-squadded' – forced to start your training again with the new intake. Not only did back-squadders have to repeat the awfulness, they were also regarded as losers. The doctor assured me the tests would only take a day, so there was no need to worry.

If I had known what awaited me, I would probably have deserted immediately and reported to the nearest prison. It was six long months before I emerged from that hospital. I remember the period as a blur of extreme pain, morphine-induced hallucinations and bedsores. The swelling had been caused by testicular cancer and had it not been detected, I might well have died. The exploratory operations and finally the removal of a cancerous testicle is not something I would wish on anybody – well, maybe one or two of the police officers I've met.

After recovering from my medical treatment, I returned to start my basic training again. Nothing much had changed; the instructors had not become noticeably more compassionate in my absence. I was once more a 'pig'. Moreover, I was now a pig who had been 'living it up, skiving in hospital'. However, I think they respected me for having put myself back into their care, when I could easily have got a medical discharge.

After completing my basic training, I was sent to Osnabruck in West Germany to join my regiment, the 5th Royal Inniskilling Dragoon Guards. I had chosen this regiment because my parents were both Irish Catholics and, being an Irish regiment, it was policy not to deploy troops to Ulster, where war was raging between Catholic republicans and Protestant loyalists. Life in West Germany was a total contrast to basic training. There was very little of the clockwork soldier routine I loathed: the marching, the parades, the spit-and-polish. It was partly because we spent our days covered in oil and grime from our vehicles. Keeping your vehicle operational was regarded as far more important than having shiny boots.

My social life in Germany mirrored my social life prior to enlistment. The main difference was that I now had a wage from the state to fund my drink-fuelled wild nights.

I found a group of people I liked – most were from cities such as Liverpool or Belfast. I found that we shared the same approach to life. It was a cocktail of drinking and fighting. Alcohol was a hobby shared by almost everybody else in the regiment, which contained its fair share of full-blown alcoholics. Before I knew it, 1980 had drifted by in a reasonably pleasant but boozy haze; however, 1981 was about to sober us all up and bring us to our senses.

* * *

In December 1980, the Ministry of Defence announced that they were abandoning the policy of not sending Irish regiments to Northern Ireland. Initially, everyone thought they would send the Irish Guards because they were foot soldiers armed with the standard self-loading rifle (SLR). Most of our regiment had not even seen an SLR, let alone fired one. As members of a tank regiment, we knew nothing about patrolling on foot and we used submachine guns. Of course, we should have had enough experience of military logic by then to know that the army wouldn't necessarily do what was rational or sensible. Within a fortnight, the news landed like a mortar among us that the 5th Royal Inniskilling Dragoon Guards were going to be given the privilege of being the first Irish regiment to be sent to the Six Counties.

I felt strangely neutral at the prospect of our tour; in fact, half of me felt quite excited about the idea. I had been in the army for two years by then and Germany had begun to bore me.

One afternoon I was told to report to the major's office in the administrative block. He said he knew my parents were Irish Catholics and that I had relations living near the border of northern and southern Ireland, where our regiment was to be sent. If I strongly objected to going to Northern Ireland, he said, I would remain in Germany. I insisted that I wanted to go, although I did not explain why. My desire had nothing to do with going to fight for Queen and country; it was far more basic than that. I just wanted to be with my friends. My loyalty was to them – I had no intention of being the one waving at the gate as they left. To me, it was like they were going out for a fight in the car park and I was going to join them.

In April 1981, I was posted to Northern Ireland to serve a five-month tour along the Fermanagh border, a notorious killing ground for the IRA. One of our jobs was raiding houses, which I hated. I remember once going into the home of an IRA man on the run. His wife was standing in the front room, her two sons, aged about eight and ten, next to her, with their arms around her. I could tell they were protecting her, rather than seeking protection. I'd clung to my own mother in the same way in the face of my father's brutality. I recognised the look on their faces, that expressionless gaze of silent hatred. At such times I felt like a Judas betraying my own kind. I wanted to reach out to them and explain: 'Look, I'm not here to oppress you. I just didn't want to go to prison, OK?' At other times, when Catholic youths would spit or throw stones, I could happily have smashed their heads open with the butt of my British oppressor's rifle.

Our job was unrewarding, sordid almost, but our methods were all about survival at any cost. On republican housing estates, we'd hand out sweets to small children, knowing that as they eagerly swarmed around us they'd effectively be shielding us. No IRA sniper would dare fire at a soldier surrounded by children, especially Catholic children.

On Tuesday, 5 May 1981, IRA Volunteer and elected MP for Fermanagh and South Tyrone Bobby Sands died after 66 days on hunger strike. The Fermanagh branch of the IRA took its revenge on the Saturday. I was on Quick Reaction Force (QRF) duty that day. For my 12-hour shift, if there was a shooting, a riot, a bomb or some other form of violent incident, it was my job, along with 11 others, to deal with it.

It was around 10.30 p.m., too early to bother trying to sleep, so I was lying on my bed in our sleeping quarters, reading someone else's tabloid newspaper. The other members of that night's QRF were likewise either lying on their beds or sitting in twos or threes around the room, talking quietly and seriously. Bobby Sands' death and our thoughts about its possible consequences had removed all lightness from the atmosphere. Everyone expected something unpleasant to happen within the next few days. As always, the Phil Collins album *Face Value*, the only music cassette we had on the camp, provided the background music. I think I heard that album in full at least six times each and every day I was in Ulster.

I half expected we would get called out at some point that night – I imagined the local republicans getting tanked up in the pubs to mark the passing of their MP and they would soon be spilling out onto the streets, looking for targets to vent their anger on. I had just thrown the newspaper down and sat up as the door flew open.

'Heli-pad! Heli-pad! They've attacked Rosslea!' a soldier shouted. We burst into activity, grabbing our weapons and running out of the door into the slumbering camp.

A few hundred yards away on the heli-pad I could see the rotors of the Lynx in full frenetic spin. I threw myself into the helicopter and huddled down in the seat behind the pilot. Within seconds, everyone was aboard and the Lynx lifted up smoothly. Then, as it passed the roofs of the watchtowers, a powerful thrust from the engine sent the sleek machine zooming off into the darkness.

'Mortar attack, Rosslea,' shouted our commander.

I felt my stomach churn, slipping an inch – I knew almost all of the soldiers who were based at Rosslea, although I had no close friends there. It was one of the smallest and most vulnerable camps, usually described as a joint RUC/Army base; in fact, it was little more than a police station based in what looked like a four-bedroom family house with four Portakabins in the garden. A barbed wire fence surrounded the camp, which stood alone, apart from a pig farm next door.

The person I knew best at Rosslea was Edwards, a Catholic from Liverpool. I had been through basic training with him and enjoyed his company. Like all Scousers, Edwards thought he was a bit of a comedian. I felt anxious for him and hoped he wasn't now 'fertiliser' – our slang for the dead victims of explosions.

The pilot was in contact with Rosslea and through the information he relayed to our commander I could tell the base was in total panic. People were shouting and screaming down the radio. I looked out of the window. At first I couldn't see anything, but within a few minutes an orange glow appeared out of the darkness. As we got closer, the glow got bigger until I could clearly make out the flames. The atmosphere in the helicopter was filled with fear and tension. My thoughts were of my mother back home in England; she would be asleep in her bed, oblivious to the dangerous situation from which her son was only moments away.

Suddenly, we had arrived. As the helicopter circled, we found ourselves looking down on a scene of devastation. The whole camp seemed alight: orange and yellow flames danced madly around plumes of grey-black smoke. I could make out figures running around the flames and felt a dryness in my mouth and a sickness in my stomach. The pilot was looking for a safe spot to land – he had to be careful, we had been told that there were unexploded mortars on the ground. As the helicopter hovered, I watched the scene below with horrified fascination. I knew there had to be casualties. Surely, the Provos could not blast the camp apart like that and not hit anyone. I felt almost hypnotised by the mayhem. In that half-trance, part of me was expecting the professionals to arrive to sort things out. Then the reality hit me: we were the professionals – we were the ones the people on the ground were waiting for to sort things out.

The helicopter landed in a field opposite the base. For a second, I felt as if I could not move, but as the others started to jump out I forced myself up. The Lynx lifted off as soon as the last person had disembarked. I don't think any of us knew what we were going to do. We all ran towards a hole in the fence, which had bits of Portakabin hanging off it. Groups of soldiers had gathered just inside the perimeter, away from the flames. Everyone looked dazed and shocked. Nearby, I saw one group kneeling over a figure stretched out on the ground.

I said to someone, 'What the fuck's happening?'

'Mortars. Some haven't gone off,' he said.

I asked if anyone was hurt.

'Edwards,' he replied, and pointed to the figure on the ground.

I felt sick as I ran towards where he was lying. The others beside him seemed to be too shocked to do anything. I knelt down beside them and could hardly recognise the prone figure. He was shaking and making gibbering noises, but what struck me most at first glance was how dirty he was; his face and clothes were covered in filth. Then I noticed his wounds. There was a gash on his face, starting on his cheek and stretching down past the jaw, but most sickeningly the right side of his chest had been ripped open. Blood was oozing out of the wound, which must have stretched for about 18 inches down his side and into his back.

'Where's the first aid kit?' I said.

I was told they couldn't find it; everything had been blown away. Even the electricity was off. The only light came from the flames.

Edwards, barely conscious, was shaking violently with shock. I thought, 'Fuck, he's going to die.' I shouted for them to get some bandages or something – anything – which I could press down on the wounds to try to stem the blood flow. Someone ran over to the wreckage and came back with something. He handed me several pairs of clean socks. I started pressing them into the wounds. Soon Edwards was lying there with socks hanging out of his side and face. I asked if they had called the emergency services. They said the fire brigade was on its way, but the ambulance service would not come this far.

'We've got to get the helicopter back to get him to hospital or he'll die,' I said.

The QRF's sergeant, who had initially been speechless with shock, got on the radio. Edwards started gibbering manically.

'Calm down! Calm down, it's me, Bernie,' I said. I was shocked to see my friend in such a state. I was terrified he was dying in front of me.

Another sergeant was telling everyone to get out of the camp and to take up firing positions in the field; he was worried about unexploded mortars and the possibility of a follow-up attack. I and a few others insisted on staying with Edwards.

The QRF sergeant was having an argument with the helicopter pilot, who was saying it was too dangerous to land. Our sergeant started screaming down the mouthpiece at him until he relented. The pilot said that he would not land too near to the camp and suggested a spot in the middle of a nearby field. During this time, someone had managed to find a stretcher. We put Edwards on it and wound a ragged blanket around his body to hold in the socks. We picked up the stretcher and ran with it through a hole in the fence. We watched the helicopter circling and heard the reassuring *dub-dub-dub-dub-dub* of its rotors as it dipped down towards us. It almost touched down a few hundred yards away, hovering a few feet off the ground, waiting for its cargo. As we ran, we couldn't help bouncing Edwards on the stretcher and he shouted out in pain. To our frustration, there was a ditch and a hedge between us and the helicopter; I told four of the others to jump over the hedge and to be ready to receive the stretcher. By this time, Edwards was moaning in pain. The rest of us stood in the ditch and lifted up the stretcher. Those on the other side grabbed one end of it and pulled. Unfortunately, none of us noticed that the ragged blanket had got caught in the hedge. When they pulled the stretcher free and started running with it, the trapped blanket held on to Edwards and catapulted him back into the ditch on top of us. Meanwhile, the others, perhaps in shock, were still running towards the waiting helicopter with the empty stretcher. As three of us lay in a heap in the ditch with Edwards moaning even louder than before, I burst out laughing. This farce amid the horror had set me off.

The stretcher-bearers soon realised they had lost their patient and came running back. They threw over the stretcher and we disentangled ourselves and stood up. We put Edwards back on the stretcher and passed it over again. This time he stayed on. I watched as they ran to the helicopter and placed Edwards inside. The helicopter lifted off and soon disappeared into the darkness.

At that moment, I felt a powerful hatred for the Provos. Edwards was a good man; he didn't deserve to die. I dearly hoped that I would get a chance to kill one of the bastards who had done that to him.

We ran back to the camp, by which time everyone had taken up firing positions outside the perimeter fence but well away from the unexploded mortars that lay smouldering in one of the fields. Within ten minutes, several fire engines had arrived. They had powerful lights, which enabled us to see more clearly, as we were now some way away from the dying flames. The firemen unreeled their hoses, but, as they turned on the water, some ammunition stored in one of the Portakabins started going off. The bullets made a *do-do-do-do-do* sound. The firemen must have assumed that the Provos had launched a follow-up attack, because as soon as they heard the bullets they dropped the hoses, jumped into their fire engines and drove off, hoses trailing behind them, spewing water all over the road.

'Get those fuckers back here!' our sergeant screamed. 'Get them back!' But it was too late, they had disappeared into the night.

Within an hour, the fire had almost burnt itself out and we were left in pitch darkness. Instead of staying put, the sergeant said we had to clear the area to create a safe cordon all round the camp. We advanced slowly through the field.

Suddenly, I heard a soldier shout, 'Halt! Who goes there?'

There was no reply.

We crouched down and pointed our rifles in front of us. I could feel my heart pounding. Was this the Provo who had maimed Edwards? Was this the bastard? If it was, he was going to die. I noticed a movement just ahead of us.

Someone shouted again, 'Who goes there?'

Still no reply.

After a short pause, we got to our feet and began advancing slowly towards the figure, fingers firmly on triggers. We surrounded it – and suddenly it ran at us. I don't know why none of us started shooting; I myself was within a millisecond of squeezing the trigger. The sheep will never know how close it came to losing its life.

We stayed in the fields until first light. As we waited for the sun to come up, I spoke to a soldier who had been in the camp when the mortars had begun to land. He said that by a miraculous fluke almost all the soldiers, except for Edwards, had been at a briefing in the one Portakabin that had escaped unscathed. Had that been struck, many men would have died.

In the morning, the fire brigade returned and hosed down the smouldering frames of the Portakabins. Then the bomb-disposal unit arrived. A short way from the camp, I could see the lorry from which the mortars had been fired: a three-ton Bedford with ten firing tubes on the back. Apparently, only three mortars had landed in the base. Those three had been accurate because they had been the first to be fired; however, they had been launched with such force that the pressure had broken the lorry's rear suspension. This had altered the trajectory of the other mortars, all of which had missed their target. One had even landed in the neighbouring pig farm. Once the area had been declared safe, a helicopter landed to bring more troops and to take us back to our beds.

My time in Ulster was spent immersed in extremely stressful and violent situations. I was dispatched to deal with rioting and shootings, and one afternoon I came close to killing a young boy who had innocently taken his father's firearm for target practice. He was aiming at cans in the countryside, unaware that we were making our way along an adjacent road. The first we knew of his presence was when a hail of bullets came whistling through a hedge. When we called out to him, he immediately began to run. Moments later, I had the boy in my sights and my finger was on the trigger.

'Halt, or I will fire! Halt, or I will fire!' I shouted. I badly wanted to shoot, but I knew something was wrong. I couldn't help myself, though; this is what we had trained for – I wanted to blast my target.

'I can see him. Target on,' I kept shouting to my commander. But he kept shouting back, 'Don't shoot! Don't shoot!' Reluctantly, I complied and gave chase.

When we eventually caught up with the boy at a farmhouse, I saw that he was no older than 15. 'You stupid little cunt! I could have killed you,' I shouted. I slapped him across the face with the back of my hand. I felt a mixture of relief and anger, like the way a mother hits her child when he turns up after she has been worried about him. He was shaking and begging us not to hurt him. I sat him down and explained my actions, which seemed to reassure him. I thank God that I listened to my commander that day; in that adrenalin-filled moment of madness I could so easily have taken an innocent life. When the police arrived at the farm to question the boy about the gun, we left to continue our patrol.

It's difficult to describe how I felt about the troubles in Ireland. It wasn't exactly a case of being torn between two sides. I knew which side I was on, I was a British soldier and I had no time for the IRA. Yet I agreed with the republican goal of a United Ireland. My mind seemed to be filled with contradiction at that time. Life was so full of injustice; everyone behaving unfairly to everyone else. That was the way of the world, it seemed to me. I'd felt this from an early age and, in some ways, I suppose this feeling helped me resolve the contradictions in my mind. I stopped getting bothered about who was right and who was wrong – everyone was right and everyone was wrong – my only goal was survival.

The army later awarded me a General Service Medal for my Northern Ireland tour of duty. For many years, my experiences there troubled me: hated by republicans for being a soldier and hated by unionists for being a Catholic. To me, my medal signified nothing but hatred and bigotry. On a drinking trip to Dublin some years later, I decided to give my British medal to the Irish. In an act of cathartic cleansing, I walked onto O'Connell Bridge and threw it in the River Liffey. It plopped into the water and disappeared. No doubt it remains there to this day. The Irish people are welcome to it.

2

LONDON CALLING

IN January 1982, I left the army, having served my time. I moved to London, where I drifted into a job normally held by the sort of professional I used to hate. I became a bailiff, repossessing goods and evicting my fellow man and woman from their homes and businesses. It wasn't an easy job and it didn't do much for my self-esteem. I felt like the man from whom my mother and I used to hide, someone trying to squeeze something out of those who had nothing. I didn't mind descending on the affluent, but having to evict single mothers and others from underprivileged backgrounds, such as my own, made my task unpleasant and at times genuinely distressing. I soon became hopeless at it. If I felt sorry for people – and quite often I did – I'd advise them about the best way to avoid payment. Then I began to lie to my employers. I'd say people hadn't been in or had moved. When they sent another bailiff to the same address and he 'succeeded' where I'd repeatedly failed, they realised I wasn't 'employee of the month material'. Eventually, they sacked me for incompetence. I didn't sue for wrongful dismissal.

I returned to Codsall in December to spend Christmas with my mother. On New Year's Eve, I went drinking with a few of my old friends. Each year the locals follow the same pattern: they walk from one pub to the next – there are only three – having a drink in each to see who's 'come home' and what's happening. I wasn't interested in doing the rounds, so my friends left me drinking alone in the Crown.

The older members of a rival clique were standing at the bar (they suffered from 'village mentality', a delusional state of mind that caused them to believe they must be harder or somehow superior merely because they were older). A girl called Diane walked past on

33

her way to the loos. She looked upset. Her brother was my brother Jerry's best friend, so I asked her what was wrong. She said she'd gone out for the evening with one of the guys from the rival clique, but they'd fallen out over something and now he'd turned nasty. Diane kept saying she wanted to go home, but he wouldn't let her. She went back to the group, but I thought he was taking the piss out of her. As his friends were doing nothing about it, I walked over and asked her 'boyfriend' what the fuck he thought he was doing. He grabbed me by the throat and tried to push me against a wall. I had a pint glass in my hand, so I shoved it as hard as I could into his neck. The glass smashed. Blood poured down his shirt. He fell to the floor and started screaming. Other people joined the chorus of screams, but I just stood over him, called him a wanker and left the pub. I regretted the incident immediately because his blood had ruined my clothes and the glass had cut one of my fingers to the bone.

Within five minutes, the police had arrived. Someone informed them that I was responsible for wounding the man and they arrested me shortly afterwards. Reluctantly, they took me to hospital, where a doctor sewed up my fingers while I stood handcuffed to a gloating policeman.

The New Year dawned for me in the cells of Wombourne police station. I'd been in and out of these cells since I was a boy. I knew I'd broken the law, but I also knew I'd received little justice during my encounters with the justice system. I regarded most of the police who'd dealt with me as petty-minded, power-crazed bullies. The only thing we had in common was our mutual hatred. As the bells chimed in the New Year, I could hear people cheering in the street outside. Alone in the cells, I felt my morale sag under the weight of other people's jubilation. Then I heard clicking on the cell block's polished floor. A police officer was striding towards me. The thought of being in the company of another human being – albeit a policeman – at such a time of communal celebration lifted my deflated spirits. Glowing in the warmth of the moment, I found my ice-cold hatred of the police beginning to thaw. I told myself they weren't all bad. Indeed, some could pass for human. The footsteps stopped outside my cell door. The uniformed bringer of festive cheer flung open the narrow steel hatch. A pair of eyes peered in at me. I found my lips forming themselves into a smile of friendship and gratitude. A voice said, 'O'Mahoney? Happy New Year, you fucking animal. Start the year as you mean to go on.' He then passed me a Jaffa Cake with a small candle stuck in it. If the bastards thought I was an animal, then I'd behave like one. I pissed on the floor and threw all my food at the walls. The following morning I spat in the face of my female probation officer after I heard her, too, describing me as 'an animal'.

The courts had closed for the festive season, so they convened a special magistrates' sitting just for me in the station foyer. The police led me out, still handcuffed. My right hand was three times its normal size because the stitches had burst and the wounds had become inflamed. The swelling caused the cuffs to rub in a way that made my wrist bleed. The prosecutor told the court that because of the seriousness of the allegation I shouldn't be granted bail. The magistrates agreed.

They remanded me in custody to Winson Green Prison in Birmingham. At 'the Green', as it's known, I was put in a cell with a middle-aged man who'd run over a traffic warden as she'd issued him a parking ticket. He'd never been in trouble before and was shocked to find himself in prison. He told everyone who'd listen, 'I'm not a criminal. I never saw her, honestly.' In the evenings, this man had the job of pushing the tea urn around. By the time he reached the end of the landing, the urn would be covered with made-up 'parking tickets'. Simple things please simple minds.

In April 1983, I stood trial at Stafford Crown Court for the glassing incident on New Year's Eve. Charged with wounding with intent, I pleaded not guilty, knowing that 'intent' is very difficult to prove. I told the jury I'd gone to the aid of a woman in distress. I'd been alone and outnumbered by a gang with a reputation for violence.

As a good citizen, I'd remonstrated with them regarding their obnoxious and antisocial behaviour. One of this gang of notorious hooligans had then grabbed me and, acting totally out of fear, I'd pushed him away, forgetting I held a glass in my hand.

The prosecution argued I couldn't 'forget' I was holding a glass. I said 'forget' probably wasn't the right word; I explained that I was also wearing a pair of trousers, but I wasn't 'conscious' of that fact. I hadn't been conscious of holding the glass either.

The trial lasted three days. My victim put on an outstanding performance in the witness box. At one stage the judge even let him sit down after he appeared to faint. I was genuinely impressed. Until then I hadn't realised I'd assaulted such a gifted actor.

However, the photographs of his injuries turned the stomachs of all those in court. He had a track of stitches along the length of his neck. His ear had nearly been severed and its remnants looked like they'd been in a dog's mouth. I could see looks of horror and disgust on the faces of the jury. I didn't fancy my chances.

On the morning of the third day, the jury retired to consider its verdict. Before leaving, the jurors had been given an alternative charge to consider: simple 'unlawful wounding', which is far less serious, as there's no intent involved. They returned after six hours' deliberation. Not guilty to 'wounding with intent', but guilty to 'unlawful wounding'. My barrister read out both the testimonial in my army Certificate of Service and a reference written by my former troop leader, attesting glowingly to my good character. I'd told my troop leader in a letter I needed it for a job. He hadn't been fooled. On a separate piece of paper he'd written, 'Hope this is OK and you get off. Good luck.' The judge told me that because of my 'exemplary' military record, society owed me a debt. He said he'd considered sending me to prison for a considerably longer period, but in the circumstances nine months would suffice. My mother was in court. Her look of anguish tore through me. It affected me more than the sentence, which I thought was pretty lenient, given the injuries I'd inflicted. I served the first part in HMP Shrewsbury, known locally as 'the Dana'. Towards the end I was moved to HMP Stafford, which had a bad reputation among prisoners, although to me it didn't seem too terrible. In both establishments, boredom reigned supreme. Life proceeded slowly and with great tedium. Contrary to tabloid myth, there were no TVs in the cells. The only TV I encountered was a long-haired, effeminate Yorkshireman called Dan – or Diane, depending on who was talking to him.

I needed the patience of a dead saint to tolerate some of the fools around me. Occasionally I'd meet an intelligent, interesting or amusing person, but by and large I found myself surrounded by idiots, fantasists, losers, bullies and the clinically insane, some of whom wore uniform and many of whom had very poor standards of personal hygiene. There was less violence than I'd imagined, but it happened now and again.

I only had to serve six months of my nine-month sentence, but it was long enough to make me appreciate my freedom. It felt good to be out: yet another new start in life. A new beginning loomed.

I returned to London and moved into the ground floor of a terraced house in Evelyn Street, Deptford, with one of my brother Paul's friends named Larry 'the Slash'. He was a rather meek man of about

5 ft 9 in. tall and thin almost to the point of frailty. He always wore a cream-coloured 'flasher'-type mac. His 'Slash' nickname came from a deep-red, angry scar that started at the bottom of his ear, ran along his jawline and tapered off under his chin. He'd picked it up one night after getting into a dispute with a man outside a pub down the Old Kent Road.

The upper floor of the house was occupied by a group of radical students who posted leaflets through our letterbox inviting us to attend anti-Nazi rallies and Rock Against Racism concerts. Most irritating, they played jazz all the time, really loud. Jazz is probably the only form of music I hate. The whole house would reverberate to the heart-sinking sound of Miles Davis.

We tried to be reasonable. At first we asked them politely to turn down the music, which they did, only to turn it up again a few hours later. Gradually, we increased our threat level ('Turn the fucking music off or we'll turn you off'). Finally, we decided we'd either bash them or burgle them. We opted for the latter on a Friday night when we knew they'd be out rocking against racism. We broke in, stole their stereo and sent Miles Davis flying against the wall. 'The Jazz Cats', as we called them, never bothered us again. They even stopped leafleting us.

A barman called Buzz started working at our regular pub, the Royal Oak, opposite Stockwell tube station. He was either extremely brave or extremely fucking stupid because he began giving evidence to the police when bad behaviour occurred on the premises. The first time, two of our friends threw a few chairs over the bar after he asked them to leave. The chairs didn't even hit him, but he still made a statement. Both our friends ended up imprisoned for a few months. Buzz had placed himself in great danger.

One evening a friend of my brother's named Ray Cartland knocked on our door. He looked a bit shaken. He said he and a friend, Colin Allabyrne, had launched a revenge attack on Buzz in the pub. During the fight, a barmaid's arm had been broken and Buzz had been repeatedly stabbed in the body. Buzz made another statement, and the police were now looking for Ray and Colin.

Ray left home and came to live with us for eight months, while Colin went to live with his dad in Stratford, East London.

After a few months, when he thought the police had lost interest, Ray started visiting his mother on Saturdays. One weekend the police swooped and arrested him. At his trial, he pleaded not guilty and refused to say who he'd been with on the night. Buzz went into the witness box and fingered him as one of his attackers and Ray was duly sent to prison.

Buzz's behaviour outraged us. He'd sent yet another of our friends to the hate factory. We felt it was a diabolical liberty that could not go unpunished.

At least once a week the pub's windows were smashed; then a shot-put was thrown at Buzz from the second floor of a block of flats overlooking the pub. It didn't hit him, but it certainly made him jump.

An old friend of mine named Hughie came down from Wolverhampton to visit and everyone chipped in to pay him £100 to 'do' Buzz. Hughie agreed, but as he didn't know what Buzz looked like he asked me to go with him to point him out. I didn't fancy it because Buzz knew me and I knew he'd grass me too, but I also wanted to avenge Ray. We'd become good friends in the time we'd lived together. One of the men we drank with, Del Boy, had an idea: he had a disguise I could use – an actor's wig. 'He'll never recognise you, Bernie,' he said with a smirk. Del Boy's masterful disguise turned out to be a cheap ginger party wig. The only actor who might have worn it was the one playing Ronald McDonald. When I tried it on, my friends wept with laughter. I kept saying, 'It looks fucking stupid,' but my friends assured me it looked good and no one would recognise me. I eventually agreed – but want to make clear here that we were all drinking at the time!

Del Boy and a man called Slippery Bill drove us to the Royal Oak and I put on the wig, then Hughie and I walked into the crowded bar. Those who saw me fell silent; a few who knew me began laughing.

'All right, Bernie. Love the wig, mate,' they shouted.

Someone started singing, 'There's a difference at McDonald's you'll enjoy.'

I pointed out Buzz to Hughie, just as he came over to serve us.

'Can I help you?' he asked Hughie, who picked up a pint glass and lunged it at his face.

Buzz saw it coming and leaned back – the glass broke across his forehead and he fell backwards. Hughie and I turned and ran from the pub.

The regulars, many of whom liked and respected Buzz, gave chase and a hail of bottles and glasses fell around us as we ran to the car.

My wig almost fell off in the excitement. Del Boy was laughing so much he stalled the car. When he finally got it going, we sped off, the angry mob shrinking in the rear-view mirror. We never heard anything from the police, so we assumed Buzz had got the message.

Ray's release from prison coincided with my birthday, so to celebrate we went up the West End to a bar called Sound and Vision. Banks of TV screens showing music videos covered the walls. A group of men from East London started behaving in a liberty-taking way, making snide comments about South London and jostling us as we walked past them to the toilets. They seemed to know the doormen, so must have assumed unwisely they could get away with the provocation. As we were playing pool, one of the men walked past and deliberately knocked Del Boy into another of our friends. I didn't say anything; I just hit the man across the head with a pool cue, then proceeded to whack his mates, too. Then both sides started throwing pool balls at one another. TV screens were getting smashed.

The doormen came to the Eastenders' aid, but we beat them back and left the bar at our leisure, jumping on the nearest tube back to South London. The only place we could find open that would let us in was a tacky bar-cum-club in Vauxhall frequented by gays and drug dealers. As we stood at the bar waiting to be served, my friend Andy said to me, 'That bloke keeps smiling at me.' I looked across to see a man on his own at the other side of the bar. He was a bit older than us and looked like he might have had one or two gay relationships in the past. The handsome stranger smiled at me, too. I told Andy to ignore him.

Andy said if the man continued to smile at him, and therefore assume he too was gay, then he was going to bash him. I said, without wishing to appear too liberal, that, as it was a sort of gay venue, then it wasn't entirely unreasonable for a gay man to assume that perhaps other male customers might also be so inclined. A few minutes later the man was on the floor, bleeding from the head, the remains of a light-ale bottle all around him.

For the second time that evening, a full-scale brawl erupted. Tables, chairs, glasses and customers flew around the room. The fight spilled out of the club and onto the street. Eventually, Her Majesty's opposition stood in the doorway, to prevent our re-entry. We stood on the road, exchanged a few insults and started to walk off up the street. Only then did we realise that Larry wasn't with us. He must have still been inside the club. We turned and ran back down the road. As we reached the club, the doors opened and Larry was launched out onto the pavement. The doors slammed shut.

One of my friends arrived with a can of petrol that he'd bought from a nearby garage. He started dousing the club's doors and windows with the fuel. Those inside could see what was happening and through the windows I watched panic breaking out. Screams and shouts accompanied people clambering to find a rear exit. But before the petrol could be ignited, a police car and van came hurtling round the corner and everyone began to run.

A policeman tackled me to the ground before I got very far. I was under arrest. I could see Larry still lying immobile on the pavement where he'd landed, a victorious policeman standing over him, informing him of his rights. I was handcuffed, bundled into the van and told to sit on the floor.

Various revellers from the club were brought to the van to identify me, but only two of them implicated me as one of the fighters. Meanwhile Larry was hauled to his feet by two large police officers. Each time they got him upright, he just collapsed again. Eventually, they gave up and carried him to the van, dumping him next to me on the floor. I tried speaking to him, but between his mumbling and a policeman telling me to shut up, I didn't get a decipherable response.

At the station, I was told I was being held on suspicion of attempted arson. Larry, still unable to stand or communicate (apart from the occasional slurred swear word), was told he was being held for being drunk and disorderly. They tried walking him up and down the custody area to sober him up, but every time they let go of him he collapsed in a heap. They took me to an interview room for questioning, while Larry was taken to the cells to sleep it off. I discovered later that, to be on the safe side, the police had called a doctor to examine Larry. He immediately summoned an ambulance. At the hospital an X-ray revealed the reason he couldn't stand up – he'd suffered two broken legs.

The police interrogated me for a few hours, but I knew I had nothing to fear because neither my person nor my clothing had come into contact with any petrol. Then the two witnesses who'd been so sure about my identity outside the club failed to appear to make statements. I was released the next day, and Larry later received a letter informing him that 'after careful consideration' no further action would be taken against him in respect of the drunk-and-disorderly allegation.

On visits from London to my mother in Codsall, I'd met and started going out with a girl named Sarah Milner, whom I called 'Millie'. It was once more a case of opposites attract: she was quiet, caring and extremely well mannered. We got on very well, and when I was with her I found myself beginning to feel like a 'normal' human being. In Millie I had found a real soulmate.

We did all the normal things that normal people do. Indeed, it was the 'normality' I really enjoyed. We just did everyday stuff together – and she never once mentioned my 'reputation'. Unfortunately, in a place like Codsall you can never escape your past.

The village gossips soon started 'warning' her parents about me and, naturally, her parents became concerned. I met them a few times. They were good, decent people and I liked them. At first they accepted me and tried to ignore the gossips, but then the rumours became more venomous and bizarre. People were claiming Millie had had two abortions. The innocent truth was that, although we'd been together more than a year, we'd never even slept together. But, as the old saying goes, a lie is halfway round the world before the truth has got its boots on.

Despite my assurances that I'd treat their daughter with the utmost respect and always ensure she came to no harm, Millie's parents made it obvious that they wanted her to stop seeing me. Both of us felt deeply hurt by the desire of some locals to destroy any chance we had of a future together, but we both knew the gossipmongers had won. On Christmas Eve 1984, Millie's father arrived at my mother's house and gave me back the present I'd bought for his daughter. He told me not to contact her again. It was an unnecessary act that really hurt me; I felt devastated. More than anything else, Millie and I were good friends who understood one another; the girlfriend–boyfriend thing was secondary.

I wouldn't have dreamt of asking her to fall out with her parents over me, so our demise as a couple just had to be. I went out that night with a heart full of hate for my fellow man. Given my mood, I decided to avoid the Crown, especially after the violent incident two years earlier during the season of goodwill. I went instead with my friends to the Wheel Inn, where I bumped into a female 'friend' of Millie's. This person's mother had been one of the gossips passing on vile rumours to Millie's parents. When this 'friend' tried to talk to me, I told her to fuck off. Her boyfriend objected. At that moment, all the resentment I felt for the good people of Codsall erupted within me. I picked up a bottle from a nearby table and smashed it over his forehead. It wasn't personal; it was just a release for my anger and frustration.

As before, I was arrested, charged with wounding with intent, put in front of a special court and remanded in custody to Birmingham's Winson Green Prison without so much as a 'Yo ho ho' or a Jaffa Cake. I spent two weeks in prison before being bailed.

I returned to London to await my trial, which had been scheduled to take place at Stoke Crown Court. I knew I'd be sent to prison again, but this thought didn't have much effect on the way I was feeling. I had treated Millie with the utmost respect but that was never going to be enough for the self-righteous busybody bastards in Codsall.

I'd had enough of 'decent citizens'. I felt I was damned if I did right and damned if I did wrong. Aged just 24, Bernard O'Mahoney had decided to stop giving a damn altogether.

3

MY WAY

After being ordered to stand trial at Stoke Crown Court, I had decided to go on the run to South Africa with my friend Colin Allabyrne. I can't remember who first started talking about South Africa, but the country of apartheid began to shine out to Colin and me as a beacon of hope and a focus for my escape fantasies.

The night before we left England I stayed with Colin at his father's house in Stratford, East London. I didn't fancy flying out of Heathrow because of my non-appearance at Crown Court; police and passport checks were less vigorous on the ferries, so we agreed to take a boat from Harwich to Holland, then fly out to Africa from there. I still laugh now when I think back to the day we left London. We were both wearing our Sunday best and behaved like robot model citizens. Very sober and correct. Indeed, as the train pulled out of Liverpool Street station, we vowed never to drink alcohol again. Alcohol only brought trouble. And we were determined to avoid trouble in our new life. Our iron-willed commitment to a new life without alcohol remained intact throughout the journey to Amsterdam. On the train, we drank only tea. On the ferry, we ordered only soft drinks. In the duty-free shop, we bought only postcards.

As we set foot in Holland, still wearing our suits, we felt pride in our self-mastery. Our abstinence had set us firmly on the road to a new beginning. In Amsterdam, we booked into one of the floating hotels at the rear of Central station, and after a shower and a change of clothes we decided to watch a football match on television.

Holland were playing Belgium, and we had to go down to the bar to see the match, but again we ordered soft drinks. We sat sipping them for ten, perhaps eleven minutes . . . Then the football chants, combined with the holiday atmosphere, began to weaken our teetotal

43

resolve. After a short discussion, we agreed it might be possible to relax our puritan restraint without compromising our good intentions. We'd proved to ourselves we could go without alcohol; now, we needed to prove we could drink in moderation.

With that goal in mind, and nothing else, we decided to allow ourselves a few beers. Just a few. Nothing to excess. There'd certainly be no relapse into drunkenness.

After a few hours' heavy drinking, we felt the agreement needed some modification. It was now all right to get drunk, so long as we avoided trouble. We were having a good time, drinking with a group of Dutch football supporters. 'Boisterous but relaxed' is how the police might have described the scene. Then a fat but otherwise nondescript young woman waddled over and, in an English accent, told Colin and me to keep the noise down. I said I didn't think we were being too noisy. No one else was complaining. She disagreed and added that her boyfriend, who'd be down in half an hour, would also take exception to the volume, especially as he was a staunch Welsh nationalist who didn't like English people. This confused me. I asked what he was doing with her if he disliked the English. 'My mum's Welsh,' she replied. We both laughed at her. Looking riled, she said, 'I'm advising you, for your own sake, not to be so loud when Dai comes.' I told her to fuck off. 'You won't say that when Dai gets here,' she said, and returned to her friends at the bar. Together they kept glancing at us, then at the door. They seemed to be counting the seconds till Dai's arrival, eager to witness the English loudmouths' comeuppance at the hands of the destroyer from the valleys.

Over the next half hour various characters came into the bar. I'd say to Colin: 'D'you think that's Dai?' Colin would reply 'Nah,' then he'd make some derogatory comment about the potential gladiator. A slightly built creature with permed, peroxide-blond, shoulder-length hair arrived. He looked like a female flatmate from an unfunny 1970s sitcom.

'That can't be Dai,' I said.

'Nah, that's Princess Di,' Colin laughed.

Then the fat woman waved at the new arrival and shouted, 'Dai!'

The two of us laughed even more. Dai spoke briefly to his partner, then turned and walked towards us. The look on his girlfriend's face said it all: 'Now, we'll see.'

Dai was a pace and a half away from me. As he opened his mouth to say something, I punched him hard in the side of the head. He fell back onto a table and crashed to the floor. As his girlfriend started screaming at me to stop hitting him, I stamped on him a few times. Dai stayed where he was. I don't think the Welsh warrior had encountered the direct approach before.

Next morning at breakfast Colin and I sat at one end of the room, while all the other guests sat at the other. Only the sound of toast being chewed broke the perfect silence. Colin and I agreed that the new life, the new beginning, would start when we reached Africa. We flew first to Cairo in Egypt, then on to Nairobi in Kenya before landing in Johannesburg at midday after 16 hours in the air. As we shuffled through passport control, I vowed never to sit in a plane again. If necessary, I'd walk back to Europe. We found ourselves an apartment suite in the rather lavish Mariston Hotel and paid for a month in advance. We wanted to ensure that, come what may, we'd have a roof over our heads. We spent our days lying by the pool or propping up the hotel bar. It was all very pleasant. You could almost forget there was a civil war festering on the horizon, though it seemed to come a little closer with every day we spent downing beers by the pool. You only had to watch the censored television news to see what was coming. The South African Army's supposed 'victories' against 'terrorists' on the borders filled those parts of the bulletins not taken up with reports of rebellion in the black townships or violent crime in the once 'safe' white suburbs.

We treated the first fortnight as a holiday, sunbathing by day, clubbing by night. Then we started looking for work. Given the shortage of whites in a country that sought to preserve their dominant status (they represented about 18 per cent of the population, while around 68 per cent were classified black, 11 per cent coloured and 3 per cent Asian), we thought it wouldn't be too difficult to find a slot somewhere. However, as we'd entered the country on tourist visas, we found the search for work more challenging than expected. Everyone asked us for work permits, which we didn't have. The South African authorities strictly enforced the permits, largely as a way to control the movement of blacks. Employers who chose to ignore the law could find themselves in a lot of trouble.

Someone told us that foreigners could enlist in a branch of the South African Army to fight on the Namibian border, and since there was a seeming absence of other employment possibilities we decided to offer our military services to the cause of white rule – although we didn't see our actions quite like that at the time; we just wanted an adventure, a bit of excitement, a journey into the unknown. To be honest, the thought of taking part in a war where the enemy wasn't very good, and therefore our survival chances were high, had encouraged us.

So, we travelled by train to the capital, Pretoria, to see if the South African Army would let us strap on the jackboots. We asked a taxi driver to take us to the main barracks, where we told the duty officer at the heavily fortified main gate that we wanted to join up. He ordered a soldier to take us to the relevant person, who turned out to be a middle-aged major sitting in a wood-panelled office, shuffling papers. We told him we wanted to enlist and fight on the border. He seemed surprised – and impressed. He asked us a few questions about our backgrounds, so I told him I'd served in Northern Ireland with the British Army; Colin had served behind the bar at the Royal Oak pub. He asked us why we wanted to join. We said we felt South Africa was a country worth fighting for. He looked at us with eyes almost moist with respect and approval.

He said he would have signed us up on the spot, if he could have. Unfortunately, he couldn't. First, we weren't South African nationals. Second, we only had tourist visas. The information we'd been given about an official South African 'Foreign Legion' was false. He regretted having to reject us; he felt the army needed more young men with our backbone and moral fibre. He said many young whites had been infected with defeatism and cowardice. Hardly anyone wanted to join the army, especially since the increase in fighting on the border. Young people were moving abroad, waking up as – spit – 'conscientious objectors', or even – horror of horrors – deserting. The country's youth was riddled with commies and conchies, pooftahs and pansies, whackos and weirdos, he said.

He told us not to be dispirited, that many Afrikaner farmers would employ an ex-British Army soldier as an armed security guard. He also mentioned a new 'private' police force that was being set up. He plucked a newspaper cutting from the papers on his desk and handed it to me. It read:

> Low-profile patrol squads plus community participation and suburban security equal a three-cornered crime crackdown unit. This equation is the brainchild of an ex-Rhodesian who heads the Johannesburg Community Crime Counteraction Squad with thousands of members. The scheme, the first of its

kind in South Africa, is based on similar operations in strife-torn areas of America. For 15 Rand per month, anyone may join the Community Policing Services Scheme, which guarantees 24-hour patrols in marked and unmarked vehicles, as well as regular house checks.

Members display a triangular board depicting a skull and crossbones to enable the crack unit and other community participants to identify their homes.

Clients are also given two 24-hour emergency telephone numbers. 'If we receive an emergency call, we send out the nearest vehicle as quickly as possible to sort out the problem,' said the company director. The car is usually there in five minutes. 'We are not Nazi pigs, thugs or bully-boys. We don't do this for fun,' he stressed. 'Our squad members are highly trained. All have police or military experience and are armed. Our job is not to investigate, but to protect. We try to use minimal force, but if my men are in a dangerous situation, they are fully entitled to protect themselves.'

About a week later we found ourselves sitting in a classroom with around ten other recruits to the Community Policing Services. At the interview, we'd been told by the company director – a Londoner by birth – that he could only offer us a position in the sales team. Later, when they'd (or we'd) recruited more customers, we could go over to the security side. He said our lack of work permits could be overlooked for the time being. The job didn't represent for me the fulfilment of a dream, but it was a start.

We spent the first week learning sales techniques. The strategy hinged on terrifying people. Instructors taught us how to play on white people's fears of violent black criminals. Every word of the spiel that we had to learn by heart contributed towards making potential customers see their homes as little more than neon-lit invitations to every passing black burglar, rapist and murderer. By the end of our training, we could have turned up at Fort Knox and made its commander feel insecure. When they finally sent us out to meet the South African public, we didn't have to work too hard to sign up customers. Apart from our newly acquired sales skills, the escalating unrest (and the resulting climate of threat and insecurity) helped us reach our sales targets quite easily. We hadn't planned on ending up as door-to-door salesmen, but in the beginning, at least, the job amused us. We had a lot of fun striking fear into people. We'd stand on doorsteps, hitting them with crime statistics (most of which we'd fabricated). Then we'd point out that 80 per cent of the state's police were engaged in fighting township violence, leaving only a pitiful remnant to protect the suburbs. Then we'd invent some awful crimes that had supposedly happened only recently in the neighbourhood, but which the authorities had hushed up to avoid scaring people. We'd bring the horror show to a climax with a 'free' security survey of their homes. Many of these homes already bristled with the sort of defences normally found at high-security military complexes, but regardless of the fortifications we'd always reach the regrettable conclusion that a gruesome fate beckoned for those who chose to live unprotected. We'd come out with lines like 'High walls don't keep burglars out, Madam, they merely hide them once they've scaled the wall' and 'Husband at work, Madam? So you're alone in your home with the children, are you? Very brave, if I may say so.' For that rare housewife who still seemed undecided, we'd glance accusingly at her children and say, 'Surely, your children's safety is worth 15 rand a month' – around £5 at that time. Hardly anyone turned us down.

However, after a month or so, Colin and I were bored. We asked the boss if we could start providing the physical protection our terrified customers now needed. Instead, he asked if we fancied working in nightclubs. He'd been approached by a few club managers after a dramatic increase in trouble at city-centre nightspots. Knife- and gun-fights were becoming commonplace; bar takings were falling fast.

In Wolverhampton some years earlier, I'd served a sort of apprenticeship in the distinguished profession of the door. I'd provided security for a friend's band and worked weekends at a town-centre pub. Since then, I'd done the job now and again, but, as with the salesman's post, it wasn't part of the dream that sustained me. However, I suspected the job would be more of a challenge in South Africa. Knives, handguns and even automatic rifles were held quite legally and openly by people, so they tended to be produced more readily in disputes.

After only a few weeks in paradise, we were fully aware that someone being shot or stabbed on the street, night or day, wasn't uncommon. The boss sent us to a nightclub in the centre of Johannesburg owned by a Greek family. Before letting us set off for our first shift, he issued us with a pair of handcuffs, a heavy rubber baton, a 9 mm pistol and – presumably for the more difficult customers – a single-barrelled, Russian-made shotgun with 12 cartridges. Everything, apart from the shotgun, was attached to a gun belt, worn on the waist so as not to restrict our mobility.

Colin and I had already spent quite a lot of time as paying customers in Johannesburg nightclubs, though we'd never encountered such heavily armed doormen. I mentioned this to the boss and he confirmed that such weaponry was unusual, but he'd promised the club manager that we'd stamp out the gang fights that were harming business. He thought the sight of us on the door would scare off troublemakers, reassure decent customers and generally encourage better manners on and off the dance floor. It was a new approach to customer service. But it worked. Gang fights ceased, and the club became very easy to manage. There were still the occasional scuffles caused by excess alcohol or wronged boyfriends (or girlfriends), but the manager and bar staff assured us that the general level of politeness and consideration to others had risen appreciably since our arrival. We moved out of the hotel into a flat in a high-rise block in Hillbrow, an area of the city centre that many considered 'rough'. Our neighbours were mostly Portuguese who'd been booted out of countries such as Angola following the collapse of Portugal's colonial empire. Technically, I suppose, the Portuguese were 'whites', but in this land of obsessive racial classification I didn't meet any whites (that is, Afrikaners, Anglo-Saxons and others with passably pale skins, preferably of European origin) who regarded the Portuguese as being on an equal footing with them. The whites I spoke to seemed to regard them as on a par with (or even slightly below) the Asians, who themselves were on a par with (or even slightly above) the mixed-race coloureds, who, like everyone else, were above the blacks, who themselves were just above the dogs, but only just. The Portuguese had a reputation – unjustified, no doubt – for being small-time criminals with a penchant for stabbing.

During the day, Colin and I would be 'stacking z's' – a popular local term to describe sleeping – or drinking gallons of the local brew, Lion Beer, in a bar called Moulin Rouge, which lay within staggering distance of our flat and was popular with British expats. Despite the French name, like most things in Johannesburg it was done out in 'American' style, with 1950s jukebox, pool table and high stools around a bar offering an array of vomit-provoking cocktails. We were popular there, at least in the sense that many customers went out of their way to make conversation with us. This may have had something to do with the fact that we were sometimes armed with the guns we were carrying to or from work. The barmaid was an absolutely stunning blonde South African who looked as if butter wouldn't melt in her mouth. She had her own little staff of 'pot-men' – blacks who'd collect and wash the glasses, clean the ashtrays and top up the peanuts, the sort of tasks a barmaid in England would perform herself. I used to watch in amazement as she slapped and shouted at the pot-men for making the slightest mistake. One minute she'd be screaming at and slapping a cowering man, the next she'd be politely serving a customer as if nothing had happened. I watched horrified one day as, for no apparent reason, she gave a pot-man a particularly vicious slap. I asked her why. 'I have to,' she said. 'If you don't let them know who's in charge, they'll turn on you one day.' She told me not to feel sorry for them, but rather to regard them as dogs. She added, 'Dogs know who their masters are. And dogs don't often bite their masters, do they?' Her views were quite common among many of the whites I met.

A lot of the younger people in the bar were English. They'd moved to Jo'burg with their parents several years earlier. The young men were whingeing about the most unpleasant consequence of the move – having to do national service in the South African Army. Most of them planned dodging it somehow, either by fleeing the country or taking up a non-military alternative, like working in a hospital. As our own attempt to join the army had been rebuffed, we used to taunt them for wanting to forgo such a 'great opportunity'.

We became friends with a group of people from Essex, which included a brother and sister, Shane and Claire, who lived with their parents in Hillbrow, and their two cousins, sisters Susan and Karen. All originally came from Romford. They also had a friend called Tim, who used to tag along. He came from Yorkshire and regarded himself as a real ladies' man. He appeared to model himself on John Travolta's character in *Saturday Night Fever*, although he lacked the looks, talent and charm of the 'Disco King'. Tim became the target for some of our more unpleasant practical jokes.

I was attracted to one of Karen's friends, Debra, who came from Basildon. She'd come over for a holiday but kept extending her stay. She'd been there around nine months when we first met and had had a few jobs in that time. During the day, she worked as a hairdresser in a downtown salon, but to earn a bit more money she'd taken on a part-time job behind the bar in a nightclub. One evening she'd refused to serve two drunken Afrikaners and an argument had blown up. One of the Afrikaners had pulled out a handgun, pointed it at her and shouted, 'I'll kill you, you bitch.' Others in the bar had wrestled the gun from him before ejecting him. Debra said she'd been speechless with shock and fear, and had left the job immediately. She was still a bit nervous when we first met.

These new friends were different from our old friends back in England. They were all reasonably balanced people with no interest in, or understanding of, the violent world in which we had roamed. At first we tried to give the impression we were nice people just like them (although obviously the weaponry we sometimes carried helped deconstruct us), but gradually the mask slipped.

One evening we found ourselves drinking with an American who claimed to be a Vietnam veteran; he was even wearing a baseball cap inscribed with the name of 'his' elite unit, the 509th Arizona Penis Pullers or something like that. At the beginning of the third hour of his story about his incredible one-man war against the Vietcong, I told him that I thought he was full of shit. He sat back on his high stool, astounded that anybody could possibly have doubted him, and said, 'Go fuck yourself, boy!' I punched him somewhere in the head. All I remember is his vet's cap flying off. Claire screamed hysterically and Colin jumped on me, piggy-back style, shouting, 'Bernie, calm down, you crazy bastard!' I was asked to leave.

The next day I bumped into Debra and Claire on the street. I mumbled a sort of apology and gave the excuse that I'd been mixing my drinks. They seemed to forgive me, but things were never really the same again. My true self had been exposed in the harsh and unforgiving light of the South African sun. Or, rather, the dim rays of the 100-watt bulbs in the Moulin Rouge, to which we soon returned without anyone mentioning 'the incident'.

Colin and I, despite our fitful attempts to hold on to our fresh-start ideals, soon reverted to our old ways. That is, boozing, then abusing people, and sometimes beating them up, as was the case with our 'mate' Tim, the wannabe John Travolta.

The problem with Tim was Tim. There was just something deeply irritating about him. One day we invited him to our tenth-floor flat and, being a fool, he came. We handcuffed him gently to the balcony railings, sprayed him lightly with CS gas, then clubbed him playfully with our riot batons until his whimpering became pitiful and decency impelled us to desist. He stopped spending so much time with us after that.

We still met up with the others, although usually in the club's alcohol-free areas, like the swimming pool. They seemed to avoid drinking with us. Claire especially seemed a little nervous around me; however, I was getting on very well with Debra. I wanted to ask her out but kept putting it off because I didn't think she'd be interested in anything more than friendship.

The success of our heavily armed approach to club security meant our job had become extremely tedious. Trouble had almost disappeared. Colin and I would sit at a table in the restaurant from early evening until the early hours of the morning, totally bored. We'd been planning to stay in South Africa and then apply for citizenship so we could join the army, but that was a long way off. Colin suggested moving to Cape Town. 'It's full of English and we'd be near the sea,' he said. I told him we could think about it. Colin said he'd only stay if the company gave him a more exciting job – the next day he told the boss he was bored and wanted to leave. He was asked to 'hang on' because something was coming up that might interest him. I didn't want to be left out, so I told the boss that I too was leaving. He told me the same thing: 'Hang on, something's coming up.' The 'something coming up' turned out to be another club, also in the city centre, but in the basement of a hotel. It was the haunt of various biker and Portuguese gangs, and it had a reputation for trouble.

It wasn't quite the new position Colin had hoped for, so he left the company, but I decided to rise to the challenge, although without Colin I had no back-up. I was expected to handle any situation that arose, alone. In fact, most of the customers turned out to be all right; it was the manager who was the problem. He was a half-witted, aggressive little shit. His decisions, always arbitrary and irrational, seemed designed to provoke. He'd point at individuals he wanted me to eject from the club, then he'd make a big show of the fact that he'd ordered their ejection. Most of these customers, so far as I could tell, hadn't actually done anything wrong. More than once I saw him, blind-drunk, threatening customers with a handgun. He'd never explain their supposed offences.

One evening he decided – again, for no apparent reason – that jeans were no longer an acceptable form of dress. Given that bikers formed the largest segment of the clientele, his request struck me as even more markedly unreasonable than usual. Not only did he order me to turn away at the door any people wearing jeans, he also demanded that I eject every jeans-wearing customer already in the club. I did as I was told, although I expected trouble.

Fortunately for me, and for the manager, almost everyone left without much fuss. Only one group of Portuguese men took exception. They felt they were being singled out. As they left, they threatened to return to smash up the club – and me. The barman told me they had a reputation and that I ought to keep my wits about me for a while.

I finished work about 3.30 in the morning and walked the half mile or so home. There was no one about. I got in the lift and stepped out at my floor. A group of men were standing around outside the first flat I reached; they were being shouted at by a Portuguese woman. I'd never seen her before, although she only lived a few doors down from me. As soon as she saw me, she ran over.

'Arrest him! Go on, arrest him!' she started shouting.

She assumed I was a policeman; our uniform was similar to theirs and, as I was also carrying a baton, handcuffs and firearms, I could understand her mistake. I tried telling her I wasn't a policeman, but she wasn't interested, she just kept gibbering on.

'I had a party in my flat. It ended. But these people want to come back in.' Her manner was agitated and she smelt of alcohol.

I told her I didn't want anything to do with her guests: 'I'm not a policeman, I live here.' I walked a few steps with her. As I got to the men, I realised they were the same men who'd threatened me earlier at the club. 'Small world,' I thought. And it was almost my last thought, ever, because the men recognised me, too. One of them stepped forward, called me a bastard and lunged at my chest with a knife. The blade cut me, but I managed to turn away, preventing it going right in. Holding the shotgun in both hands, I swung round and belted the man with the knife across the head with it. The wooden butt crashing into his skull made a wincingly loud noise. He fell to the floor, unconscious and injured. I raised the shotgun and pointed it at the others, making as if to shoot. They tore off down the corridor.

The woman was standing there, muttering in Portuguese. I wasn't sure what to do with the man on the floor. His head was bleeding quite badly; one of his eyes had closed completely. I grabbed his feet and dragged him to the lift. I ferried him down to the ground floor, then dragged him out into the street, where I left him alongside the rubbish, then took the lift back up. The woman was still standing near her flat, alone. She started shouting in Portuguese and seemed angry with me. I couldn't understand why. After all, I'd got rid of her unwanted guests. I told her to calm down. I walked with her to the door of her flat. Her alcohol consumption that evening had really started to kick in and she was becoming abusive. I'd had enough. I was bleeding too, my stab wound was starting to hurt and I wanted to go to bed. I grabbed her by the arm, pushed her into her flat and told her to fuck off, then I walked off down the corridor. She followed a few paces behind me, screaming abuse.

Colin was awake when I got in. He said he'd heard a row but hadn't realised I was involved. I warned him that if the Portuguese man ended up in hospital we'd probably get a visit from the police. And, whether or not he made it to hospital, we'd probably get a visit at some point from him and his mates.

I washed and cleaned the wound in my chest, then put the knife I'd picked up from the floor, and my torn shirt, into a bag and went to bed. I slept uneasily with the guns by my side. I was expecting either the police or the Portuguese men to burst through the door, but no one came.

Early next morning the company telephoned to say they needed every available body to attend an incident near the black township of Soweto. An hour or so later I was picked up by a company van, which drove at speed out of the city. I hadn't realised we had customers in Soweto. I couldn't imagine how we'd recruited them. Perhaps we'd scared them with stories about the white police ('Flimsy shack, Madam? That's not going to stop a determined Boer in uniform, is it?') In fact, I discovered our customers were the South African police. They occasionally called on freelance help for 'non-political' incidents when they were overstretched. I was told in the van, which contained around ten other heavily armed colleagues, that two black factions had been fighting over ownership of a shebeen, an illegal drinking den, often a venue for gambling and prostitution. When I first heard the word shebeen, I thought it was native South African. Only years later did I discover it comes from an Irish-Gaelic word for 'bad ale'.

By the time we got there, a gang fight had already taken place. One young man of about twenty had been trapped by rivals, put against a wall and stoned. He lay there motionless, blood spattered all over his broken body. I thought he was dead. Another man had been stabbed in the head. He was reeling around the street, clutching his wound and screaming in pain. After a while, he collapsed. A police pick-up truck arrived and a few officers got out, grabbed hold of the two men and dumped them both into the back of the truck like sacks of rubbish. They drove off, leaving us standing in a cloud of dust.

When I got back to the flat, I found an anxious-looking Colin waiting for me. He said that armed police had raided the flat. Apparently, the Portuguese woman had alleged I'd assaulted her. Colin said the police had made plain they planned to arrest me.

I decided to seek legal advice. As I left the building, two policemen suddenly stood up, guns drawn, from behind a car near the entrance. Pointing their weapons at me, they shouted, 'Raise your hands and turn around.' I wasn't going to argue. They came over, searched me, handcuffed me, then asked me where my guns were. I said they were in the flat.

They told me to get into their car. As we drove off, one of them said they were taking me to John Foster Square police station. It had a worse reputation than my bikers' club. Numerous prisoners had died after 'jumping' from windows on the upper floors during interrogation.

Sweating – and not just from the heat – I was taken into a detention room, where I waited on my own for a few minutes before a detective entered the room. He asked me about the events of the night before. I told him the truth and added that I still had the knife and torn clothing at home. He produced a statement made by the Portuguese woman. She had claimed that, for no reason, I'd grabbed her by the arm, pushed her about, threatened her with a gun and even sexually assaulted her (although she'd given no explanation of how). I was furious.

'Why the fuck would I attack someone who lives on the same fucking landing as me without reason? I'm not fucking stupid, mate,' I shouted.

I needn't have worried. The detective said he didn't believe the drunken woman and he wasn't going to look into the matter any further. He said she was known to the police, then added, 'Be careful of these people. They're dangerous and they're trouble.'

He wrote out a statement for me, asked me to sign it, then told me to go home and forget about it. Less than 30 minutes after being arrested, I was released. I thought that was the end of the matter; in fact, it was only the beginning. The company heard about my arrest and the boss didn't like having any bother with the police, so he decided I needed a break from the nightclub. He thought that, between us, the manager and I were causing more trouble than we were preventing. He said he wanted to transfer me temporarily to 'patrol work' – that is, driving around the suburbs of Johannesburg in a pick-up truck.

I was owed a few days off, which I took before starting my new duties. During this time, I spoke a lot with Colin about moving on to Cape Town. The luxurious Blue Train connected the two cities and we agreed we'd make the trip in style if or when we left Jo'burg – although it was most certainly becoming a case of *when* rather than *if*. Debra said she would like to travel with us, too. It was December by now, and she was missing her family, as she'd been away from England for almost a year – they had thought she'd only be gone for a month or two – so before travelling with us, she wanted to go home and spend Christmas in Essex. We booked three train tickets for Cape Town due to depart Jo'burg on 14 January. I don't know why, but something told me I wouldn't be on it. I just couldn't look forward to the journey (and the new 'new start') because subconsciously I knew it wasn't going to happen.

Debra planned to leave for England in the second week of December. I told myself I'd ask her out for a meal the night before she left, but I bottled out of it. I thought she'd make some excuse and decline my offer. She had planned a farewell drink with her friends, and they did invite Colin and me, but I said I had to work. I hoped to pop in to see them at some stage, but I never did. I don't know why. The following morning Debra came round to say goodbye. I was surprised at how sorry I felt to see her go, even though she'd only be gone for a month. We said our goodbyes and she promised to return for our trip to Cape Town. I knew I was going to miss Debra, but thoughts of romance soon receded when I started my new duties patrolling the suburbs. Until then, I foolishly thought I'd seen it all.

4

PSYCHO KILLER

'LET'S get this straight, Bernie. Kaffirs are fucking vermin. They're not human, OK?'

Dougie, my senior colleague in the pick-up truck, was explaining the cornerstone of his world view as we drove around the tidy and well-tended suburbs of white Johannesburg and the less tidy and less well-tended suburbs of coloured Johannesburg. Most of the blacks we encountered were either domestic servants or – at least in Dougie's eyes – potential criminals. Our job was to answer emergency calls from Community Policing Services customers. We had white and coloured householders on our books, but calls from whites tended to be treated with the greatest urgency. These whites were usually calling to report suspicious people near, on, or in their properties.

Dougie was in his mid-30s, was slightly built and not very tall, but he bolstered his otherwise unimposing presence with an arsenal of weapons which were strapped all over his body. I don't know if he was an Afrikaner or an Anglo because we didn't have the sort of conversations in which I could have asked a question like that. Any details about his background emerged incidentally, through anecdotes he'd tell about his past, which tended to describe his beating, shooting and humiliating blacks ('kaffirs', as he and most other South Africans preferred to call them). He said he'd shot his 'first kaffir' as a teenager. He'd been cleaning a handgun in his house when he'd heard his sister screaming in the garden. He'd run out with the gun, seen a black man standing over her and fired twice. The first bullet hit the man in the shoulder; the second slammed into his head, killing him instantly. He'd told the police the man had been attacking his sister. And that was the end of the matter. No charges, no inquest, no nothing. I didn't really believe him. Naively, I thought he'd have to have been

57

lying, or at the very least exaggerating. After a few days with him, I changed my mind.

On one of my first shifts, we were called out to a coloured person's house in the west of the city. The householder had reported five black youths trying to force their way in. Apparently, they'd smashed his windows with sticks and were now trying to break down the front door. We pulled up leisurely at the address. The youths were still there, throwing rocks against the door and trying to shoulder it open. Dougie didn't say anything. He just jumped out of the truck and started shooting. The youths skedaddled. Dougie ran up the path towards the house, firing his pistol wildly at the fleeing figures. He wasn't just shooting in the air for effect: he seemed to be aiming his shots. Luckily for his targets, he couldn't shoot well on the move and, anyway, the juveniles were probably running faster than his bullets. I'd jumped out of the truck and was running behind him. His behaviour left me speechless. Everything was happening too quickly for me to say or do anything. We started chasing the only youth still visible. He was streaking down the road with the velocity of an Olympic sprinter. Dougie fired again and, as he did so, a police car came round the corner. The terrified youth ran straight up to it. Without even stopping to talk to the policemen inside, he opened the rear door and jumped in. It must have seemed a better option than summary execution.

For the second time in a week, I found myself back in John Foster Square police station. The fact that shots had been fired meant a bit of paperwork had to be completed. I expected a hard time from the police, who I assumed would be keen to discover why a security guard had been shooting at a member of the public in a residential area. But, apart from a few questions from a bored sergeant that were the very opposite of probing, no one seemed too concerned. We could have been reporting a stolen bike.

I told the police I'd been talking on the radio when the shooting started. I'd only just got out of the vehicle as the police arrived, so I couldn't throw much light on the events. However, Dougie didn't just tell the full truth, he exaggerated the more illegal aspects. I knew security guards could get away with a lot, but I'd also been told the law was crystal clear about self-defence. You could shoot if you considered your life in danger, but not if that danger had passed. Someone whizzing gazelle-like (or even Springbok-like) down the road away from you could not be regarded as a threat.

They released me and Dougie stayed to make a statement. I thought he'd be charged with something, and perhaps suspended, but next day he was waiting for me as usual at work. He said the police considered the matter closed. It seemed that even if he'd shot someone dead – so long as that someone was black – they wouldn't have done anything. Dougie had obviously learnt early on what he could get away with. What I thought had been tall tales were probably faithful depictions of reality.

I began to feel very uncomfortable working with Dougie. He had a spitting aggressiveness fuelled by paranoia, suspicion and hatred. I knew a lot of violent people, and I wasn't particularly gentle myself, but Dougie was different. I could never feel at ease with him. Not only would he start waving a gun about for little or no reason, but he'd also threaten and beat blacks just for fun. His brutality astonished me. I'd often tell him to ease off, but he'd just look at me as if I was mad. I think he regarded me as some sort of humanitarian goody-goody.

Over the next few weeks, I came to realise the law didn't exist for blacks as something they could call on for help. I'd witnessed the official contempt for black lives every hour of every day. I'd seen a policeman kung-fu kick a black man in the chest on a crowded street for no reason. I'd attended an incident where a white man who'd knocked down a black man in his car was asked by the policeman if the victim had caused the vehicle any damage. It was an odd, brutal world that seemed on the brink of boiling over into a bloodbath. I soon felt that I could no longer stomach the misery and injustice I was witnessing. I would see a black family living in an abandoned car surrounded by corrugated iron, and watch the black women and children sharing a meal of thin gruel from the paint tin they'd cooked it in. Yet only a few miles away white families lived in bloated luxury. I was beginning to think like a *Guardian* reader. I thought I was cracking up.

One night while Dougie and I were on duty, we had been whiling away our shift drinking outside the Moulin Rouge. Of course, we should have been patrolling the streets in our truck, but we had pagers with which the company contacted us in emergencies. Claire was sitting with us. Normally, she tended to avoid me when I was drinking, but she'd arranged to meet someone, had arrived early and didn't want to wait on her own.

My pager started bleeping – we were being called to a reported burglary. The address was just round the corner, so we got up to leave. I told Claire we wouldn't be long. She asked if she could come along because she didn't fancy sitting on her own, and so foolishly I let her jump in with us. We arrived at the address quickly.

A young white woman told us the offender had only just run out of the house. She gave a brief description of a black man wearing jeans and a T-shirt. Dougie ran one way, I the other. I bolted down the street and round the block but couldn't see anyone, and after a few minutes I made my way back to the house. A few hundred yards away, I could see Dougie frogmarching someone in my direction. Before long the two of them reached me. On Dougie's face was a smirk; on his black prisoner's was blood. Dougie then suddenly belted the man across the back of the head with his pistol. He crumpled to his knees. Dougie then started to pistol-whip him.

'Leave it out, Dougie,' I said. 'Leave it out, man.' But he was in a real frenzy.

'Dirty kaffir! Dirty fucking kaffir!' he spat, as he booted the man, who was by now curled up into a defensive ball. I heard the sound of somebody pounding their fists on a window and looked up. It was Claire. She'd been watching everything from the truck. She looked distraught. Banging on the window with both hands, she was crying her eyes out, shouting at Dougie to stop.

Dougie eventually tired and pulled his blood-smeared victim to his feet. He forced the man up the path to the house he'd allegedly burgled. Dougie rang the bell, and the young woman who answered let out a scream. She didn't scream because she recognised the quivering man, she screamed because his face was a mask of blood.

Dougie told her to call the police. Within a few minutes, they'd arrived in a van. 'I've got a burglar for you,' Dougie said. The police didn't ask how the alleged burglar had ended up in such a state. Trivial points like that didn't interest them. Dougie said he'd attend the station to make a statement. The police pushed the man into the van and drove off. We drove Claire back to the Moulin Rouge. She was still upset but had stopped crying. She asked Dougie why he'd had to hit the man like that. 'He was a burglar,' he said.

We dropped her off and drove on. I didn't feel well. It struck me that the man hadn't been wearing jeans and a T-shirt. He didn't fit the householder's original description. I asked Dougie if he could be sure he'd got the right man.

'Do you really think he's the burglar?' I said.

Dougie laughed. 'Don't be stupid. Of course he isn't.' He'd seen the man walking up the road with his girlfriend, he said, and he'd asked him where he'd been and the man had 'got lippy'. Dougie had then pistol-whipped him on the spot. 'Fucking kaffir. His black bitch got a kicking, too,' he added. He claimed that as he was kicking her she'd wet herself. Her urine had gone all over his boots and trousers. 'That's why he got what he got.'

I felt sick, just sick, and dirty. I asked myself what I was doing with such an animal. I was holding the shotgun in my hands and felt like smashing the butt into the side of his head. I really wanted to damage him, but I didn't. He was white. The law would have punished me severely for harming a hair on his head. I felt like going to the police and telling them the man was innocent, but I guessed my intervention wouldn't make any difference. The man was black: as far as the police were concerned, he had been born guilty. It seemed to me that so long as some black man was in custody for an offence, it didn't matter to the police if he was the right or wrong one. Dougie would make his statement and 'the burglar' would probably receive a lengthy prison sentence. The next day I went into the office and told them I didn't want to work on patrols any more.

Some people might think I'm exaggerating the way things were for blacks. I'm not. The more independent papers were full of stories of astonishing official cruelty. One story in particular has stuck in my mind. It involved the so-called 'Pabello 26'. Pabello is a black township. A policeman had been murdered outside his home by demonstrators who'd just been dispersed from a nearby football pitch with tear gas. He'd been struck on the head with his own rifle after he'd shot indiscriminately, paralysing an 11-year-old boy. The courts convicted 26 blacks of having played a part in the murder. Six received community service, six were sent to prison, and fourteen were sentenced to death. The controversial law of common purpose had been used to convict all of them without ever having established who'd actually struck the policeman. It subsequently emerged that five of the blacks sentenced to death had only been arrested by chance. They'd been stopped at random in the street seven months after the murder and asked to make up the numbers in an identity parade. The police witness had picked out all five of the innocent men. Despite the public outcry, all were hanged. I knew, too, that injustice wasn't reserved for non-whites. I heard enough stories to know that anyone who displeased the authorities could be locked up without charge, fitted up and, in extreme cases, even murdered.

The boss found me another nightclub. It was neither as big nor as busy as the last one I'd worked in, but it shared a similar biker clientele. The bikers were older, mostly men in their mid-30s to early 40s, and were involved in most things criminal. Mercifully, however, my new manager didn't indulge in provocative and irrational behaviour, so life became easier. On my second weekend at the club, Colin visited me for a drink. We shared more than a few beers together over the next couple of hours, until the manager came over. He said a group of men had started bothering customers outside the club. Even though Colin wasn't working, he went with me to the door. Rather foolishly, I left the shotgun behind at the reception desk upstairs. I recognised the troublemakers – four of the Portuguese men I'd last seen on the landing near my flat. Their number didn't include the knifeman I'd battered with the butt of my gun – I hoped he was still in hospital. I explained politely that they should return forthwith to their slums, but one of them stepped forward and kicked in the glass door. The others ran at us. We backed off into the foyer, and they followed, picking up chairs and tables. Furniture was soon flying through the air towards us. I grabbed one of the chairs and began to smash it over anyone within striking distance. Unfortunately, in the confusion I smashed Colin over the head, too. The blow knocked him out – and down a flight of stairs. Now alone, I knew I could lose. Only my shotgun could save me. I ran back up the stairs to reception, grabbed the gun from behind the counter and spun round to level it at the Portuguese charging up after me.

The police arrived before the situation could deteriorate any further and drew their guns. I was pleased to see them, but I sensed the feeling wasn't mutual – I think the police had had enough of me, the English holidaymaker. They ignored the Portuguese men and arrested me. I saw Colin still lying comatose downstairs as the police marched me out to the van.

Once again I found myself standing in front of the desk sergeant in John Foster Square police station. I felt I'd been treated unjustly. I was also worried about Colin. These feelings combined to make me less polite and respectful than usual. I kept interrupting the desk sergeant, who then said something insulting about my mother. I lunged at him, but before I could grab him, his colleagues brought me down to the ground with a crash. Several of them dragged me along the floor to the cells, punctuating my journey with kicks. They opened a heavy metal door and shoved me into what seemed more like a cage than a cell. The door slammed shut and for a moment I lay still on cold concrete. Looking up, I could see the stars in the night sky. The architect had forgotten to sketch in a ceiling. Only the security bars offered protection from the weather. The cell was about six paces wide and twelve long. At one end sat a broken, stinking toilet. At the other was a small round hole in what appeared to be a coal bunker. In fact, the hole was the entrance to the sleeping area, which contained no beds, only a few flea-infested blankets. Crawling through the hole made me feel like a dog entering its kennel. I managed to fall into an uneasy sleep, but the unbearable heat from the rising sun soon made that impossible.

In the morning light, I could see that around the wall of my cell ran a cast-iron gutter containing water for drinking and washing. You had to pull a chain to set the liquid flowing. I didn't fancy catching amoebic dysentery, so I avoided the water.

The accommodation had one other drawback – I had to share it with five others. I introduced myself to my cellmates. All had been arrested for drink-driving.

Breakfast was served at sunrise. It consisted of one scoop of cold porridge on a piece of dry bread. I asked the policeman on breakfast duty if I could use the phone.

'Yeah, sure. I'll bring it to you. I'll just fetch it out of my arse,' he replied, then slammed the door shut with a sneer.

I didn't have the stomach for breakfast and I gave my meagre portion to one of the others. I sat and pondered my options. I hoped Colin was all right, because I knew he represented my best hope of finding a way out. He was probably the only person in the entire country who'd be concerned about my well-being. I needed to contact him to tell him to get me a lawyer.

One of the other prisoners, a Welshman (no relation to Dai, I prayed), was to be released that morning, so I scratched Colin's telephone number on the back of his belt buckle. He assured me he'd ring him to let him know where I was.

During the afternoon the police came and moved me to another cellblock. It was marked 'Category A: Serious Crimes'. This worried me, to say the least, because I didn't think a brawl in a club represented a serious crime. The policeman opened the door to my new cell. It looked much the same as the other one; it just smelt a bit more.

I relaxed a bit when I met my new cellmates. None had committed any serious crimes. Johnny had been arrested for using a stolen chequebook. He'd been in custody for seven months and was still waiting for other matters to be investigated before his case could be heard. Mario was in for drink-driving and driving while disqualified. Two teenagers were in for burglary and theft. The fifth man, Andrew, didn't know what he was in for because he'd lost his memory. He said the police had told him he'd be staying put until he started remembering things. My colleagues told me to abandon any great hope of getting out swiftly; I could expect to be held for a long time while 'investigations' continued. They told me the police kept some people in custody indefinitely for no reason other than some officer had taken a dislike to them. I wished fervently I hadn't tried to grab the desk sergeant – I hoped he wasn't the type to bear a grudge. I wondered if it was too late for an apology.

Some hours later, as the others dozed, Johnny whispered that I should be wary of Andrew, the supposed amnesia sufferer. 'He's a cop,' he said. Apparently, the police moved him from cell to cell to gather information. Normally, I'd have considered such a suggestion ridiculous, but nothing done by these upholders of the law could surprise me now.

Around two in the morning, a policeman called me from the cell. He led me to a room that was empty apart from a single chair in the middle. He told me to sit on it. I assumed I was about to be interviewed.

I sat there for around 45 minutes before the policeman returned. He ordered me to follow him. He took me straight back to the cell, slammed shut the door and walked away. I felt a bit unnerved. I asked Johnny if this procedure was normal. He laughed and said, 'Anything is normal in this place.'

During the day, the heat in the cell was unbearable. It didn't matter where you moved; you couldn't escape it. In the early evening, the rain fell heavily for about an hour, flooding the floor. The clouds cleared and the sun beamed down again, turning the cell into a Turkish bath. It stank.

The one other meal of the day, delivered late afternoon, wasn't any more appetising than breakfast. It looked like a bowl of hot water with some sort of plant life floating on top. And more dry bread. Again, I let one of my cellmates have it.

The police came for me around seven that evening. Once again I was led to the room with the single chair. After half an hour a detective came in and told me to follow him. He was in his mid-40s and looked mean, very mean. I was thankful I wasn't black. He took me into an office, sat me down and stared at me.

'You English bastards,' he said. 'You're worse than the bloody blacks.'

That was all I needed: an anti-English racist.

He began questioning me about the guns that had been in my possession when I'd been arrested. I explained they'd been issued to me by the company. I admitted I didn't have a work permit. 'What? No fucking permit?' he said. 'You're a tourist and you think you can stroll round our city, armed to the teeth, assaulting and threatening our citizens? You've come to the wrong place, sonny.'

Come what may, he said, he'd make sure I was deported. He seemed to take my presence in his country very personally. I'd really upset him. I prayed the desk sergeant wasn't his mate.

He questioned me about the assault on Colin and about my threats to kill the Portuguese, which he said I'd shouted during the disturbance. He seemed to be fishing around to see what charges he could bring. I tried to explain that everything stemmed from the incident some weeks earlier when I'd been cut by one of their mates outside my flat. This seemed to turn on a light in his head. He left the room and returned a moment later with a file. He sat there reading it for a few minutes. Then he held up the statement I'd signed regarding this earlier incident.

'Is this yours?' he asked. I said it was. He then tore it up into about eight pieces, threw the remains in the bin and said, 'Well, we won't be needing that, then.' He led me out of the room to the reception area, where I was charged with assaulting the Portuguese woman two weeks earlier. I was gobsmacked. But for the moment there wasn't much I could do.

The detectives told me they'd be seeking my deportation and therefore needed my last address outside South Africa. I didn't want to give them my English address in case they contacted the English police, who'd no doubt inform them of my wanted status, so I gave them the address of a friend in Amsterdam. I was told that when the time came I'd be deported to Holland. They photographed me, fingerprinted me and noted all distinguishing marks on my body before returning me to my cell. The other prisoners told me I'd be taken to court the following morning now that I'd been charged.

At night, the cell turned into a fridge – the frozen-food

compartment. As I sat shivering in the darkness, my mind swirled with countless ifs and maybes, and I couldn't sleep. The cells never fell silent. The slamming of doors and the despairing cries of prisoners didn't stop. Around midnight I heard shouting outside. A woman started screaming. Then I heard the door of the adjacent cell being slammed shut. As the jailer's footsteps faded, I could hear a woman sobbing uncontrollably. I called out to her and asked if she was all right.

'Please help me! Please help me! The guards have threatened to rape me!' she said. In her voice was a sense of absolute terror. I told her they were just trying to scare her, that nothing would happen to her; she shouldn't show she was scared because they'd just play on it. In truth, I couldn't be sure nothing would happen to her. As Johnny had said, and as I'd already found out myself, in this place anything was possible and everything was normal. She said she'd been arrested for 'stealing' a car that she had bought legitimately from a showroom two weeks earlier. 'They want me to say I stole it. I've never broken the law in my life. I'm married with children. Please help me.' I spoke to her on and off throughout the night and she became a lot calmer.

I never found out what happened to her because in the early morning I was loaded with several other prisoners into a truck with a wire-mesh back door. About 15 minutes later, the truck drove into a courtyard. We all got out. Police led us into what seemed like a long tunnel under the courts. For the first time since my arrest, I found myself sitting with black prisoners. One black youth sat there sobbing. He had a gaping wound in his side. It had been dressed, but badly. I was told he'd been shot by police as he ran from a car that had been broken into. Another man stood there completely naked. His clothes had been taken away, supposedly for forensic examination, and hadn't been replaced.

I kept thinking about my ex-colleague Dougie and the events I'd witnessed, the events I'd allowed to happen. No doubt the black victims of our patrols had ended up down here, bewildered, humiliated and terrified, yet guilty of nothing usually. I felt like scum. I wanted to fly a thousand miles away from that demented country. I could hardly believe that only a few weeks earlier I'd wanted to embrace the system and way of life.

After a few hours' waiting, I heard my name being called out. A jailer escorted me upstairs to the courtroom. I looked up into the public gallery and saw Colin. For the first time since my arrest, I felt a surge of relief. He indicated with hand gestures that he'd got me a solicitor. There was no system of legal aid in South Africa: either you paid for justice or you didn't get it. That was another reason so many black people ended up being railroaded to jail – or the gallows.

I couldn't understand what was being said because my solicitor and the court officials spoke in Afrikaans, but after a few minutes of what was to me incomprehensible jabber my lawyer leaned over and said, 'You can get bail if you're willing to surrender your passport and pay 1,000 rand in cash.'

'Tell them it's done,' I said. I told him to sort out the cash with Colin. Moments later I was being led back down the stairs into the tunnel. It's hard to describe the awful atmosphere below. The air stank of sweat and fear. Everybody sat staring at the floor, looking troubled. Some looked desperate and defeated. I could barely imagine the suffering this miserable place had witnessed over the years. You could sense it in the heavy air.

I'd relaxed considerably because I thought I'd soon be walking out; however, to my alarm, the police loaded me back into the truck and said I was being taken to the notorious Deepcliffe prison. I kept saying I'd been granted bail, but no one wanted to listen. My heart sank to my toes. In the truck, I sat near the exit, looking through the wire mesh as the driver pulled out of the courtyard. Then, a little morale booster brought my heart back up: Colin was following in a car. I had one of those strange, dreamy moments when everything seems peculiar. Here I was, being taken through the streets of Johannesburg in the back of a prison truck on a beautifully sunny day with my friend in desperate pursuit. It was hardly the new life we'd dreamed of.

We reached Deepcliffe in an hour or so. They unloaded the prisoners and led us into a reception area. One by one, we were called forward. When my turn came, I had to stand on a wooden box and answer a series of mundane questions from a screw standing behind a counter. Name, age, address, religion, birthmarks, mother's maiden name. I told him I shouldn't be there. 'I got bail, mate,' I said. 'Check with the courts.'

He gave a look of mock concern and answered, 'Oh, really? Don't tell me – we're swapping you for Barabbas! Put this name badge on, hold these papers, stand over there and shut up.'

I had to stand for another half-hour whilst they documented everyone. Then they led us through the prison. I'd just about resigned myself to another spell in custody when I heard my name being called. I was taken back out to the reception area and into the office of a man I assumed was the prison governor.

'Your bail's been paid, O'Mahoney,' he said, 'and your passport's been lodged with us. Do you understand that if you don't appear in court, the friend who paid your bail will lose his money?' I said I did. I wasn't concerned about the money; I'd told Colin to take it from my own account. I signed a form and in two minutes I was walking back out the main gate as a free man. Colin was waiting for me. It was 30 December 1985. I had only one thought in my mind: flee the country as soon as possible.

Trying to travel without a passport presented a significant hurdle, but I had an idea. I drove with Colin to Pretoria, where a few months earlier we'd tried to enlist in the army. I already had an open return ticket, so I went to a travel agent's, showed them my ticket and said that I had to get back to England as soon as possible because of a bereavement. The earliest available flight, leaving on New Year's Day and taking me as far as Brussels, involved flying via Nairobi, Cairo, Madrid and Geneva. 'No problem, I'll take it,' I said.

Ticket in hand, I went to a nearby police station. I told them I'd been visiting my sister to help her pack. She was moving back to England to get married. Unfortunately, I couldn't find my passport. I had a horrible feeling I'd accidentally packed it away in my sister's belongings, which were now on their way to England. I had to fly out the day after tomorrow. What could I do? I showed him my ticket. He walked off, returning moments later with a lost-property form. He filled it out, stamped it and told me to take it to the British Embassy down the road. At the embassy, they checked I held a valid passport before issuing me with an emergency 'one-way' passport. This 'passport' was, in fact, just an A4 piece of paper declaring my right to travel on one journey only from Johannesburg to England.

I now had all I needed – apart from the certainty that I'd get out of the country. I knew if they carried out a thorough check at the airport they'd rumble me; I'd be arrested and wouldn't get bail until my case had been dealt with. I imagined the next year stuck on remand in a South African prison cell.

I'd let a few people in on my plan, and not everyone thought it was a good idea. Someone suggested it might be better to cross a river on the northern border, but I discovered the river was crocodile-infested

– and the far shore a haven for anti-apartheid guerrillas. Someone else suggested travelling to Durban or Cape Town and stowing away on a ship.

On balance, I felt my own plan was the best, so long as I kept my head and didn't appear suspicious at the airport. The next day, New Year's Eve – the day before my planned departure – I went to a huge street party in the centre of Johannesburg with Colin and a few of our friends. The city was celebrating its centenary and the streets were packed with people – white people. The city centre became a black-free zone in the evening. Black people lived under a curfew. Apart from those with special work permits, all blacks had to be back in their townships by ten at the latest.

Cheers went up as the New Year swept in. A few glass bottles fell to the ground. The police, always keen to over-react, decided that they had a potential riot on their hands. Using loudhailers, they ordered the crowd to disperse. Nobody paid any attention. Everybody kept partying. The occasional bottle could still be heard crashing to the ground and I watched as a line of riot police formed up across the street. Again, the police used their loudhailers to order the crowd's dispersal. Again, everyone ignored the order. Suddenly, the police started firing tear gas into the crowd. Then the riot police began advancing, batons in hand. I suppose it was a fitting end to a century of oppression.

I didn't enjoy my last night in South Africa. I walked the streets alone until five in the morning. I went into a couple of bars but felt so sick with worry that I couldn't even drink. I knew if I was caught, I'd have no legal rights. They could pretty much do with me what they wanted, for as long as they wanted. There'd be no civil rights lawyer to read the police the riot act on my behalf. I wouldn't just be dealing with a few bent Old Bill trying to give me a hard time; the whole fucking system was in on this one.

The next day I packed my bags and went to the airport with Colin and a few other friends. I checked in for my flight, handed over my luggage and went for a drink in the bar in the hope of steadying my nerves. I kept looking at my emergency passport, that pathetic piece of paper. I thought any official with a spare brain cell was bound to check it out. My 'passport' seemed to grow more laughably, transparently bogus with every second that ticked by.

My time came. Colin was flying home to England in a fortnight: I told him I'd see him either in half an hour – being led back to the cells – or in two weeks' time. We said our goodbyes and I walked off towards passport control. I asked myself if I was walking too fast or too slow. Being normal is easy. Trying to act normal is a nightmare. I didn't know where to look or to put my hands. I stood in the queue, trying vainly to control my sweat glands. Then it was my turn to show my passport. The man at the gate gave it a quick glance – and waved me through. I'd done it. I'd fucking done it. I felt elated. Then more doubts. I wouldn't be safe until the plane had taken off. Surely some Nazi bully-boy could still jump on and do a spot check. I sat shaking in my seat on the plane. I just wanted the 747 to move, to fly off, but it just sat there. I really began to believe they'd checked all the names on the boarding cards and had identified me as a fugitive from justice.

Then the stewardesses shut the doors. Relief.

The plane began to ease itself backwards, away from the terminal. More relief.

It taxied onto the runway and came to a halt. Then the engines began to roar. Finally, my metal bird of freedom accelerated up the runway and zoomed off into the clouds. I knew I was safe. I was going home.

5

OUT OF THE FRYING PAN

THE following day I arrived in Brussels. I didn't fancy making the last leg of my journey by plane, as I believed I had a better chance of slipping unnoticed into England on a ferry. When I say *believed*, I actually mean *hoped*. It was a vain hope, however; a very vain hope, indeed. I couldn't have made myself more conspicuous if I'd have had rabies.

Unlike my fellow foot passengers, each of whom carried at most a rucksack and a few plastic bags of duty free, I was laden with three large suitcases and a bulky sports bag. And, compared with their pale complexions, my skin had been burnt so brown the Afrikaners could have classified me 'black' and allowed Dougie to shoot or hack me to death.

When the official requested a look at my passport, therefore, it came as a disappointment, but not a surprise. My disappointment intensified when I saw Debra at the other side of the barrier. I'd rung her in Brussels and explained my situation. She had agreed to pick me up in her car. We had exchanged a few letters and phone calls since we had last seen each other some weeks earlier. She had been disappointed I hadn't asked her out in Johannesburg – now, she would have to wait even longer for our first date.

The official looked at my A4 piece of paper. 'One moment, sir,' he said, then walked into a nearby office. A few minutes later, he reappeared, accompanied by two men in suits.

'Bernard O'Mahoney?' said one of the detectives.

'That's me,' I said.

'Are you aware there's a warrant out for your arrest?'

'No, there must be some mistake.'

'Make it easy for us, Bernard. You're not going anywhere till we've checked it all out. So do everyone a favour.'

In a cell at Dover police station, Debra and I shared our first kiss. The police had allowed us a few minutes alone together when they'd discovered that she'd driven down from Basildon in Essex. They had also given her permission to take my luggage. And they'd even let me phone my mother. If this decent treatment had continued, I could well have turned into one of those pub bores parroting, 'British justice? Best in the world, mate.'

Within 12 hours, I found myself sitting in a cell beneath Stafford Crown Court, agreeing to a prosecution deal that involved my pleading guilty to 'unlawful wounding' in return for their dropping the 'wounding with intent' charge and others relating to my failure to appear. Later in court the judge told me a custodial sentence was unavoidable. 'You cannot go around Staffordshire beating people up at your leisure, Mr O'Mahoney,' he said. 'You will go to prison for 12 months.'

As a result of my lifelong reluctance to conform, I ended up in six different prisons during the six months I served of the twelve-month sentence. First was Shrewsbury, then Birmingham; after that I went to Ranby in Nottinghamshire. From there, I went to Lincoln, then back to Birmingham and finally Stafford. I hadn't been at Ranby long when they put me in solitary confinement for allegedly trying to escape. It was, of course, nonsense – I'd merely gone for a stroll in an out-of-bounds area – but the screws wouldn't listen. They refused to let me shatter their fantasy. They'd foiled an escape attempt – and not even the truth could be allowed to detract from their achievement.

It was my first experience of solitary. My new apartment suite had been fitted out to minimalist standards. The bedroom consisted of a slab of concrete, the bathroom a plastic bucket. I was permitted the following possessions, although not all at the same time: the prison clothes I stood in (minus shoes) and bedding (pillow, sheet and cover). At night, in order to get the bedding, I had to hand over my clothes. In the morning, I had to exchange the bedding for my clothes. I had nothing to write with or read, not even the Bible, and certainly no telly or radio. You'd have provided more home comforts for a dog. A small, high window made of thick frosted glass ensured I could barely distinguish night from day. The cell had obviously been designed to destroy any traces of humanity remaining in its occupant.

My only human contact – and I'm probably stretching the definition here – was with twisted screws. Mercifully, this didn't last for more than a few minutes each day. I came to understand how silence could sometimes be described as deafening. The dirty beige walls seemed to close in on me. Hearing the jangle of keys would make my heart jump. I'd hope the screws were coming to let me out. And they knew it. One screw used to put his keys in my door, take them out again and laugh.

I didn't want them to think they could get to me, so when I heard them coming, I'd sit cross-legged on the floor with my back to the door. I wouldn't even turn round at meal times, when they'd slide a tray of slop across the floor towards me. It really used to annoy a few of them. 'You think you're fucking clever, don't you, O'Mahoney?' one used to say. 'I bet that when the other kids wanted to play cowboys and Indians at your school, you insisted on being a fucking Mexican!' Eventually, they moved me to HMP Lincoln, back to Birmingham, and finally Stafford, where I returned to normal prison life.

On 8 July 1986, a prison warden unlocked a door in the main gate and I stepped out onto the street.

'See you soon, O'Mahoney. Next time bring a friend,' he said.

I turned to answer, but the door slammed shut in my face.

Striding away from the prison gate towards the station, I was free to think all the philosophical shit you have to think when you come out of an institution: a fresh start, a new beginning, no more trouble. Futile crap, I know, but essential to raise your expectations and give yourself some sort of hope for the future. On the train journey south to Basildon, I sat in silence, staring out of the window, considering my prospects. Debra had been very loyal to me, visiting me in every penal dustbin I'd been sent to. Loyalty is of paramount importance to me; I believed that we would be very happy together.

My first sight of Basildon new town was Laindon station and the Alcatraz Estate, so-called because of the warren of alleyways and Legoland-type flats that it's made up of. I spent an hour walking around identical streets, hopelessly lost, before I finally found Debra's home. I was, to say the least, extremely pleased to see her. Unfortunately, the Home Office do not allow for such feelings. I had to report to my probation officer within one hour of reaching the town. I've had several probation officers in my life, so I know the pointless ritual.

Sit down.

Smile.

'How are you?'

'Fine.'

'How are you feeling?'

'Fine.'

'Do you regret the crime?'

'Every moment of every day.'

'Do you think you'll be in trouble again?'

'Who? Me? Never!'

'Congratulations, Mr O'Mahoney. You've just won your freedom. See you again next month, goodbye.'

Probation, in my humble opinion, is about as much use as tits on a bull.

Coming out of prison and trying to go straight is extremely difficult. Employers tend to shun you and socially you are deemed tainted, or somehow unacceptable. Despite these problems, Debra and I did eventually manage to settle down in what most would consider a 'normal' life. Debra had her own hairdressing business and I used to commute to London every day, where I worked as a heavy-goods vehicle driver.

The estate we lived on was as rough as a bear's arse. Parties would rage on through the night, making sleep impossible. I would leave the house for work at quarter to five in the morning and return at seven in the evening. More often than not, I'd fall asleep on the train on the way home and end up in Southend, having missed my stop. One of our female neighbours would host a party whenever she found a new boyfriend – so I could rely on her disturbing my sleep at least three times a week. The bark of her dog would accompany the pounding music. Revellers would urinate, fornicate, vomit and argue on the stairs outside my front door. Despite my pleadings for a little less late-night noise, the parties continued.

One night, I reached the end of my short tether. Around two in the morning, the sound of a screaming girl involved in an argument tore me from my sleep. I put on a pair of boxer shorts and opened the front door. My neighbour and her latest boyfriend stood in the stairwell trading insults. I walked the few paces over to them and said to the boyfriend, 'I'm not having a debate about it, mate. I get up in two hours. Fuck off now or I'll kill you.' He just grinned at me moronically. The alcohol fumes from both of them could have put me over the drink-driving limit.

I'd had enough. Bang. I chinned him. He flew backwards down the stairs. His girlfriend started screaming. I told her to shut up, closed my door and went back to bed.

A short time later, someone began banging loudly on my front door. I got up again, thinking, 'If it's the boyfriend, he's going over the balcony.' I opened the door to a stern-faced policeman. Several other officers stood in the background with dogs. I could see my neighbour and her boyfriend, the latter bleeding from facial wounds. As soon as he saw me, he shouted, 'That's the cunt! Arrest him!' The officer said he wanted to question me about an alleged assault and threats to kill.

'For fuck's sake, mate,' I said. 'Unlike most of the scum round here, I work for a living. I'm up in less than two hours. How can I not react when these people are pissing, puking, fucking and fighting on my doorstep all night?'

The policeman looked at me in my boxers, then looked at the drunken boyfriend – who'd now begun to scream obscenities – and told me to go to bed. My neighbour soon found herself a new boyfriend. But the partying continued.

In the end, I broke into the offending woman's flat one day when she was out and smashed her stereo to bits, stamped on all her tapes and tried to hurl her snarling dog over the balcony. The hound sensed my hostile intentions, however, and scampered around the flat. It bared its teeth whenever I got near and stayed just out of my grasp. I was making too much noise, so to avoid being caught I abandoned my mission. The dog lived to bark another day, but my neighbour became quieter.

In June 1987, Debra gave birth to our son. I named him after a good friend of mine, an armed robber named Vinney Bingham from Huyton in Liverpool. Our son Vinney brought us a lot of happiness. Our pretty uneventful lives suddenly had meaning. Vinney was our world, a labour of love rather than an unwanted chore, which was what most of the kids on our war-torn estate appeared to be. Two years later, Debra gave birth to our daughter, whom we named Karis. We loved her equally. The Beatles penned a song that claimed money can't buy you love, but it's equally true to say that love doesn't pay your bills or put food on the table. I was working as hard as I could to provide for my family, but I knew that it was not a lifestyle that I could sustain for any period of time.

The stress and strain of travelling to and from London every day and working long hours in between with two small children in the house to greet me when I got home began to tell. All I wanted to do during the eight hours I had free each night was sleep, but with screaming neighbours and howling kids it was impossible. To preserve my sanity and my relationship with Debra, I decided to seek out additional income locally. Through a friend, I was told about a vacancy for a nightclub doorman at a venue called Raquels in Basildon town centre. The day after my 30th birthday, Friday, 16 March 1990, I telephoned the manager of the club and he arranged for me to meet the head doorman the following Wednesday. The bar was fairly quiet when I went in, but I thought it would be the type of venue that would get busy at weekends, as it was an annex of the main club. Revellers usually meet up in such bars before moving on to clubs later in the evening. On a small stage, there was a white grand piano, a memorial to the man who had tried to introduce culture into Basildon. He had called the place 'Strings'. It was done out like a fancy cocktail bar, the clientele were mainly middle-aged heavy drinkers and peroxide blonde Essex girls teetering about on white stiletto shoes. The long-since redundant pianist had been replaced by a DJ who dumped his record decks on the piano lid and wrapped flashing rope lights around the legs. A culture vulture he clearly was not.

I asked the barmaid where I could find Dave Venables, the head doorman. After being subjected to the 'who wants to know?' routine, I was finally introduced to him. Venables was six foot tall, balding and very powerfully built. He told me that he had a partner named Nicky Cook and they ran a couple of clubs and most of the pubs in the Basildon area. Venables looked me over, asked a few questions and then told me I could start work the following weekend. The wages, he said, would be £40 per night, cash in hand.

I remained at the bar for a short while, talking to Venables about things in general. He told me things were not going too well for the local bouncers; I was entering the Basildon nightclub security scene at a time of change following a spate of retirements, deaths and public disorder. A bouncer named McCabe who was once all-powerful had recently died in a road accident and the infamous West Ham United football hooligans, known as the Inter City Firm, had smashed, slashed and stabbed the hardcore of Basildon's doormen at a rave that had been held in the town. Madness had reigned that night, Venables told me. The ICF had come prepared with coshes, hammers, 'squirt' (industrial ammonia), tear gas and knives. The unwitting doormen had nothing to defend themselves with other than their muscle-bound bravado and reputations. They soon lost them both. The ICF rampaged through the hall, hacking, slashing and stamping on the retreating bouncers, whose crime it was to have had one of the ICF members ejected over a trivial remark.

Being a good doorman isn't about going to the gym and throwing your steroid-bloated frame about, it is about diplomacy and trying to understand the psyche of the psychos you encounter. The Basildon bouncers were now learning this valuable lesson. Those who avoided the lecture in the main hall were captured in the car park and given the most brutal of tutorials. They were beaten and their flesh ripped open with Stanley knives; one blood-soaked bouncer was thrown into a lake. It was a miracle nobody died. Many of those who avoided hospital 'retired' immediately from the security industry.

Things had changed. Lager louts with bad attitudes had been replaced by smartly dressed, drugged-up, knife-wielding villains. Commuting to Essex from the East End of London, these crooks wanted to flood the county with the 'love drug' Ecstasy. Disco versus rave, bouncer versus firm member, pints versus pills – they were all on a collision course and, without realising it, I was stepping into the epicentre. I thanked Venables for the job and told him that I would be at the club the following weekend.

That Friday I drove into town looking for what had resembled a trendy bar during daylight – at night it looked like some sort of night shelter for down-and-outs and the clinically insane. Dodgy-looking geezers and even more dodgy-looking girls hung around outside the bar entrance. Like moths, they seemed drawn to the blue neon light that announced, or warned, you were about to enter Strings. I later learned these former customers were barred from entering for a variety of unpleasant offences, but they still turned up every night and huddled beneath the light to spit abuse at customers entering the bar and attack those who objected to the insults.

It's bad enough at the best of times to be surrounded by drunks, but when you're a doorman whose job it is to try and be rational with the fools the experience is even more unpleasant, so on my first night I was pleased to learn that I was going to work in Raquels, the nightclub next door. The only trouble was, I discovered it was there that the real heavy drinkers washed up when the pubs closed, and it was there where most of the trouble occurred.

Venables introduced me to my fellow doormen. Most of them

were there, like me, just for a bit of extra cash. They didn't seem like a proper firm, to me. I wasn't exactly confident of their ability to sort out any major trouble if it came, but I kept my thoughts to myself and started work. About two hours into my shift, a pot-man, the guy who collects the empty glasses, came over to me and said somebody was causing trouble on the dance floor. He pointed to a growling, bearded man who was towering over everybody else in the club. This Neanderthal giant was squeezing a man's throat and showering him in phlegm whilst threatening him.

I went over to the bearded man and said, 'Leave it out, mate, or you'll have to go.'

'It's all right, I know the score, I'm a doorman,' he replied.

'It's not all right,' I replied, 'and if you are a doorman and you do know the score, then you will leave it out. If you wish to fight that guy, you will have to do so outside.'

He let go of the man and started walking down the stairs, with me following him. We went down one flight of stairs and he stopped at the cloakroom and began talking to a female – I assumed it was either his wife or girlfriend. I was insistent. 'I'm sorry, you've got to leave,' I said.

'Who the fuck are you, anyway?' the man shouted. 'No fucking Northerner tells me what to do.'

I grabbed the man in a headlock and tried to force him down the stairs. He struggled and so I began to punch him in the throat and face. His sheer size sent us both crashing to the floor and we both rolled down the stairs. When we reached the bottom, the female who was with him hit me across the nose with a champagne glass, then took off her high-heeled shoe and began beating me across the head with it. I must admit I felt overwhelmingly relieved when we crashed through the doors into the club reception area. I knew five or six of my fellow doormen were on duty there and it would only be a matter of time before they came to my aid. But amidst the flying fists and the pecking stiletto heel, I looked up to see Venables' partner Nicky Cook laughing at me. I remember wondering, why the fuck aren't the other doormen helping me fight this not-so-jolly giant? After what seemed an age they did intervene and the man and his female friend left the club shouting and threatening reprisals. I was absolutely livid.

'What the fuck do you think you're doing?' I shouted at the other door staff. 'Do you work on your own here or what?'

Cook calmly explained to me that the man I had been fighting with was a member of the door team, but it was his night off. It wasn't the best impression I've made on my first day in a new job, but it certainly didn't do my reputation any harm.

Raquels was a very violent club. I would expect to be involved in at least two fights each night I worked there. However, it wasn't all doom and gloom. One evening the manager had booked a fire-eater to perform a stage show. When he arrived, the fire-eater was clearly drunk and unsteady on his feet. During the show, he tipped flammable fluid into his mouth and blew out a large cloud of fire into the air. Because the man was intoxicated, he unwittingly spilled some of the flammable fluid down his chin and chest and so the next time he wafted the flame around his body he burst into flames. Waving his arms frantically, he fell off the stage backwards into a large pair of velvet curtains that were also then engulfed by the flames. The club's fire alarm was activated and the door staff were dispatched to tackle the fires, which they soon stamped out. Sitting smouldering in the office later, the entertainer almost wept with pain as he nursed his broken ribs and nose with his badly burnt hands. 'Fucking hell, lads,' he whined. 'You surely didn't have to stamp that hard on me to put the flames out?'

One Saturday night, I was working on the door at Raquels with a man named Larry Johnston. He was one of the few doormen I felt safe working with. If a fight broke out, I knew instinctively that Larry would be alongside me in the thick of it. The problem with Larry was he always had to go the extra mile. When the fight was over, he couldn't resist one last spiteful kick, or stamping on one of the bruised and bloodied bodies that lay motionless on the floor. I was convinced that one day Larry's over-enthusiasm for the job would result in somebody's death.

On this particular evening, a group of men who had left the club minutes earlier approached the door and asked to be readmitted. The club was due to close and so I told them that wouldn't be possible. The men were very drunk and became abusive. I wasn't particularly bothered because if you work on the door you endure that kind of nonsense all the time. You have to accept it goes with the territory. I stood watching them in silence. People were standing around listening to the men giving me abuse and it wasn't doing much for the team's image, so I thought the best thing to do would be to go inside and close the door for a while.

I was hoping they would grow tired of their juvenile name-calling and walk away, but they seemed to be getting more and more hyped up. As soon as I'd gone inside, the men, obviously getting braver because of my lack of response, had started kicking and banging on the door. Larry smiled, pushed the door open and we both ran outside.

The men began to run. Neither Larry nor myself were built for jogging around Basildon town centre, so we stopped and stood in the road. The fleeing men, who had been desperate for a fight moments earlier, also stopped running and stood facing us several yards away. They started shouting, calling us wankers and chanting, 'Kill the fucking bouncers! Kill the fucking bouncers!' Rather surprisingly – or unsurprisingly in Basildon – they were joined by several other men from a nearby burger van queue. This group, who had no grievance with us whatsoever, began to hurl pallets and iron poles that were used to make up the market stalls that stood adjacent to the club. Bottles, stones and anything else the men could lay their hands on rained down on us. It was pretty pointless standing there waiting for their aim to improve, so Larry and I went back into the club and closed the doors.

Whenever a fight broke out in the club, either bar staff, the DJ or those in the reception area activated an alarm. A light on the DJ's console would tell him which alarm button had been struck, so he could then announce over the PA system 'Door to reception' or 'Door' to wherever. Nine times out of ten, it was 'Door to the dance floor' because a jealous boyfriend was attacking somebody who had dared to look at his girlfriend. In this instance, it was 'Door to foyer'. When the other doormen arrived, the siren was blaring and the blue emergency light on the ceiling was flashing.

There were eight of us in total. Everyone armed themselves, some with pickaxe handles and washing-up bottles filled with industrial ammonia – family size, of course. Others chose smaller weapons, such as knuckle-dusters or coshes, which were easier to conceal should the police turn up. I had a sheath knife I always carried and an Irish hurling stick, which is a bit like a hockey stick but with a broader striking area. I always found it particularly useful when dispersing crowds. When everybody was ready, we opened the door and ran back into the street. One of the men ran towards us, screaming hysterically, carrying an iron bar. I swung the hurling stick, bringing it crashing down across the top of his head. He lay on the floor where he fell, bleeding but motionless. Larry ran over and kicked the man in the head and body several times. This spiteful act incited the crowd and they ran at us. Within minutes, the street had turned into a battleground strewn with debris and bodies. Unbeknown to me at the time, there were actually three separate groups fighting. The men who had asked to re-enter the club wanted to do so in order to fight another group of men who had assaulted one of their friends earlier. When the alleged assailants had walked out of the club at closing time and into the disturbance in the street, the group to whom we had originally refused entry had attacked them. The third group was made up of bystanders from the burger van queue who had joined in for the hell of it.

We didn't know who was who and so we resorted to hitting everybody who appeared to be involved in the fighting. Within a few minutes, the police arrived on the scene, but rather than restore order their presence seemed to make matters worse. The crowd backed off at first but then re-grouped and started throwing missiles again. The baying mob was now about 100 strong, their number having been swelled by revellers turning out of a nearby club and people queuing for taxis.

Nobody could see much point in standing in the street being used as target practice, so, along with the police, we retreated into the club foyer to await reinforcements. As we did so, two officers stumbled on a wooden pallet that had been thrown into the middle of the road and the crowd charged. Soon they were surrounded, being kicked and struck with weapons. Their colleagues inside the foyer asked us to help them, so we all went outside and managed to retrieve the two officers from the crowd. It wasn't long before police reinforcements arrived, their blue flashing lights and wailing sirens creating panic among the crowd, which dispersed in all directions.

'You'd better lose that,' one of the officers said. I still had the blood-stained hurling stick in my hand. I wasn't surprised he had chosen to advise me rather than arrest me, as it had been an extremely dangerous situation we had faced together; the officers who had fallen could easily have died.

On Monday, the *Basildon Evening Echo* published a story about the incident headlined 'Policeman Injured as Youths Fight'. It read:

A policeman was taken to hospital after a disturbance outside a nightclub in Basildon. Acting Inspector Ian Frazer was injured when youths turned on police as they tried to break up a string of fights in the town square near Raquels disco. Scuffles broke out among 100 people at 2.15 a.m. yesterday and back-up police crews were called from Basildon, Billericay, Wickford, Southend and Grays. Mr Frazer was treated in Basildon hospital for cuts and bruises but not held overnight. A man charged with assault is due before magistrates today.

It was not an exceptionally violent incident for Raquels. The lunatics who got drunk out of their tiny minds in there thought nothing of stabbing, cutting, glassing or even shooting those who displeased them. I can recall one unfortunate man who was out on his stag night being pushed into a fire exit, where he was repeatedly slashed with a Stanley knife. His crime? He had unwittingly shown a local idiot 'disrespect' by accidentally bumping into him. The would-be groom needed 160 stitches – a lesson in 'respect' he will undoubtedly never forget.

Once I had settled in at Raquels, it became quite clear to me that things were not running the way they should be. It was as if a handful of local hard men were running the club and not the doormen. Local men with reputations would fight in the club and the following evening they would be allowed in – because, as the other doormen would say, 'It's not worth the trouble.' The doormen were worried about barring one of the local hard men who regularly caused trouble, believing £40 a night simply wasn't enough to invite trouble into their everyday lives and the lives of their families. I was of the opinion that if you were going to do a job, then you should do it properly, and if these people wanted trouble, then they could fucking have it.

I liked Dave Venables – we became good friends – but I could never understand why he tolerated the local people who took liberties with him. One brief war to put them in their place was surely preferable to entertaining trouble each and every weekend.

By January 1992, I had reached the end of my tether with many of the local hard men and had become more vocal about the need to deal with them.

One of the pubs that Venables and Cook provided security for was called the Bullseye. One evening Venables received a telephone call to report that a man named Shaun Dunbar had been asked to leave the premises by the manager but had refused. He rang me and several other doormen and we all raced towards the pub. Let's put one thing straight here: none of us considered Dunbar to be a threat. It was a different story for the Bullseye's clientele, however. Located in Basildon market, the pub attracted the desperate, the deranged and the mentally unstable. When things kicked off in the Bullseye, you did well to walk away unscathed.

When we arrived, there was a scuffle with Dunbar, as he tried to resist being ejected. Doorman Tim Whidlake punched him – the single blow broke Dunbar's jaw. He was deposited on the pavement still out cold and we all went our separate ways. The following evening, while Tim and another doorman, Ronnie Downes, were working in the Bullseye, a local man who had taken exception to what had happened to Dunbar walked into the pub carrying a plumber's bag. He put it down by the bar, ordered a drink and sipped it silently. A few minutes later, six other men entered the pub, ordered drinks and sat at various tables. Downes and Whidlake didn't think anything untoward and carried on chatting at the door adjacent to the bar. All of a sudden, the man with the plumber's bag stood up and called out to the others in the bar to attack the doormen. As they passed him to advance on Downes and Whidlake, the man opened his bag and handed each of them a machete. Whidlake knew he was going to suffer a severe injury or die and so he turned and fled; Downes, foolishly but to his credit, stood his ground. Suffice to say, he suffered terrible injuries, but he remained on his feet throughout the battle.

Once more, Venables' door staff were summoned to attend the Bullseye. When I arrived, I was of the opinion that we should go after those responsible and sort it out there and then, but Venables suggested that we should sort it out later. I really felt that it was the wrong way to handle the situation.

The following evening a man named Les Murphy came into Raquels. Venables claimed that he was one of the men responsible for the attack on Downes and Whidlake. I wanted to attack Murphy straight away, but again Venables insisted that I should refrain from doing so. I wasn't prepared to work in a place where the customers could cut you up and drink in there the following day as if nothing had happened. I watched Murphy until he went into the toilets and then I told Whidlake to confront him as he walked out.

'Downes got cut up for you, so it's down to you to sort Murphy out,' I said. As Murphy walked out of the toilets, Whidlake told him to leave. Picking up a glass ashtray from the bar, Murphy replied, 'The only cunt who's leaving here is you.'

Somebody – I don't know who – squirted industrial ammonia at Murphy, hitting him in the eyes. He screamed, clutching his face, and fell against the bar. He was then hit over the head with a five-litre water jug, kicked and beaten. He suffered head injuries and, we later learned, was permanently blinded in one eye. The incident confirmed what I had always believed: combating violence with violence was the only way to maintain complete control of the club.

Nicky Cook quit immediately after the incident. He had had enough of trouble on the doors and went to work on his father's farm. Cook is one of the most able fighters that I have known. One minute somebody would have their hand raised at him, the next they would be lying on the pavement out cold. Venables had relied on Cook's reputation a lot over the years and with him off the scene cracks began to appear in his confidence. Incidents at Raquels became more frequent and more serious. One man who refused to be searched returned to the club and petrol-bombed the front doors.

Jason Riley, a local man and a friend of mine, put a gun to someone's head on the dance floor. The management barred him when the customer said he was going to the police. (To help him out, I told the manager Jason had been to a fancy dress party earlier that night as a German soldier and that the firearm had been an imitation – but he was not fooled. In fact, this particular gun belonged to a member of Raquels door staff. Jason had ordered it but had still not paid for it, although it remained in his possession.)

The next week Jason came back to the club and asked if he could come in. We explained the situation to him regarding the management and suggested he go over to Time, another local disco, for a couple of weeks until things died down. Jason agreed and left with a friend, Simon Wally.

Jason and Simon were in Time later that evening when a girl accused Jason of pinching her backside. He vehemently denied that he was responsible, but the girl didn't believe him and complained to a male friend. He marched over and punched Jason in the face.

Jason fought back, but soon the doormen were on the scene, pulling the men apart. Jason was duly ejected. Naturally, he was livid because he felt that he had done nothing wrong. He threatened the doormen and the man who had attacked him and vowed, 'I'll be back.' It's a phrase people who work on the door hear at least once a week; few take any notice of it, but everybody should.

Jason jumped into a taxi and told the driver to take him home. He was out of control. Simon joined him in the taxi to try and calm him down. When the taxi arrived at Jason's home, he told the driver to wait before disappearing inside. He returned with a gun in his pocket. Simon was telling him to calm down, but he kept saying that he was going to 'shoot the bastards'. Jason shouldn't have said what he did in front of the cab driver, and he should have listened to Simon, but he had abandoned common sense. Jason went back to Time, walked up to the front doors and into the reception area. Those who had assaulted him were still there, talking to the bouncers. Jason pulled out his gun and opened fire. One man was hit in the ankle; another, who put his hand up to protect himself, was hit by a bullet in his wrist, which exited through his elbow.

I got a phone call at Raquels shortly afterwards and was told what had happened. I had a flat in London and, because one of the door staff owned the gun with which Jason had committed the crime, I thought I should help.

Venables and I went over to Time. Everybody was saying it was Jason Riley who had shot the two men. I rang Jason's girlfriend and told her to tell him to stay wherever he was and we would be in touch. When Raquels closed that night, Venables and I met Simon Wally and Jason's girlfriend outside a pub not far from Jason's house. I told Simon that he should go to Jason and tell him to meet me nearby at an agreed time. I would take him to my brother's flat in South London. On the way, we could dispose of the gun and wait until the dust had settled. He would then be in a far better position to offer a defence if and when the police caught up with him.

At that time, we were the only people who knew where Jason was. Shortly afterwards Venables said he had to go home and so he left us. I went to the agreed meeting place to pick Jason up, but he never arrived. Nobody knows how the police knew where to find him, but armed officers stormed the house where he was hiding and he was arrested. Jason's friends believed it was Venables who had told the police where he was. It may, of course, have been a calculated guess by the police. Nobody will ever know. Jason was later sentenced to twelve years' imprisonment for two attempted murders and firearms offences.

Venables used to work at Epping Forest Country Club on Wednesdays. The venue, once owned by football legend Bobby Moore, was a magnet for celebrities. For whatever reason, Venables announced that he no longer wished to work there and so he asked me if I would take his place. It was whilst working at Epping that I first met Dave Done, a fanatical bodybuilder from Romford. We got on very well and, shortly after being introduced, he came to work at Raquels.

They began to play house and rave music on Sundays at Epping, which proved to be extremely popular. It meant more staff were needed and so I was asked to work Sunday nights as well. Many of the door and bar staff who worked Friday and Saturday nights in East London and Essex used to go to Epping on Sundays, so it wasn't long before I got to know many people involved in clubland throughout the capital. One of them was called Tony Tucker.

An up-and-coming face in the Essex underworld, Tucker ran a very well-organised, well-respected door firm that supplied security at clubs in Essex, Suffolk and London. He was a very abrupt and rude man to those whom he deemed below him – and that was most people. If somebody he didn't know tried to strike up a conversation with him, Tucker would glare at them as if they were mad or stupid.

One evening while working at Club UK in Wandsworth, South London, Tucker confronted a group of black doormen. They were meant to be working with him but had congregated for a chat on a stairwell that led to the fire exit. Never unsure of himself, Tucker began shouting abuse at them, calling them useless and lazy. One of the guys objected, pulled out a CS gas canister and sprayed Tucker with it in the face. The group then pounced on him and beat Tucker senseless before leaving via the fire exit. The following night, Tucker arrived at Epping, seeking help from everybody he knew; he was ranting and raving that he wanted bloody revenge. He asked me to accompany him – I suppose that was the nod that started our close friendship. Despite working with the men and knowing they were from Brixton, Tucker never did find the doormen who had beaten him up. Some said he wasn't keen on looking too hard, just in case he tracked them down. Despite his reputation, many close to Tucker considered him to be no more than a bully and a coward. I wouldn't have agreed at the time, but my views did change.

Tucker had warned me about Dave Done. He claimed that he was unreliable, but I told him that I preferred to judge people myself. That doesn't mean I ignored Tucker's advice; I scrutinised Done whilst he was working, but he always seemed to be on the ball. After a few weeks, however, Done started arriving late for work or leaving early, relying on our friendship to ensure no questions were asked. If they were, I would make excuses for him.

My colleague Larry Johnston took exception to the favours being bestowed upon Done and started making comments about him being a 'part-time doorman on a full-time doorman's pay'. The atmosphere between the two became quite hostile. One evening as Done prepared to leave early, Larry asked if he would give him a lift home. Done said he couldn't, he was going the opposite way, so Larry kicked the door panel of his car. Done jumped out of his vehicle and started shouting. Larry responded by pulling out a knife. I couldn't believe how quickly the situation was escalating. I asked Larry to put the knife away, but he told me to fuck off and keep out of it. I see very little or no point in holding talks with deranged men wielding knives, so I took out my bottle of industrial ammonia and squirted him in the face. Larry was temporarily blinded and then permanently sacked. David Done remained.

I was annoyed we had fallen out because I liked Larry, but what choice did I have? I couldn't stand by and watch a friend kill another friend. Larry was an extremely dangerous individual, more than capable of doing the deed. Three years later he took exception to a doorman's attitude after being refused entry to a pub in Romford and stabbed him to death. He is currently serving a life sentence for murder.

David Done's obsession with bodybuilding resulted in him having a serious problem with steroids. His addiction to these performance-enhancing drugs meant he was always short of money. He had even had to resort to being a pizza delivery boy to help finance his drug craving. He refused to listen to reason and his addiction began to affect his judgement.

One Monday morning, Done rang me up and told me that he had been sacked from Epping for allegedly selling drugs. I knew this was false – Done had nothing to do with drug dealing. I said I would pick him up and we would go and see Joe, the head doorman, to see if we could sort matters out.

When we arrived, I asked Joe who had told him Done was dealing. He said the club had received an anonymous telephone call. I got quite annoyed and reasoned that if the person who alleged Done was a dealer didn't do it openly and with some evidence to back up his claim, then he shouldn't be believed. Eventually, Joe relented and Done got his job back. That evening, I received a phone call from Venables, who said the management at Epping wanted me to be sacked instead of Done. No reason had been given. What particularly annoyed me was that now I had been sacked, Done refused to stand by me. He said that he needed the money – the fact I'd lost my job was unfortunate, but there was nothing he could do. I was livid, and my friendship with Done became at best strained.

Done worked at the Ministry of Sound in South London occasionally and, in an effort to patch up our friendship, he got me a job there to replace the nights I had lost at Epping. The Ministry door team were a powerful and feared firm: nearly every man was capable of extreme violence.

Done was a good friend of Carlton Leach, a former football hooligan. Leach had once been the head doorman at the Ministry of Sound, but he had recently been sacked and his door team removed from the club. Two brothers from South London, Tony and Peter Simms, had taken over and there was immediate conflict between Leach and the brothers. I asked Done if Leach minded us working for Tony and Peter because I felt our loyalty lay with him – he was, after all, Done's friend and a good friend of Tucker's. Done said he had discussed it with Leach and he was fine with us continuing to work there.

A few days later, I learned that Done had lied to me. When he had approached Leach about continuing to work at the Ministry, he had been told that it would be appreciated if he left. When Done had explained that he needed the money, Leach told him he would pay his wages not to work there. Done decided he would take money from both the Simms brothers and Leach. I told Done I wanted nothing more to do with his deception, so we ended up falling out once more.

I was still seeing a fair bit of Tony Tucker. He asked me what the problem was between Done and I, so I told him. Tucker was incensed; he said he was going to go to the Ministry and stab Done. I told him Done wasn't worth it, so instead Tucker simply informed Leach that Done had been taking wages from him and the Simms brothers. When he was confronted, Done denied the allegation and slagged me off, claiming that I was a liar and had been trying to cause trouble. I rang Done up and taped the conversation to prove that not only had he taken the money from Leach and the Simms brothers, but also the things he had said about me to cause trouble were untrue.

Around the same time, an article appeared in the *News of the World* about two doormen who had worked at the Ministry of Sound – Mark Rothermel and a South African named Chris Raal. Rothermel had left the Ministry long before I had started work at the club and until I had read the *News of the World* article I had never heard of him, but Raal was still there, working alongside Done and me. Raal was on the run from the South African police after it was alleged he had shot dead a nightclub manager in Johannesburg. The Ministry of Sound had at that time won one of its many awards and the article was making a big issue about men with violent pasts being employed there.

In November 1989, Mark Rothermel had been imprisoned for assisting in the disposal of a body. He had been working at Hollywood's in Romford – one of Tony Tucker's doors – with another man, Pierre St Ange. Pierre and Rothermel had got into a dispute with a DJ there named Bernie Burns. They had lured him to a flat in Ilford, where Burns had been strangled. His body was wrapped in a blanket, put in the boot of a car and taken to a quiet wood near Chelmsford. It was there that Rothermel took an axe to the man's body; he hacked off the head and both of his hands, so it would be difficult to identify. Rothermel was reported to have told a friend, 'The hands came off easily, but the head was more of a problem because of the veins in his neck.' Burns was buried in a shallow woodland grave; his head and his hands have never been recovered. Police found the mutilated corpse after a tip-off and arrested Rothermel at the same time; he was hiding in a pond, up to his neck in water, near the grave. Rothermel was found not guilty of murder and not guilty of manslaughter; he received six years for disposing of the corpse. Pierre St Ange was found not guilty of murder but was sentenced to ten years for manslaughter.

At first, people blamed Carlton Leach for tipping off the newspaper about Rothermel and Raal's association with the Ministry of Sound – the Simms brothers thought Leach might have been trying to discredit their door team. Meanwhile, Done was telling people that it was me who had gone to the newspaper. I felt it was a childish and dangerous thing for him to have done; Rothermel and Raal were no fools and were obviously extremely dangerous men.

I was initially unaware of what Done had been saying, but the next time I worked at the Ministry of Sound it was apparent something was not quite right. Raal was unusually abrupt with me and you could have cut the atmosphere with a knife. However, it soon became clear that it wasn't the atmosphere that certain people wanted to cut. I immediately guessed I was under suspicion concerning the *News of the World* article and was pretty sure who had planted the seeds of uncertainty in people's minds. I went out to the front door and asked Done what the fuck was going on. He looked at me rather sheepishly, but said nothing. I could tell by his manner that whatever was going on, he was behind it. Despite the atmosphere, nobody accused me of anything, so I decided to sit it out and see what developed. I worked until the end of the night and then left as normal.

The following day I rang Tony Tucker, since he knew all of the characters involved; both Rothermel and Raal had worked for him. I told him what had gone on. I said there was only one way to sort things out: ring Leach, ring Rothermel, ring Raal, ring Done and arrange a meeting. A 'meeting' is not a democratic discussion; it's where each person says his piece and whoever is not believed does not get to leave the room under his own steam. Later that day Tucker rang me and said the meeting was on for the following morning. It was to be held in a Portakabin at a car front in Essex.

I was ready to leave for the meeting the next morning when Tucker rang and said it had been called off – they had been unable to get hold of Done. Another meeting was arranged and this time they had been able to contact Done, but then he said he didn't wish to attend. The matter, I was told, was therefore closed. I found it hard to contain my anger. This had all started because I had suggested Done should show some loyalty to his 'friend' Leach. As a result of that, people had been plotting to attack me for no reason and now I was being told to forget it. I decided I *would* forget it and carry on working for the Simms brothers; if people didn't like it, it was their problem. I have not seen or spoken to Done since.

One night while working at the Ministry of Sound, I hit a man in the face with a lead cosh. He had been threatening another doorman and me: we had refused him entry because he was drunk. We had politely asked him to go away several times, but our good-natured requests had fallen on deaf ears. Eventually, we told the man, 'Fuck off – or else.' His response was to step forward with a raised fist. Smack! The sound of the lead cosh making contact with the man's jaw and cheekbone echoed all around us. I knew something had broken in his face; I knew I had hurt him. Then he fell motionless to the ground. Ronnie, another doorman, advised me to disappear. The following day Peter Simms rang me and said that the man had suffered a broken jaw and a fractured eye socket. 'Management would prefer it if you didn't return,' he said. Peter and his brother Tony are decent men and had been good to me; I didn't want to repay them with grief, so I said I understood.

Back in Basildon, Raquels continued to be a cauldron of trouble which would simmer then boil over every night without fail. Trouble came not only from the customers but also increasingly from those I worked with. Venables seemed to be losing more and more confidence.

A local doorman called Paul Trehern, who used to work with us, announced that he was getting married and planned to take 30 other doormen from various clubs into Raquels for a drink. He was considerate enough to tell us that he would be having his stag night there, but I told Venables that he should explain to Trehern that there would only be four or five of us working and it would be inconceivable for us to control thirty door staff. We would expect Trehern to supervise his own friends, in which case they would be most welcome at the club. Venables, however, discussed it with the management and together they decided that Trehern and his friends would not be allowed in. I thought it was ridiculous.

On the night of Trehern's stag party, he and his friends arrived at the club and were quite rightly disgusted to learn that they were barred. Trehern ended up grappling on the floor with Venables, but he and his friends were eventually allowed in. Apart from the scuffle with Venables, the stag party behaved exemplarily. I was embarrassed to be working with doormen who turned other doormen away for no reason whatsoever, particularly doormen who had worked with us.

The following night Venables didn't come into work. He knew I had the serious hump with him. That night Dave Godding, a good friend of Venables, and a man named Joe were involved in a fracas in Strings. Joe hit a man and dislocated his arm, and Godding insisted that an ambulance be called. I refused because if an ambulance is called, the police get involved as well. Godding went behind my back and rang 999. He said he was also going to ring Venables. I went berserk and told him what I thought of Venables. Godding got nervous and left the premises at about 1 a.m.

The next day the manager of Raquels asked me to call in and see him. He told me Venables had resigned that morning because, he said, he didn't think he could work with me any longer. He offered me the security contract at the club and I accepted it on the condition that the door would be run my way. The manager shook my hand and said he didn't have a problem with that. Before I'd arrived at the club, people had taken liberties all the time: I decided to use excessive violence to combat violence. By doing so, I thought that I would reduce the amount of trouble: people would think twice about starting anything in the club. It's easy to say with hindsight, but I should have realised that excess would eventually be met with excess.

6

MONSTERS INC.

AWAY from Raquels, I led a far from orthodox life. Rather than watch the news and tut when I heard of a tragedy, or say how terrible the world was, I tried, where possible, to physically assist, if I were able. I have no intention to blow my own trumpet, or attempt to make out that I am some sort of saint, but people are not one-dimensional and even I have some good traits.

To this day, if I read in my local newspaper that an elderly person has been mugged and lost £70, for instance, I will give him £100. I have never embarrassed the victim by handing the money over personally; I donate it via the newspaper that reported the story. I once met a gentleman in a pub who told me that his father had died in a Japanese prisoner-of-war camp. His father was buried in the Far East, but he had never been able to afford to visit his grave. The Royal British Legion organises subsidised trips for bereaved families to visit the graves of fallen soldiers and the man said he was saving hard to go on one, so I walked out of the pub, into a bank and withdrew £500. When I gave it to the man, he wept. Several months later his grandson contacted me and showed me an album of photographs, proving his grandfather had used the money to visit his father's grave. I said it wasn't necessary, but he said his grandfather had worried that I might have thought I had been conned. I explained I hadn't doubted the man's story for a second, which is why I felt compelled to help him. It's the way I am, and I'm proud of the fact.

Some people feel strongly about global warming, the war in Afghanistan or the government's legislation concerning student loans. Me, I loathe the sub-humans who harm innocent women and children or the elderly. I don't need an overpaid psychiatrist to tell me that my strong feelings are probably the result of my own experiences at the hands of my psychotic father. I have never understood why he – or anybody, in fact – would feel the need to harm a woman or child. Some abusers use the excuse that they had a shit childhood, but surely that should strengthen their resolve not to put their loved ones through a similar nightmarish experience. I think that if a man's children have a better childhood or life than he has had, then his life has been worth living. If not, then he has failed. We are, after all, here to advance the human race, aren't we?

Given my staunch views, it is rather surprising that I found myself befriending a monster who had murdered thirteen women and attacked a further seven. It's impossible to gauge how many children the Yorkshire Ripper's murderous campaign affected, but I have no doubt many of his victims were mothers. The winding road that led me to write to Peter Sutcliffe began in Johannesburg. A ten-year-old boy named James Fallon was struck by a car that had been taken by an unlicensed driver without the permission of the owner. James suffered horrific injuries. He was totally paralysed and couldn't breathe without the aid of a ventilator. The Fallon family had lived in Codsall, where I had grown up, but they had emigrated to South Africa in the mid-1980s. In a country with no free National Health Service, the Fallons had struggled to afford the specialist medical attention James needed. Their plight was reported in a local newspaper and, after reading it, I decided that I would try to help. I wrote approximately 120 letters to football clubs, celebrities and anybody else I thought might send me something I could auction in order to raise money for James. The Rolling Stones, Tina Turner, The Who and U2 all sent signed records. Arsenal, Manchester United, Wolverhampton Wanderers and West Ham United sent signed footballs and shirts. The most surprising response came from two prisoners, Ronald and Reginald Kray. During the 1960s, the Kray brothers controlled the criminal underworld in London's East End. In 1969, they were convicted of two murders and sentenced to life imprisonment, with a recommendation that they serve at least thirty years. Reggie had telephoned me to say he and his twin brother Ronnie had been touched by James's plight and wished to help. With the Krays' assistance, I organised a boxing event. Sadly, James passed away just a few days before it was to be held. It was decided that the boxing show would go ahead and any money raised would be given to the Fallon family.

I became firm friends with the Krays during our efforts to assist

James and I would visit them regularly. Ronnie Kray was being held at Broadmoor hospital for the criminally insane. Peter Sutcliffe was held on the same ward as Ronnie and he would often sit at an adjacent table in the visiting room. One morning I received a telephone call from a man who introduced himself as Gary Jones. He said that he was the chief crime reporter at the *News of the World* and he wanted to know if I could help him with a story he was working on, concerning a spate of gangland murders. I had been involved in numerous violent incidents since moving to Essex but certainly no murders. Jones told me that he didn't really wish to discuss matters on the telephone and suggested we meet. I was curious why anybody would think that I could help them in relation to a spate of murders, so I agreed.

I met Jones at the Tower Bridge Hotel, which is adjacent to the famous landmark that shares its name. After a brief conversation, it soon became apparent to Jones that I could not help him with his enquiries, but rather than head straight back home we had lunch. I recognised Jones from a recent television programme I'd watched called *Hard News*. The programme had questioned the methods he had used to infiltrate a gang of vile paedophiles he was trying to expose. I told him I thought the programme was a joke and that any method was worthy if it stopped that type of sub-human from harming children. As we were talking about children, I mentioned what I was trying to achieve for James Fallon and the fact that the Kray brothers were assisting me. I also mentioned that I often visited Ronnie Kray at Broadmoor hospital. Jones suddenly became very interested in what I had to say. He wanted to know if I ever saw the Yorkshire Ripper, or if I ever heard of anything that he was up to. He explained that the *News of the World* were planning to publish a feature on Sutcliffe and his crimes and so were trying to gather as much fresh information on him as possible. I told Jones I often saw the Ripper in the visiting room, but apart from Ronnie making the odd rude remark about him he was never acknowledged. I suggested that if Jones wanted to find out what the Ripper was up to, he should ask him.

'Yeah right,' Jones laughed. 'I can see Peter Sutcliffe giving the *News of the World* an interview.' I felt a little embarrassed – it was a rather naive remark.

I tried to save face by saying I had meant something completely different. 'I didn't mean he would sit down and answer your questions personally, but if you wrote and befriended him, I bet he would answer them in a letter.' I don't know what made me say it, it just came out, but it suddenly made sense. The Kray brothers wrote to me, why wouldn't the Ripper? Jones remained sceptical and so, in order to prove a point, I said I would write to the Ripper myself. Jones assured me that if I were successful, the *News of the World* would pay handsomely for any letters I received.

On the way home, I began to think about what I had talked myself into. Being wrong isn't something I enjoy, so I wanted to prove to Jones that I could pull it off. I wanted to show him that I was right. It was true the Krays had written to me without knowing who I was, but they had replied for James's benefit not mine. What cause or type of person would make a man who had murdered 13 women want to respond? What could I possibly say that would be of interest to him? Bernard O'Mahoney, a scar-faced thirty-something-year-old burly bouncer would hardly appeal to him. Sutcliffe, I imagined, would warm to a meek, vulnerable, obedient little woman who knew her place. The thought of such a woman admiring him in spite of the awful crimes he had committed would surely massage his ego. I began to believe I could achieve my aim. I would write to Sutcliffe posing as a female. On that journey home, barmaid Belinda Cannon was born.

In my first letter, I told Sutcliffe I had wanted to write to him for a very long time, but I hadn't been able to pluck up the courage to do so. I had been living at home with my father, 'an overpowering man who wants to run every aspect of my life'. I didn't have the nerve to tell my father how I felt, so I changed jobs just so I had an excuse to move away to another area. Now I was free of him and had my own address, I could write without worrying about anybody seeing the letters. I told Sutcliffe that I remembered the hysteria that had followed his arrest, trial and conviction and I had always wondered what sort of man he really was. To me, he had always looked handsome and kind, certainly not the ogre the media had portrayed.

Five days later, the Ripper replied.

I telephoned Gary Jones. He was surprised that the Ripper had not only replied, but had also talked openly about his past, the present and his hopes for the future. We agreed that I would keep the correspondence going and see just how much the Yorkshire Ripper would reveal about his crimes. Over the next 12 months, I exchanged more than 80 letters with Sutcliffe, during which he talked openly about the murders and what had led him to committing them. He also talked about his life, his family and everything from his favourite football team to his favourite music and colour. Sutcliffe asked his imaginary friend if he could telephone her and so the *News of the World* supplied a female reporter to take the calls, which were recorded. I reached a point where there was little else I could ask Sutcliffe, so I concluded that the correspondence had run its course. I gave the letters to Gary Jones for use in the proposed *News of the World* feature on Sutcliffe. Unbeknown to me, however, a *News of the World* journalist named Barbara Jones had befriended Sutcliffe's wife Sonia and subsequently wrote a book called *Voices from an Evil God* based on what she had learnt. Instead of using Sutcliffe's letters for the feature, the *News of the World* decided instead to serialise Barbara Jones's book. Naive to the workings of the newspaper world, I asked Gary what I should do with the letters; he advised me that most, if not all, of the tabloid newspapers would be interested in purchasing them. The first newspaper I called was the *Sunday People*, who immediately offered to pay £4,000 for the letters. It didn't seem a bad return for a bit of stationery and a few stamps, so I said I would accept their offer. I was asked to produce my passport as identification for 'payment purposes'. I was also asked if I could provide a girl who would be prepared to pose as 'Belinda' so they could put her photo alongside the Ripper's letters to 'spice the article up'. I told the journalist that no woman would want her picture alongside the Ripper correspondence and therefore he was wasting his time. 'Don't worry about her being identified,' he said. 'She can wear a wig, heavy make-up, whatever. We don't mind.'

My brother Michael and his girlfriend Carol were visiting London at the time and so I suggested splitting the £4,000 with them if Carol was prepared to stand in as Belinda. None of us was taking the task in hand seriously; in fact, we all thought it was a bit of a laugh that would earn both parties a couple of grand. We went to Camden Town and bought Carol the kind of wig that would look out of place on a clown, never mind 'Belinda, the bubbly barmaid'. Michael and I reassured Carol through outbursts of uncontrollable laughter that she looked absolutely fine. Carol is most definitely not the type of girl one could call brazen, brash or forward; in fact, she is quite shy, so it was obvious to Michael and I that her heart wasn't in it, but we persisted and eventually Carol agreed. We bought hairclips, a hairband and a dodgy plastic hairbrush in the hope we could turn the cheap wig, which resembled an ongoing catfight, into a presentable hairdo. Michael and I ended up crying with laughter. Carol, too, was reduced to tears when she saw herself in the mirror.

After much persuasion, we eventually managed to bundle Carol through the doors of the newspaper offices, where the journalist greeted us. When we all sat down, he asked Carol for her real name. I immediately sensed something was wrong and told her to remain silent. I asked the journalist what was going on and he started asking ridiculous questions he already knew the answers to. 'Does Belinda really exist? Why did you make it all up?' he asked. I told Carol to take the wig off – we were no longer going through with the charade. Carol did so and we all left. Three days later the following article appeared in the *Sunday People* under the headline, 'Killer Sends Love Notes to Barmaid Who Turns Out to Be Bouncer'.

Evil Ripper Peter Sutcliffe has fallen for a sexy barmaid who's really a man. For the past year the 13-times killer has been sending love notes with 'big juicy hugs' to show how much he cares for passionate pen pal Belinda Cannon. But the *People* can reveal that the mad mass murderer's 'sweetheart' is really a beefy nightclub bouncer called Bernard! After we rumbled tattooed Bernard O'Mahoney trying to sell Belinda's love letters from Sutcliffe, he confessed, 'I had to con the Ripper because I wanted to get inside his mind and he wouldn't write to me as a man. But he loved my letters so much that he really believes Belinda exists and has totally fallen for her. For the past year he has been writing every week, pouring out his heart and expressing his love.'

Six-footer O'Mahoney tried to sell 'Belinda's' love letters to the *People* for £4,000. Sutcliffe, who was jailed for 30 years in 1981 for murdering 13 women, sent the romantic notes from top security Broadmoor hospital in Berkshire. He also posted signed pictures of himself smothered with kisses. In one of the handwritten letters to 'dearest Belinda', he swooned about how she brought 'sunshine into my life'. And he signed off: *Take extra special care of your most dear self, my sweet – be happy, lucky and in love! Much love and fond thoughts always! Pete XXXXX*

Crop-haired O'Mahoney, from Basildon, Essex, also tried to sell taped conversations between Sutcliffe and a woman he claimed was Belinda. Then to try and prove she existed, he brought a gorgeous blonde into our office and said, 'She will tell you everything.' But O'Mahoney had to swallow his words as soon as she opened her mouth. For the woman talking on the tapes had a cockney accent – and the blonde claiming to be Belinda had a Brummie twang. When we told her she had been rumbled, the red-faced girl pulled off a wig to reveal a head of jet-black hair. And she confessed, 'Belinda doesn't exist. Bernie asked me to pretend I was her and I thought I was going to be paid. I'm just a friend.' O'Mahoney then admitted: 'Belinda exists only in Sutcliffe's mind – but the tapes and the letters are genuine. And that's what I wanted. I wrote the letters as barmaid Belinda asking Sutcliffe every question that I thought would one day be saleable as a story. I asked Sutcliffe his views on crime, sex, religion, everything . . . and he happily wrote back, answering them all. It was obvious from his letters that he was falling in love with Belinda. He then wanted to talk to her on the phone. So I persuaded a girl to do it. I thought there was no way he would ever find out. Unfortunately, you have.'

I really could not believe what I was reading, nor could I understand why the journalist had preferred to turn a story that gave an insight into Sutcliffe's mind into a tacky non-story. I had produced my passport to the journalist when we had signed the contract concerning the purchase of the letters. The journalist knew exactly who I was and how and why the letters had come to be in existence. I was upset, to say the least.

I contacted a solicitor and was told that as they had used extracts from the letters as per the contract, they would have to pay me some, if not all, of the agreed fee. Eventually, after an exchange of letters between my solicitor and their legal department, the newspaper was forced to pay. The experience taught me a valuable lesson concerning journalists and it was simply don't trust them!

I thought it would be wrong for me to keep the original family photographs that Sutcliffe had sent me, so I returned them with a covering letter, using my real name. A week later, Sutcliffe replied:

Dear Bernard,
You're not so bad.
I did know but was curious who was behind that scam.

I didn't know it at the time, but Sutcliffe was the first of many to find out that I was behind what many in the media would call a 'scam', but what I would call a legitimate search for the truth. While the journalists who condemned me posed as clients to expose prostitutes or homeowners to snare unethical plumbers, Gary Jones and I worked together coaxing child murderers into making confessions concerning their heinous crimes.

* * *

In the summer of 1991, Ken and Julie Pearson moved approximately 15 miles from the industrial city of Middlesbrough to the quaint seaside town of Marske. They wanted their children to grow up in an environment where they believed drugs, muggings and other inner-city-related crimes rarely, if ever, were committed. The family settled in quickly and the children soon became friends with other children in the area.

Seven-year-old Paul Pearson soon befriended a local boy whose parents kept an allotment. The boy's parents were friendly with a man named Richard Blenkey, who tended an allotment adjacent to theirs. Paul had been introduced to him by his friend's parents, so felt safe in his company. Blenkey, who always made a point of chatting to the local children, picked peas with Paul and gave them to him to take home. Any warnings Paul had been given about talking to strangers were now null and void in relation to Blenkey: responsible adults had introduced him to Blenkey and he had been present when his own mother had spoken to him. Paul had not been told Blenkey was a danger, and Blenkey had not displayed any behaviour to Paul or his mother that indicated he was a threat.

Thirty-two-year-old Blenkey was known locally as a bit of a loner; he was an 'oddball' who had never had a girlfriend, but because he came across as friendly he was accepted as a harmless individual. He organised security for allotment holders and would take his turn staying overnight to stop intruders and vandals damaging crops and property. Blenkey lived with his widowed mother and spent most of his time on the allotments, where he looked after his chickens and a vegetable patch. He was obsessed with his chickens: he used to talk to them and had given them names. Blenkey told friends that he found it extremely difficult when he had to kill any of them.

What locals did not know was that Blenkey had a morbid interest in young boys. In 1978, he had been convicted of a breach of the peace after forcing a young boy to go with him up a hill into a wooded area. The terrified youngster had kicked Blenkey in the shin and run to his father, who reported him to the police. Blenkey pleaded not guilty but was convicted and fined.

In 1988, Blenkey molested several local youngsters, but instead of the police being called, their parents beat Blenkey up. He was not prosecuted and, as a result, his unnatural behaviour escaped scrutiny by the proper authorities. I can understand the parents' reaction, but their reluctance to deal with Blenkey via the proper channels probably cost Paul Pearson his life because at the relevant time Blenkey could have been where he belonged: behind bars.

At 3.45 p.m. on Wednesday, 14 August 1991, just two weeks after arriving in Marske, Paul Pearson went out on his red BMX bike to play with a friend. Always conscientious, he promised his mother that he would be back for his tea at six o'clock. It was the hottest day of the year and the children were enjoying their school summer holidays. Paul was playing on his bike in a field less than 200 yards from his home; he was not near any road, so he appeared to be in one of the safest environments for a child. He soon tired of riding his bike in the summer heat and so went to the allotment of his friend's family to play. Not forgetting his promise to his mother, he set off home later that afternoon for his tea.

Paul's journey was to take him past Richard Blenkey's allotment. At teatime, his mother was surprised that he hadn't returned, but as the family had eaten a late lunch and it was hot she concluded Paul must not be hungry. When Paul still hadn't arrived home by 8.15, the Pearsons reported him missing. As darkness fell, concern for Paul's safety grew.

The following day the holiday mood that normally buzzed through the tiny seaside town was dampened, as a huge search got under way for the missing boy. Police, coastguards and concerned civilian volunteers, many of whom had abandoned their day out on the beach, began a systematic hunt through the surrounding area. A team of 80 detectives interviewed holidaymakers on a caravan site close to the spot where Paul was last seen. It was as if he had vanished off the face of the earth.

On Friday, 16 August, Paul's mum made a tearful plea for help at police headquarters. But as Julie and her husband Ken faced the TV cameras in a bare, drab police station, a horrific discovery was being made. A member of the public had found Paul's body at the bottom of a 50-foot ravine overlooked by the Pearsons' home. He had been strangled with a piece of red twine. His BMX bike had been found earlier in long grass near a bridle path. Paul was wearing a T-shirt and tracksuit bottoms that were inside out. His body was covered in chicken droppings and pieces of straw. The fact that Paul's tracksuit bottoms were inside out indicated that he had been stripped of his clothing at some stage and there was also evidence that he had suffered a serious sexual assault before being murdered.

Just minutes after making their emotional plea, detectives broke the news to the Pearsons. Scarcely able to believe what they were hearing, the couple were told that their son had been dragged off his favourite red bike and murdered in broad daylight. A stunned detective told the media: 'There is not an officer in Britain who is not totally disgusted by it all.' Police immediately launched a murder inquiry.

It was not long before police established where Paul had spent the day playing and inquiries in and around the allotment area soon began to focus on the oddball loner Richard Blenkey. He was arrested shortly after Paul's body was found and quizzed for nearly 12 hours. He denied even seeing Paul that day.

The following morning police charged Blenkey with Paul's murder. He made a brief appearance at Teesside Magistrates Court and was remanded in custody to await trial. As I sat in my house thinking about Paul's murder, I began to consider my correspondence with Sutcliffe and how easy it had been to extract information from him. Surely Blenkey would not fall for the same ruse. Surely Blenkey, who had endured hours of police questioning, would refuse to discuss the case with a stranger.

I rang Gary Jones and asked him what he thought about the chances of Blenkey disclosing anything of evidential value. Gary laughed at first, saying Blenkey would never risk putting anything in writing about his case. I agreed, but nagging doubts in my head made me wonder if we were both wrong. I ended the conversation saying, 'I'll give it a go, Gary. See what happens.'

The plan was simple; I would befriend Blenkey and see what, if anything, he would tell me about the murder of Paul Pearson. Alone in my room, pen in hand, the task ahead seemed immense. I stared at the blank page in front of me. How would I go about befriending a man who had abducted, sodomised and then murdered a seven-year-old boy? What does a man who could do that to a child enjoy reading about, what interests could we possibly share? My mind was flooded with countless questions, but there were no obvious answers. Outside in the street I could hear the shrieks and laughter of children playing. It seemed to make my task all the more difficult, but all the more important. It disgusted me, having to write the words required to forge our 'friendship', but if I was to succeed I would have to create a character Blenkey would not only feel comfortable with, but also on whom he could depend.

Unlike Sutcliffe, Blenkey was clearly interested in males, so I saw no point in using a pseudonym; I decided I would use my own identity. Picking up my pen, I began to write the first of what would be 36 letters. I didn't present myself any differently: my only falsehood was that I said I wanted to help him.

Desperate for a friend, Blenkey immediately wrote back:

> May I say a big thank you. It was nice to get a letter from someone I don't know. Every time I feel low, I read your letter. It helps me. Now I am in prison I am terrified, but I will get through it somehow, as I know I did not have anything to do with it.

Blenkey insisted he was innocent for months. Then towards Christmas he started blaming someone else for the crime, a demented down-and-out by the name of 'Mr Punk'. Blenkey claimed that he had asked Mr Punk, 'How could you kill so easily?' Mr Punk allegedly replied, 'After once or twice, it is easy.'

Over the next few weeks, Blenkey forwarded me a series of hideous, obscene messages signed by Mr Punk. All were transparently composed by Blenkey himself, but I didn't point that out. Instead, I played along. Once or twice Mr Punk proposed a clandestine rendezvous to discuss the case, so for a while I was reporting back on my failed attempts to meet someone even more fictitious than myself. Despite the mind games, however, and a strong forensic case against him, Blenkey was still insisting into the summer of 1992: 'I am going to plead not guilty, as I am not the murderer.'

The trial date was nearing, but then my 36th letter, written in October, yielded this: 'To tell you the truth, well, I don't remember killing him, but I must have strangled him. I did not have sex with him. All I remember is moving the body.' I immediately contacted Gary Jones, who rang the officer in charge of the case. Later that same night we met the policeman and a colleague in a pub in East London, where I handed over all of the letters.

At Blenkey's trial, which was expected to last a week, he was shown the letters and, after flicking through them, he changed his plea to guilty. Blenkey was sentenced to life imprisonment and Paul's family were spared the ordeal of having to listen to their son's murderer lie about his final moments.

* * *

On 30 June 1994, three-year-old Rosie Palmer popped out to buy a lolly from an ice-cream van only yards from her home in Hartlepool. Shaun Armstrong, who lived opposite Rosie, had spent the day celebrating his 33rd birthday. He returned to the street where they lived just as Rosie was returning from the ice-cream van. Armstrong lured the child to his flat on some pretext, then attacked, raped and murdered her. When the terrified child began to scream during the attack, Armstrong's dog bit her repeatedly. In a final act of humiliation, Armstrong disposed of Rosie's tiny body in a bin bag.

One innocent life had been taken; several others were ruined. In the wake of his grand-daughter's murder, Rosie's grandfather stabbed an innocent man whom he believed was responsible for the murder. Her mother suffered a mental breakdown.

When I read about Rosie's murder, I knew that I would have to write to Armstrong. I wasn't fooling myself – I knew I was not some sort of self-taught shrink or an expert in the workings of a paedophile's mind, but the fact remained that I had talked Blenkey into confessing to his crime and, although unlikely, it was possible that I could do it again. I decided I would have to try because if I did not and Armstrong was released on a technicality, or following a dubious not guilty verdict, I would wonder for the rest of my life if I could have coaxed him into confessing.

I sat down with the newspaper reports concerning Rosie's murder spread out on the table in front of me. There had been blanket coverage of the case, but the kind of information that might have been of use to me was extremely limited. I thought it likely that paedophiles would take a keen interest in other paedophile cases and so I had to assume that Armstrong would have read about Paul Pearson's murder. He would therefore be aware of my letter-writing ruse and might even remember my name in connection with the case. I realised I would have to think of a pseudonym to use.

Unlike Blenkey, Armstrong was attracted to females rather than males, but what female would want to write to a man who had sexually assaulted and murdered a three-year-old child? Sutcliffe's fictitious ex – Belinda Cannon – would hardly warm to Armstrong, nor he to her.

It took me several hours to come up with a solution. I eventually settled for Lauren Stephens, a liberal, young, fit, educated dance instructor from London. Over 11 months, I exchanged more than 60 letters with Armstrong. Initially, he refused to accept that he was responsible; however, slowly but surely I began to talk him round. When I suggested that he should plead guilty, Armstrong replied, 'They haven't got a cat in hell's chance of a guilty plea to murder.' As time went on, Armstrong became more infatuated with the fictitious Lauren and confided in her: 'You deserve a straight answer, so here goes. Yes, love, I am responsible for the crime I am accused of. Both mentally and physically I am as fit as a fiddle.' However, Armstrong later claimed he was guilty of manslaughter rather than murder on the grounds of diminished responsibility:

> If I plead guilty to murder, there would be no extenuating circumstances and I'd get life with a recommendation of 25 to 30 years. That, my love, is exactly what would happen if I were to go there without a story of how drunk, how ill and down I had been. Even the fact that I had been on my own totally for three years, without even a damned date, and that it was my birthday, all go towards cutting the amount of time I will do. You are the first person to get the full story. Even my solicitor doesn't know, but I figured I owed you an explanation of why I am so insecure and terrified of losing you.

In several letters, the beast joked about how he planned to beat the legal system. He wrote:

> I cannot remember going home or the crime. My legal team are preparing psychiatric reports that I was not responsible for my actions at the time and that I had a temporary breakdown.

They are trying to extend the reasons for my breakdown so I have to do less time, a hell of a lot less. I have given them full rein to do and say whatever the hell they have to – to get me off with as little time as possible. Love you, kiddo. As you said, doll, if we were honest we would be okay. Well, this is as honest as it gets. You are the only woman I've trusted in years and years. Believe it or not, love, you now have my life in your hands. I thought I had better trust you. You are the only one who knows.

Armstrong was convinced that his vile secret was safe, but a week before his trial I contacted the police and handed them the letters. Copies were passed to Armstrong's legal team, who gave them to their client to consider. Realising that he had been duped into telling the truth, Armstrong pleaded guilty to murder and was sentenced to life imprisonment.

* * *

Another case my correspondence was instrumental in solving was that of nail bomber David Copeland, a man in his early 20s with a clutter of extreme right-wing views. On three dates in April 1999, Copeland planted bombs in various parts of London, each containing about 1,500 nails, timed to an alarm clock.

The first bomb went off in a street of shops in predominantly black Brixton. Fifty were injured, including two people who lost an eye; one toddler was left with a nine-inch nail embedded in his skull. Copeland's second device was planted in Aldgate, the centre of London's Bangladeshi community. A passer-by put the bomb in the boot of a car just before it exploded. There were eight serious injuries and five others suffered minor injuries from flying debris.

The third and most devastating bomb exploded at the Admiral Duncan pub in Soho. Three people were killed, including a pregnant woman, while one hundred and thirty-nine others were hurt, some of whom later required amputations. After scouring hours of street surveillance camera footage, the police arrested Copeland.

Unlike the majority of others to whom I had written, Copeland wasn't a paedophile, but he had murdered a woman and a baby, and had maimed many other innocents, including the small child whose skull had been pierced by a nail. Copeland had the audacity to say that these people were collateral damage in his efforts to start a race war. The more I read about him, the more I despised him.

I didn't need the police's description of him as a 'loner' to know he'd turn out to be a bit of a loser. Inevitably, there would be some sort of serious disturbance in his background, something that had probably destroyed his childhood. Inevitably, also, whatever had wounded him as a child would have left him with a deep-seated grievance against the world – and the belief he had the right to hit back violently.

I decided to write to Copeland; the challenge was creating a female character that would appeal to him. Whilst searching the Internet for background information on Copeland, I'd noticed that far-right magazines often featured photos of blonde women wearing stockings, suspenders and Waffen SS regalia. They'd often be bound, gagged or in some way restrained: in other words, vulnerable and helpless. I decided, then, that my character had to be young, attractive and, most importantly, vulnerable. That way she wouldn't be a threat to him. Copeland could feel in control. I settled on a slim, blonde secretary called Patsy, a naive, curious 20-year-old English rose. The name Patsy appealed to me because it's also an American slang word for a sucker.

Shortly after being remanded in custody, Copeland was sent to Broadmoor hospital for psychiatric tests. Despite a plethora of damning evidence against him, Copeland decided to plead not guilty to murder. He confided in Patsy that he intended to fool the doctors in the hope that he could plead guilty to manslaughter on the grounds of diminished responsibility. 'This place is a joke and so are the doctors,' he wrote. 'They are as stupid as the fools in here. I can't believe that I have fooled them all.'

At Copeland's trial in June 2000, the letters were entered as evidence for the Crown. It was Michael Wolkind, Copeland's barrister, who broke the news to him that Patsy was fictitious. The depth of Copeland's reaction, he says, was impossible to gauge: 'He was under so much stress, heavily drugged up. He was listening to me with blank eyes.'

The judge condemned my letter writing as a 'shabby ruse' and prosecutor Nigel Sweeney called it a 'low trick', but that didn't stop him from stooping to use its fruits. Sweeney read extracts from the letters, asking the defence witness Dr Andrew Payne, 'Where, in all these letters, is there a sign of mental illness?' Dr Payne said there was none. Perhaps, he said, Copeland was pretending to be sane to impress Patsy. This theory sank without a bubble within the jury. There was no mood to go soft at a trial where amputees were haunting the gallery.

On 30 June, Copeland was convicted of murder and sentenced to six life terms.

* * *

For every child murderer who confessed, there were numerous others who refused to change their plea but were later convicted. The police have used my letters as evidence in numerous high-profile cases, including that of Soham murderer Ian Huntley, Sarah Payne's killer Roy Whiting and Moors murderer Ian Brady. I am astounded that sections of the media and the authorities criticise what I have done: innocent people awaiting trial do not send detailed letters to strangers confessing to murder. Trials cost millions of pounds of taxpayers' money and so do appeals – defendants who plead guilty to their vile crimes don't require either. More importantly, the families of the victims do not have to endure the heartache of sitting in court, listening to pathologists explain in gruesome detail how and why their loved ones died. Nor do they have to listen to the animal who took the loved one's life lie and see him trying to squirm his way out of facing the consequences of his evil deeds.

Although I am astounded and disgusted by the comments made by so-called respectable and professional people, their views will do nothing other than strengthen my resolve. I say that because it is the victims' families that have to live with the horrors of child murder and their views do mean a lot to me.

Speaking after Blenkey's trial, Paul's mother Julie told reporters: 'It makes things a lot easier knowing it was definitely him. I know the police had a very strong case, but it was good to hear there was no doubt. I gasped when he pleaded guilty in court. It was such a shock. It meant a great deal to us.'

Her husband Ken, added: 'We'd have had a week of torment if he hadn't changed his plea, though that's nothing to what Paul went through. I never had any doubt in my mind that he did it, but you never know how trials will go. I'm pleased Blenkey has been sent down for a long time. I'd hate to think another child would have to go through what Paul did. It's been a long time to wait. But on Monday it was worth it. I have maximum faith in the police. I used to run a neighbourhood watch and realise what a good job they do. But I had to hear, from Blenkey's own mouth, the word guilty.'

7

THE UNWASHED BITCHES

IF my brother Paul hadn't been charged with wounding and assault, I wouldn't have become involved with the Taylor sisters. Paul had fallen out with a friend, and the falling-out had resulted in violence. He'd been remanded in custody to Belmarsh prison in London after police told magistrates they feared he might try to interfere with witnesses. I wanted to help my brother escape the charge and so I set about contacting potential witnesses on his behalf. Within a week or so, I'd gathered together enough 'new evidence' to enable Paul to make a credible application for bail. He was given a date in July 1992 to have his application heard. The venue was the Old Bailey.

I had decided to attend the hearing, and so duly arrived in London on the set date. I was dismayed to learn that my brother's hearing had been adjourned. I didn't fancy heading straight back to Essex in the congested traffic, so hung around. Like most people reading newspapers at that time, I'd been following the Taylor sisters' trial. It was a lurid tale of obsession, sex and violence that had ended in murder. By coincidence the Taylor sisters' trial was also being held at the Old Bailey, so I went and sat in the public gallery to observe.

Michelle and Lisa were sitting in the dock. In the flesh, they seemed unlikely murderers. They just looked like nice ordinary girls, although there was one detail that, to my cynical eye, made Michelle seem a little more cunning and worldly than she might at first have appeared: she was holding a Bible, a picture of Jesus Christ and what looked like a chain with a small crucifix attached. Nice touch, I thought – a show of Christian piety for the benefit of the jurors.

Seasoned criminals had over the years taught me several courtroom tactics for swaying gullible jurors – using a walking stick for sympathy, dressing nerdish to destroy the image of hardened criminality, crying

'No! No! No!' when the victim gives particularly damaging evidence. I assumed Michelle had received similar guidance from fellow prisoners whilst on remand. As I sat waiting for the proceedings to begin, I read the latest instalment of the story in a discarded copy of *The Sun*. It helped me clarify in my mind the details that had so far emerged.

John Shaughnessy was born in Dublin in December 1961 and moved to London to work – first as a porter, later as purchasing manager – at the Churchill Clinic, a private hospital in Kennington, South London. He soon established a reputation for being something of a 'charmer'. He met his future wife in October 1986 at the Archway Tavern in North London. Alison was 16 and worked at Barclays Bank on the Strand in central London. She was a shy girl but extremely pretty. Shaughnessy was Alison's first boyfriend and she was completely besotted by him. In the spring of 1989, they became engaged.

Shaughnessy meanwhile had met Michelle Taylor, who was a cleaner at the Churchill Clinic. In February 1989, she invited Shaughnessy to her 18th birthday party. They began sleeping together soon after. Like Alison, Michelle was a virgin. And, just like Alison, she fell hopelessly in love with Shaughnessy.

Michelle was devastated to learn of his engagement and broke off their affair; however, it quickly resumed, with regular sexual encounters on Monday nights when John worked late, arranging flowers at the clinic. Following their wedding, Alison moved into John's room at the clinic. The room next to John and Alison's belonged to Michelle's friend, Jeanette – or 'JJ' – Tapp. Michelle spent a lot of time in there, leaning against the paper-thin walls, eavesdropping on the newlyweds. The couple's happiness tore Michelle's heart. She tried to distance herself from John, but she was weak.

On 1 October, Shaughnessy took Michelle to a shed in the grounds of the clinic for sex. 'I hate the feeling after,' she wrote in her diary. 'I feel sick with myself.'

Early the following year, John and Alison moved to Vardens Road in Battersea, South London. They began to talk about starting a family and moving back to Ireland. This news, the prosecution alleged, had tipped Michelle Taylor over the edge. If the Shaughnessys moved to Ireland, the affair would be over – and the man of Michelle's dreams would be lost forever. Alison, Michelle decided, would have to go.

The Taylor sisters were charged with the murder of Alison Shaughnessy on 7 August 1991 and the case was brought to trial in July 1992. Michelle was just 21, Lisa 19. Sitting in the dock, they looked very young and radiated innocence.

The evidence was hard to refute. First, there was the motive. Michelle was John Shaughnessy's mistress, she was obsessed by him and terrified of losing him. Her diary provided ample evidence of her hostile feelings towards Alison. In one entry, Michelle wrote, 'I hate Alison, the unwashed bitch . . . my dream solution would be for Alison to disappear as if she had never existed so I could give everything I want to the man I love.' Alison had suffered 54 stab wounds, an indication that the attack was personal rather than the work of a stranger.

Then there was the evidence of two witnesses. The first, James Hewitt, remembered seeing a white Sierra like Michelle's parked around the corner from Vardens Road at the time of the murder. The second, Dr Michael Unsworth White, reported seeing two young girls hurrying out of Alison's flat at around 5.45 p.m. on the day of the murder. The girls were carrying what appeared to be a large plastic laundry bag.

Importantly, there was also one piece of forensic evidence. In separate statements, Michelle, Lisa and their mother Anne Taylor were all adamant that Lisa had never been to the flat on Vardens Road. She had absolutely no reason to have visited the flat and even told police she thought it was in Clapham. Yet her fingerprints were found inside the flat door. These were fresh fingerprints, according to the forensic expert.

However, the most damaging evidence was the sisters' attempt to manufacture a false alibi.

The Taylors told police that on the day of the murder they had spent the afternoon shopping in Bromley, returning to the Churchill Clinic at 5.15 p.m., when they saw Jeanette Tapp. As Alison left work at 5 p.m., arriving home at 5.35 p.m., this would effectively rule them out of the murder. Jeanette Tapp's evidence was, therefore, crucial.

When originally interviewed by police, she said she arrived at the clinic at 5 p.m. and saw the Taylors shortly afterwards. However, she later withdrew her previous statements and stated in court that she returned to the clinic no earlier than 7.15 p.m., when she was immediately approached by Lisa Taylor, who told her she and

Michelle had been waiting for her since 5 p.m. They asked to leave a laundry bag, apparently full of clothes, in her room. Jeanette Tapp's mother and two sisters both confirmed this later version of events.

Tapp said that Michelle returned to collect the laundry bag the next day and pressurised her into giving the false alibi, saying it didn't matter, as she and Lisa had been at the clinic anyway.

The Taylors' story of an afternoon shopping in Bromley was proved to be false. They had no receipts to indicate that they had been shopping, no one remembered seeing them and they failed to appear on any of the CCTV footage covering the streets and shops. Even more damning – despite insisting she'd been in Bromley from 3 p.m. until returning to the clinic at 5 p.m., Michelle's bank card had been used at 3.20 p.m. to withdraw £10 from a bank a couple of minutes' walk from the clinic but a 30-minute drive from Bromley.

Michelle had first stated in interview that she had taken her card to Bromley but hadn't used it. When confronted with the evidence of the cashpoint withdrawal, she accused Jeanette Tapp of stealing the card and using her PIN number to obtain cash. Michelle's explanation smacked of desperation when coupled with the undisputed fact that Tapp used her own card to draw out £50 at 3.44 p.m. – just 24 minutes later – from a cashpoint on Kennington Park Road, some distance from the 3.20 p.m. transaction.

Tapp's evidence was indirectly supported by two other witnesses. Carol Healy, a nurse at the Churchill Clinic, saw Michelle Taylor driving out of the clinic car park in her white Sierra just after 4 p.m., with Lisa sitting in the passenger seat. Healy was certain of the time, as she had just finished her shift. Another clinic employee, Valerie McDonald, told police that she saw Michelle and Lisa returning to the clinic at 6 p.m. Again, the witness was certain of the time, as she had also finished her shift.

The tabloid newspapers were claiming that this was the trial of the century. The story was undoubtedly a media dream. A spurned lover, helped by her loyal sister, had apparently murdered the wife rival – a real-life *Fatal Attraction*.

'Love Crazy Mistress Butchers Wife' screamed the headlines. Over a photograph showing Michelle kissing John on the cheek at his wedding to Alison, it read 'Killer at Wedding'. It was this sort of sensational newspaper reporting that concerned me; Michelle in particular was being referred to as a 'cheat' and a 'killer' long before the jury had been asked to consider her fate. If jury members were reading the same newspapers as I was, then I was in no doubt that they would have been influenced by content that didn't form part of the prosecution case.

On the train home that evening, I decided to write to the sisters to point out the biased way I thought their trial was being conducted. It was a short letter, which read in part: 'I can only hope that your legal representatives are studying the text used by the tabloid press and considering your position in relation to it. They are all but saying that you are guilty. I do not normally put pen to paper to voice my views, but I feel that your treatment is bordering on criminal.' I have regretted sending that letter more times than I could possibly recall, because Michelle replied and thereafter we became friends.

After two long weeks of hearing evidence, the jury unanimously found Michelle and Lisa Taylor guilty of murder.

The day after the guilty verdict, Michelle phoned me from prison and asked if I would help her win her freedom. Rather foolishly, I agreed. That same day, I launched a campaign to free the Taylor Two, as they became known.

I suggested that their father, Derek, and I should challenge the police timings. Alison had arrived home at approximately 5.35 p.m. A pathologist had given evidence stating that the attack would have taken no more than two to three minutes. Police estimated the drive from Vardens Road to the clinic took 11 minutes 20 seconds, thus allowing Michelle and Lisa to return at 6 p.m., when they were seen by a work colleague. My intention was to prove that the journey between Alison's flat and Michelle's workplace took far longer than the police had claimed. If I could do so, doubt could be cast on their convictions. Derek and I videotaped the journey, with a stopwatch to verify the timing – but the exercise backfired spectacularly. We were able to complete the journey far quicker than the police. Even keeping rigorously within the speed limit, we managed the first run in just 8.23 minutes. Derek and I looked at the stopwatch, looked at each other and said, 'Fuck it. If the police can lie, so can we.' After several attempts over several weeks, more than a third of the video timings had to be destroyed because the results supported the police case. The remaining footage, which supported our version of events, was handed over to the legal team to form part of possible grounds for appeal.

The bank card evidence, which initially seemed irrefutable, was undermined when I managed to track down a Liverpool solicitor called Dennis Whalley who specialised in computer banking errors. He was able to provide evidence that thousands of errors concerning withdrawals are caused by cash machines and therefore that particular evidence could no longer be relied upon.

Jeanette Tapp was the real problem, however, as her evidence was damning. I decided that she had to be pressurised into changing her statement. Her home telephone number was obtained by one of Michelle's friends at the clinic. I rang her and attempted to talk her into making a fresh statement, but she broke down, sobbing uncontrollably, and assured me that she had told the truth. I advised the Taylors that Tapp would likely go to the police if she was contacted again, as she was extremely emotional. It was agreed that she would be left alone, but I later learnt that she had become the recipient of a stream of silent phone calls. The Taylors' mother Anne then claimed to reporters that she had received an anonymous call, which she just happened to have taped. The female caller said she'd been talking to 'JJ', who had allegedly admitted she had lied in court and was now feeling 'guilty and frightened'. This backfired when a journalist later reported, 'Despite the potential importance of such a statement, Anne Taylor showed no interest in tracing the mystery caller.'

Whenever people convicted of a crime claim they are innocent, one of the first question asked is, 'If you didn't do it, then who did?' It was a question the Taylors were asked regularly, so I set out to provide them with an answer.

At the time of Alison's murder, Graham Baldwin, who worked with the homeless in London, had rung police to report that a down-and-out called David Wylie had told him he'd killed a girl. Baldwin's call was duly logged and the details appeared in the unused evidence. I tracked Baldwin down and suggested numerous scenarios and things that might have been said until he had convinced himself that Wylie was Alison's killer. Before long the broadsheets were running stories about Baldwin's dramatic new evidence and he appeared on television more than once to repeat all that I had suggested to him.

Eleven months after being sentenced to serve life sentences, the Taylor sisters appeared at the High Court to have their appeal heard. The guilty verdict was declared unsafe, and due to the 'prejudicial press coverage' a retrial was deemed impossible. Michelle and Lisa Taylor walked free.

I cannot deny that I was elated, and I cannot deny that my feelings of joy were for myself rather than the Taylors. I realised that my efforts had not been for the sisters; deep down, my motive had been to prove the police, who had caused me so much grief in my life, wrong. Numerous newspapers and publishers offered the sisters deals to tell their story, but they asked me to assist them in writing their book. I took it as a compliment at the time, but I now realise they didn't want to answer the kinds of awkward questions a stranger might have raised.

I drove home to Basildon and Debra. She was in the kitchen doing the washing up. She'd already fed the children and put them to bed. 'So, they're out then?' she said. I told her they were. We chatted about how the day had gone. She was genuinely pleased I'd achieved my aim, but I could tell she was relieved that at last I could forget about the Taylor sisters. Over the last 11 months we'd had countless rows about the time I was spending on the campaign. She was always accusing me of putting strangers before my own family. In the early days of my involvement with the Taylors, I'd tried to explain to Debra what was driving me, but it was hard to put it into words. I often felt surprised myself at the obsessive hold the case had over me. Debra broke off from the washing up to make me something to eat. There was silence for a little while. Then she asked me what the sisters were going to do now. I said they were going to write a book. She asked me if I was planning on having something to do with it. I knew I was about to trigger a row, but I wasn't going to lie. 'I'm writing it for them,' I said.

I could see Debra's jaw dropping, as she opened her mouth and said in a tone of final-straw exasperation: 'You have got to be joking.' I said I wasn't. She tried to reason with me: I had achieved my aim and now I should get back to looking after my own family. 'They're out now, Bernie. You've done what you set out to do. Now move on.' I didn't try either to justify my intentions or to make them in any way more palatable to her. I had decided, and that was that.

I soon realised I'd pushed her beyond her threshold of tolerance. She'd had enough. She said if I did the book, then our relationship was over: 'You forget them – or you go.' Pig-stubborn and self-righteous, I wasn't going to argue with her. I just left. I suppose I didn't honestly think our relationship was over. I was angry; she was angry. In my heart, I thought we would probably get back together again. But I wanted to make her understand that I had no intention of compromising my plans to write the book. Older, wiser and with hindsight, I find my total insensitivity towards Debra astonishing.

As well as the media deals that flooded in, the Taylors also received a lot of hate mail, including a parcel which, when opened, covered them in flour. The attached note warned them that the next parcel would be a bomb. It was signed 'Kilburn IRA'.

We agreed it would be in everyone's interest if we moved in together for a short time. I could get the book written by having their undivided attention – and they would feel more relaxed and secure by having me around in case someone did try to attack them.

One evening, after a fruitless day's work on the book, Michelle said that she wanted to get away from everything for a few days because it was all getting her down. I said it would be a good idea because, in her current state of mind, working on the book was pointless. She asked me if I'd go with her. I agreed and we decided on North Wales as our destination. For some reason, we ended up in Colwyn Bay, where we found a cheap hotel near the seafront. We'd chosen a room with two single beds. Michelle chose the one near the window; I put my bag on the other. It was early afternoon, so we decided to go for a walk around the town.

Michelle was a different person. She seemed really happy to be away from London and her various troubles. We had a bargain meal in a cafe, then headed for a pub. We couldn't be bothered trying to find Colwyn Bay's finest, so we settled for some barely tolerable dive. There were only about six people inside. No one paid us any attention as we settled in for a drinking session. Michelle talked about prison. She told me she'd cracked up before the trial because she had been left alone when Lisa had been granted bail. She said she'd barricaded herself in the prison chapel and refused to leave. The staff had finally coaxed her out. She was sent to the prison psychiatrist because she couldn't sleep and felt she was on the verge of a complete breakdown. The psychiatrist had given her a tape to listen to at bedtime. One of the songs was by The Temptations, entitled 'Just My Imagination (Running Away with Me)'. I laughed. She asked me what was so funny. I said that her imagination running away with her had been what had got her into trouble in the first place: if she hadn't transferred her negative thoughts about Alison into the diary found by the police, the case against her would have been even weaker. She smiled, but didn't join me in laughter. She said she'd never keep a diary again.

The afternoon swayed into the evening and, before long, they were ringing the bell for last orders. We were both very drunk when we ambled back to the hotel. That night we slept together for the first time. I woke up before Michelle the next morning. As she lay beside me, snoring fitfully in a way that fanned her beery breath towards me, I felt like a condemned man waiting for the sun to rise. I knew I'd crossed a line, and I just wished that I hadn't. I told myself it wasn't going to happen again: I'd tell Michelle that we had to be friends and friends only. But I didn't. When she awoke, she oozed happiness, almost skipping out of bed to the bathroom. If she'd shown just one sign that she was feeling even a smidgeon of regret, then perhaps I'd have had the courage to tell her my true feelings. But I'd never seen her so happy: she was almost cooing with delight. Most worryingly, from almost her first sentence that morning she was talking as if we were a married couple of long-standing.

I couldn't face breakfast. I had an urge to get out of the hotel, so we went for a walk down the town. All the time, I wanted to tell her that what had happened was nothing serious and that we should forget about it, but she was so happy I didn't have the heart. I was, however, determined not to spend any longer than I absolutely had to in the situation I was in.

Around midday I told her I'd phoned a work colleague and something had cropped up at Raquels that required my immediate return. I could tell she was disappointed, but she didn't make a fuss. On the drive back to London, I could think of nothing but ways to ensure things wouldn't become more complicated. I didn't want to get into the habit of sleeping with her, and although I knew she'd expect me to share the one bedroom in the house, I also knew that my late nights on the doors would give me an excuse to avoid getting too intimate. I assumed that, in time, things between us would just wind down naturally. It didn't take long for me to realise how wrong I was.

Inevitably, despite my resolve after Colwyn Bay never to sleep with her again, it did happen occasionally. Many relationships have a honeymoon period before they decline into bitterness and arguments; well, Michelle and I bypassed the former and zipped straight to the latter. I always regretted sleeping with her because no sooner was the act over than she'd demand to know how I felt about her. Did I care for her? Did I love her? Did I even want to be with her? Whatever answer I gave was the wrong answer. If I said I cared for her but stopped short of saying I loved her, she'd subject me to abuse: 'I fucking knew it. You're only using me. You're no better than John,' she'd scream. If I let her browbeat me into making an untruthful declaration of love, I got a mouthful of abuse anyway: 'You're a liar. You're just saying that. If you did, you wouldn't stay out all the time.' I couldn't tell her the truth because it wasn't what she wanted to hear, and anything she didn't want to hear was a lie. No matter how honest I intended to be, I always ended up playing games with words, neither entirely dismissing her barking deluded fantasies about 'the relationship' nor being so honest that the ramshackle structure of our togetherness collapsed in a mushroom cloud of dust and debris.

I knew I was being a bastard. I knew she wasn't being entirely unreasonable in expecting more than I was willing to give. In a sexual sense, she was right: I was only using her and leading her on. I knew we could never be an item, because I didn't want us to be one. I decided that once the book was complete I would move out of the flat and out of the situation I had so foolishly walked into.

Four months later, in October 1993, Michelle was visiting her mother while I remained in the flat, researching the book. I'd flicked through a lot of the material before and I wasn't expecting to come across anything of use, so I wasn't totally engaged in what I was reading. All the same, I was moving through the documents methodically, if not with any great interest. Then, in the space of perhaps 20 seconds, I read a document that changed my life. If a fist had come up from the box and punched me in the face, I couldn't have been more shocked. What I discovered was a letter from a solicitor's firm, dated from the early days of the case, not long after the sisters' arrest. The letter referred to Michelle's having made 'certain admissions' in the light of which Lisa was being advised to give evidence on behalf of the prosecution. The letter may have been couched in legal phraseology, but I knew instantly what it meant. Michelle had told her legal representative that she was guilty of murdering Alison Shaughnessy.

For a few minutes I just sat there, barely moving. The activity was all in my mind. I felt everything – shock, anger, embarrassment and disbelief. However, what truly devastated me was the knowledge that I'd been conned. Michelle had pleaded with me not to make a mug of her in love. Yet from the very beginning she'd made me the biggest mug of all. I thought of all the time and money I'd spent on the Taylors, all the risks I'd undertaken on their behalf, all the misery I'd inflicted on Debra and my own children. And throughout that time Michelle and Lisa must have been secretly laughing at me.

I don't know how long I sat there thinking like that. Suddenly, I heard a key in the front door. It had to be Michelle's. I heard the door close behind her. I heard her footsteps. With the legal letter in my hand, I got up off the floor and sat on the settee. I'd begun to shake with temper. I was ready to confront the murderer.

When Michelle walked into the front room, I remained on the settee, perhaps three yards from her, holding the letter like a weapon. My face must have signalled something was wrong because she stopped walking as soon as she saw me. I waved the letter at her and said sarcastically; 'You'd better get rid of this, hadn't you?' She looked puzzled. 'Go on. Explain it. Explain it,' I said. I handed her the letter. She looked at it quickly but didn't read it properly. I could tell she didn't need to. Her face grimaced with recognition. It was her turn to look shocked. She screwed up the letter and threw it on the floor. All the time, I kept saying, 'Come on, then. Let's hear it. Explain it, Michelle.'

She was silent, then anger erupted from within her. She started screaming abuse at me, calling me a bastard. 'You have never believed in our innocence!' she screamed.

'Oh, yes, I did,' I said. 'Until now I fucking did.'

She strode past me towards the door at the other side of the room, screaming at me all the way. She practically goose-stepped out of the door into the hallway leading to the bedroom. Then she shouted 'You fucking bastard!' at the top of her voice before slamming the door furiously behind her.

There was silence for perhaps 30 seconds, then the lounge door flew open with a loud bang, as if she had kicked it. She stormed back into the room and shouted, 'John Shaughnessy is twice the man you are.' I suppose this was meant to hurt me, but at that moment I couldn't have cared less what she said about me or John. I gave a sarcastic laugh and knelt over to pluck the screwed up letter from the floor. In a voice loud enough to be heard over her shouting, I said, 'Yes, but explain this. Go on, explain it!'

Her face was red with the effort of hurling abuse at me, but then she did something I'd never seen her do before – she started crying. Full sobs replaced her shouts. She sat down on the settee; I didn't want her near me, so I stood up. Still sobbing, and wiping away the tears that had begun to stream from her eyes, she said, 'It wasn't my fucking fault. It was Alison's.' I didn't say anything. She continued, her voice quieter but distorted by the sobs. She said that Alison had told her that she and John planned to move to Ireland to live; they were going to have a baby and make a fresh start. Michelle said she had questioned John about it, but he had told her he had no plans either to return to Ireland or to start a family. She indicated that in her mind Alison had therefore been lying to her in order to hurt her. From my own recent experience with Michelle, I thought that if John had ever said those words, or anything like them, he would have done so in empty pillow talk or under duress caused by the sort of persistent and remorseless questioning to which Michelle had so often subjected me. I knew myself that with her on your case you would say whatever you thought she wanted to hear to get her to drop the subject.

Michelle said the situation with John and Alison had begun to make her ill. She had lost weight and had difficulty sleeping. She said that on the Monday of the killing she'd told Lisa she was going to have it out with Alison. Lisa had said that she would go with her. Michelle, without Lisa's knowledge, had taken from among her father's tools a steel ruler, one end of which had been sharpened to a knife point. Michelle said they had driven to Vardens Road and parked near the Roundhouse pub. (Anyone parked in this position has a clear view of people walking up or down Vardens Road.)

Michelle interspersed her story with lots of swearing and interjections such as 'I couldn't fucking stand it no more.' Michelle said that when they saw Alison walking up the road, they got out of the car and went to meet her. When they reached her, Michelle told her that John had sent her to collect some plant pots for the clinic that were too heavy for him to take on the train. Alison opened the main front door and then opened the door to the flat. Lisa stood at the second door and held it open as Michelle walked into the flat behind Alison.

Michelle had been crying throughout the story, but at this point she became distraught, sobbing violently and wiping tears frantically from her face. She kept saying, 'I only meant to scare her, I only meant to scare her.'

'Well, what happened?' I said.

'I don't know what happened,' Michelle cried. 'I grabbed her from behind, I stabbed her and everything else is a blur.'

Michelle couldn't look at me; she kept her eyes focused on the floor. She said they'd put 'all our stuff' (by which I understood her to mean any blood-stained clothing and the murder weapon) into a bag and run from the flat to their car. They had then driven back to the clinic. She stopped talking and, with her head in her hands, just sobbed. I looked at her for a few seconds in silence, then swore at her and walked out of the flat, leaving the letter behind. Furious at the betrayal, I vowed never to speak to Michelle again and returned to my family – the book about their 'innocence' abandoned, my loyalty to their cause destroyed.

Subsequently, fearing that I would reveal what I knew, the Taylors began a court action to prevent me from publishing any of their letters. The case – which the Taylors asked to be held in private – quickly grew into a dispute as to whether Michelle had confessed to murder. Michelle and Lisa denied that any incriminating letter had ever existed, or that Michelle had confessed. For nearly three years, I fought the sisters at the High Court in London. For long periods, I represented myself. Then, in October 1997, the matter came to a climax when Mr Justice Neuberger made an order compelling all the Taylors' legal representatives to swear affidavits that they had no knowledge of the alleged incriminating letter. No such affidavits were forthcoming and the Taylors attempted to suspend their action against me. However, the courts insisted on the matter being brought to an immediate conclusion. The case against me was struck out and I was awarded my costs, but more importantly I was free to tell Alison's family and the world of the Taylors' guilt.

8

PARTNERS IN CRIME

WHEN I wasn't trying to avoid the affections of murderers or coaxing confessions out of monsters from the comfort of my own home, I was trying to convince violent lunatics to behave themselves at work. Dave Venables and his forgiving attitude had left Raquels, but his departure had only resulted in another problem loitering with intent on the horizon. The club's door team was still made up of local men, who harboured the same fears about the local hard men who had earned their reputations in the playground. And, as far as the door team were concerned, they were going to take those reputations to their graves. I had to concede that, despite the fact the majority of these doormen were good decent people, the only way I was going to keep the troublemakers out of the club was if I sacked them and brought in fresh faces from out of the area. But, for now, the local doormen were all I had and I would have to make do.

I have to admit that I was nervous about my position, but controlling the door of a nightclub is all about front. I couldn't show my fear or walk away after criticising Venables: I was going to have to stand my ground and do what I needed to do. The legacy of the last door firm was over and I was determined not to make the same mistakes as my former boss. As soon as I started to employ my rather abrasive tactics, more and more people began to get seriously hurt; knives and other weapons were regularly used. Before too long, revellers were commenting on the decrease in violence, but behind the scenes those who wished to cause trouble were paying for it dearly.

In one incident, a local man came to the front door and became abusive because I insisted that he be searched before he entered the club. He went away and returned with a rounders bat. Maurice Golding, a doorman from Bristol, was hit across the head and the man ran away. We all chased the bat-wielding assailant, and the manager followed, trying to reason with me to calm down. We caught the man 500 yards away from Raquels outside the local bingo hall. The doorman who caught him began to hit him, but I told him to stop. I kneeled on the man's chest and cut him twice with a sheath knife: once on the face, once on his upper thigh. The manager was outraged. I posed the question: if he had chased Maurice and Maurice had fallen over, what would he have done with the rounders bat? It was only right that he got a bit of his own medicine.

Another night, a man from Leeds was refused entry because he was drunk. He produced a knife and began waving it and shouting obscenities. I told him to put the knife down, but he kept shouting, 'Do you want some? Do you want some?'

'It's up to you which way this goes,' I said. 'Last chance: put the knife down.'

He refused. He was slashed and left with a deep open wound to the left-hand side of his face. Again, I justified this by asking what would have happened if I had walked towards him without a knife and he was still brandishing his? I've always said the aggressor dictates the way things go. If they put their hands up, I'll put my hands up. If they pull out a weapon, I'll pull out a weapon. It's entirely their choice. Violence is a messy business.

One Sunday evening, I arranged to go to Epping Country Club with three drug dealers from Bristol named Steve Curtis, Nathan Kaye and David Thomkins. I had met them in the Ministry of Sound and had agreed to introduce them to Tony Tucker because he was trying to recruit new dealers for his clubs. I'll always remember introducing the trio to Tucker. He asked if they had any drugs with them. When they said they had cocaine and wanted £40 a gram for it, Tucker looked at me, looked at them as if they were mad and started to laugh. 'Tell them to hand over two grams or I'll take the fucking lot,' he said. This was typical of Tucker – he wasn't in the habit of paying for things, particularly his drug habit.

Whilst in Tucker's company, I decided to put a proposal to him concerning the situation at Raquels. I explained about the trouble that I was having with inadequate doormen and said I needed the back-up of a strong firm. I told him that if he went into partnership with me, I would run the door and he could reap whatever benefits there were to be had from providing invoices and any other 'commodities'– drugs, protection, debts and so on. I would not bother him with the day-to-day running of the club. The only time I would call on him was if I had a severe problem and needed back-up. In return, trouble or no trouble, he would make money each week from the club. Tucker nodded in agreement, shook my hand and said we had a deal.

On 4 September 1993, Tucker and I began our partnership together at Raquels. The agreement brought new faces onto the scene. Men who worked for Tucker in East London and were looking for a change would come and work for me in Basildon. They had never heard of the local troublemakers therefore their reputations and threats meant nothing. They were dealt with like anybody else: reasonably at first, but if that didn't work they were subjected to extreme violence and barred.

One evening, I got a call from a doorman who said his mate, Gavin Spicer, was looking for work. Apparently, Gavin had been sacked from a club in Ilford after sending a customer to hospital. The man said he'd already spoken to Tucker on Gavin's behalf but had been told that there weren't any vacancies. This struck me as odd because I'd already mentioned to Tucker that I needed an extra man. I suspected he had another reason for saying no.

The politics of the door is worthy of academic study. The microcosm is a catty little world built on bubbling jealousies, stifled resentments and long-borne grudges. One week someone was in favour, the next he was a grass, a bottler or a wanker. People won't speak to each other for years for quite petty reasons. Perhaps someone sweated on their towel in the gym or tipped over their nail varnish. Many bodybuilders are better manicured than Jordan and Cheryl Cole put together. If you could calculate which groups spend the most on sunbeds, leg-waxing and hairdos, you'd find it a toss-up between call girls and bodybuilders. I hated all that doorman politics. I like to take people as I find them, not as they're 'generally known'.

I rang Tucker and asked him about employing Gavin. He said he didn't really like the guy, although he couldn't, or wouldn't, give a reason. In the end, he said, 'It's up to you, Bernie. If you need someone, then take him on.' I rang my contact back and told him to tell Gavin he had the job.

When I got out of my car at Raquels that Friday evening, I noticed an Asian-looking bodybuilder locking up his car. I was always very vigilant when entering and leaving the club; I felt that was the time at which a doorman was most vulnerable to attack from people seeking revenge. The Asian man walked towards me and asked, 'Are you Bernie?' When I said I was, he stuck out his hand and said, 'All right, mate. I'm Gavin.' During the evening, I asked Gavin why certain people seemed so set against him working with us. He explained that Tucker had once turned up at a club where he was working and hadn't wanted to queue, pay or show any sort of respect to the doormen. That would have been typical of Tucker. He'd walk to the front of any nightclub queue and when asked for money would look at the door staff as if they had just asked him for unnatural sex. When he had done so at the club where Gavin was working, Tucker had not only been refused entry but was also beaten up. Word soon got round about the incident and Tucker lost face – an unforgivable outrage in the world of the door. It was because of this that he didn't want to employ anyone who had been part of that door firm.

I liked Gavin from that first evening I met him. Quiet and uncomplicated, he meant what he said and said what he meant. His catchphrase with leery customers was: 'What's your problem, mate?' Then he'd usually try reasoning with them. If they remained unreasonable, he had no hesitation in creating new patients for the NHS. He didn't care for reputations – and could certainly fight. In fact, he turned out to be the most reliable and able doorman that I ever employed. Within a short period of time, Gavin became the man I relied on most when war broke out. Away from Raquels, he became my closest friend.

One Saturday night, two skinheads with tattoos on their heads and necks came to Strings. They arrived with four non-skinhead friends. I could see them looking at Gavin, making snide remarks and laughing. Then they started doing the same to me. When they thought they were getting away with their moronic behaviour, they began to get braver. One of the clowns stood behind me, aping me, so I spun round and grabbed him by the throat, pushing him backwards as I did so. He fell back and hit his head on the corner of a glass pillar, which shattered – as did his tattooed head.

Gavin heard the sound of breaking glass and ran from the other side of the bar with a bottle in his hand. He told me later that he thought I'd been attacked with a glass. He saw my 'attacker' on the floor but couldn't see the gash in the back of his head. Gavin whacked his bottle a few times over the skinhead's already skewered skull. Then we both pulled him up and manhandled him towards the exit. His mates seemed too stunned to do anything.

With my brothers Paul (left) and Jerry (right), and mother Anna, Dunstable, early 1960s.

Aged 16, with Carole Lett,
the mother of my son, Adrian.

In the army, aged 19.
Taken in Catterick, North Yorkshire.

On the run in South Africa, 1985.

With Debra, after arriving in Essex, 1986.

At Tony Tucker's birthday party, where I first met Craig Rolfe.

With Reggie Kray in Maidstone prison, 1994.

With the Taylor sisters – Lisa (left) and Michelle – June 1993.

THE RETTENDON MURDER SCENE, 7 DECEMBER 1995

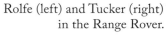

Rolfe (left) and Tucker (right)
in the Range Rover.

Pat Tate slumped in
the rear of the vehicle.

Fighting with John 'Gaffer' Rollinson, 8 May 1999.

Emma and I on our wedding day.
We were married at Peterborough Cathedral, 16 July 2004.

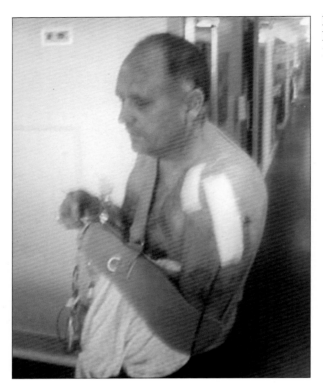

In September 2005, after I had been stabbed with a 14-inch blade.

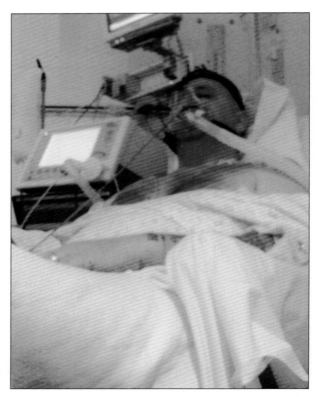

Fighting for my life in a Birmingham hospital, December 2006.

I married Roshea at Alnwick Castle in Northumberland on 20 September 2009.

My mother Anna, with Roshea, Codsall, August 2009.

At the *Bonded by Blood* premiere, 31 August 2010. The film was based on my book of the same name. (L–R: my son Vinney with his partner, Hayley Barnet; Roshea and me; my son Adrian; and my daughter Karis with her partner, Sean Conlon.)

My son Paddy O'Mahoney, aged 10 months, November 2010.

As we were dragging him across the floor, we threw him into one of the glass doors, which also smashed, cutting his upper arm. He was still struggling a bit, so we beat him before throwing him down the stairs. His mates followed him meekly, only shouting abuse when they'd got safely outside.

About half an hour later, customers near the main doors began screaming and shouting 'Fire! Fire!' Gavin and I ran to the stairwell and saw flames leaping up from the bar entrance. I told the manager and staff to deal with the fire, and then Gavin and I ran out through the flames into the street. We found the skinhead with the sore head standing in the middle of the road with a red petrol can in his hand. Perhaps the earlier beating had slowed his reflexes because, although he looked surprised to see us, he didn't run immediately, a significant mistake on his part.

I sprinted across to him, an Irish hurling stick in hand. The skinhead dropped the petrol can and pleaded, 'It wasn't me, it wasn't me.' He turned to flee, but I hit him across the back with the stick. He fell to the ground. Gavin began kicking him in the head with his steel boots. The skinhead begged us not to beat him any more, but the time for debate was long gone. I hit him with the hurling stick so hard across the back that it broke, and Gavin stamped on his head. By this stage, there was little point in administering any further treatment: the skinhead was no longer moving; he was unconscious.

We picked up the petrol can and doused him with the remaining fuel. Another skinhead, who'd run a short distance away, began screaming, 'Please don't burn him! Please don't burn him!' We told him to come to us and assured him that we were not going to do anything. He wasn't stupid; he remained exactly where he was. When we bent over his prostrate friend and gave the impression that we were going to ignite the petrol, the man became hysterical. Having had our fun and taught two Basildon citizens a valuable lesson in manners, we threw down the petrol can and walked back to the club.

A week later, the skinhead who'd run away returned to the club's front door, pissed out of his head, asking for 'that fucking Paki'. When we were made aware of his presence, Gavin and I dashed downstairs to deal with the dissatisfied customer.

'What's your problem, mate?' said Gavin.

'You, you Paki cunt,' said the skinhead. 'You're going to get this.' He then produced an axe from the inside of his jacket. But before he could use it, I'd squirted him in the face with ammonia, and Gavin had slashed him across the head with a blade. We threw him outside amid a flurry of kicks and punches, then slammed the door shut. The skinhead lay howling outside in the gutter. Eventually, he got up and disappeared into the darkness, whimpering.

We regularly received death threats and warnings from various sources, but the skinheads never did come back.

Not all of the customers were violent misfits. Many were just amusing freaks. One character I warmed to was an awesomely thin creature in his late teens. Around six feet tall with lizard-like features, he'd gulp and stutter violently when he tried to talk. We named him Disco Dave.

On Mondays, we used to hold an under-18s night, which attracted 300 potential and actual juvenile delinquents from the local estates. We wouldn't sell them alcohol, but that didn't make any difference: they'd just get pissed before they came into the club. Like their sociopath parents, these kids would then spend the evening indulging in brawls, beatings and drunken gropes.

One Monday night the door staff got called to a disturbance on the dance floor. As I approached, I noticed a heap of around ten writhing, spitting kids. They appeared to be attacking someone who lay on the floor beneath them. We dragged the kids off one by one to find a bleeding man cowering in fear. This was my first meeting with Disco Dave. Apparently, he'd taken off his shirt to expose his grotesquely underdeveloped body. A group of youths had objected. Disco told them to fuck off and they'd steamed into him.

I cleaned him up and suggested he go home and come to the adult nights instead, as it was now a few years since he'd been under 18. He said he didn't have enough money to get into the adult nights or to get home.

I agreed to give him a lift when the club closed and he waited patiently for me. Every time I tried to talk to him, he became engulfed in violent gulping and stuttering. In the end, I decided silence was the best policy. I told him to sit in the back of my car when we left to prevent idle chat.

On the way to his house, I was stopped by the police. This wasn't unusual: they were always on my case. When I saw the flashing blue light, I told Disco to let me do the talking because I wanted to get home at a reasonable hour. The policeman walked up to the driver's door and asked me the usual questions. 'I've been to work and I'm going home,' I said, 'and before you ask, he's fuck-all to do with me. I'm just giving him a lift.'

The officer then asked Disco for his details. Disco was so nervous that he gulped, stuttered, spat and blinked for so long that in the end the policeman said, 'It's all right, mate. Forget it. Off you go.'

I suppose I adopted Disco Dave as a sort of club mascot. I knew he had no money, so I used to let him in for free. I could see this made him feel important. One evening, I told him that in the future he should ignore the long queues, march straight to the front, walk past the door staff, cashier and those searching, and if *anybody* said *anything* he had to say, 'My name's Disco Dave. I don't pay. And I don't give a fuck.' Nothing more. Nothing less.

This amusing scenario worked well until the company directors and other VIPs decided to visit the club. They were all standing around the reception area when Disco walked in wearing trainers. One of the directors looked at Disco, looked at me, and stood waiting for me to say something. I just shrugged.

The director decided to intervene. 'I'm afraid you can't come in wearing trainers, sir,' he said. Of course, Disco looked straight at him, gulped and, with the pride and arrogance of a gladiator, stuttered out the words: 'My name's Disco Dave. I don't pay. And I don't give a fuck.' He then marched past the director and all the door staff and disappeared upstairs.

'Who on earth is that?' the director asked, aghast.

'Don't even go there,' I replied. 'He's a fucking psycho nightmare.'

When our visitors went upstairs later, they saw that Disco was dancing on a raised podium with his shirt off, looking like a complete fool. Indirectly, he'd helped us rebuff recent allegations that we'd become too violent towards customers. Indeed, the director thought we ought to impose our authority a bit more firmly. He hadn't liked our completely hands-off approach to a stuttering, skeletal representative of the undead who'd pushed his way into the club without paying.

Since our partnership had begun, I had seen a lot more of Tony Tucker socially. He invited me and all the other doormen from Raquels to his birthday party at the Prince of Wales pub in South Ockendon. He also asked me to take along Steve Curtis, Nathan Kaye and David Thomkins, the drug dealers whom I had introduced Tucker to, so that there would be a supply of drugs for him and his guests. Tucker was in a very good mood that night. The party was a real success. Doormen from as far afield as Brighton and Manchester were there. Most were out of their faces on cocaine, Special K or Ecstasy, or a cocktail of all three and more.

In the early hours of the morning, I was sitting on the floor of an upstairs room with Steve and Nathan. A man in his early 20s pushed open a door, which struck me. I looked at him, waiting for him to apologise, but he just smirked and asked me what my problem was. 'You've just knocked the fucking door into me,' I said.

'Well, you're a doorman, aren't you?' he replied.

It was a stupid thing to say because it was obviously intended to incite trouble. I got up and strode towards him. The man walked out to the kitchen and I went after him. Friends of Tucker's also followed us, but before I could teach the wretch manners, others intervened. It was only later I learned that the man was Craig Rolfe, Tucker's closest friend. I was told that Rolfe was extremely possessive over his friendship with Tucker.

The next time we met, I told Rolfe that, out of respect for Tucker, he shouldn't have tried causing trouble at his birthday party. Rolfe seemed to accept this and we tolerated one another thereafter, but he never did lose his 'couldn't give a fuck' attitude. When I explained to Tucker what had gone on, he told me why Rolfe was so bitter and appeared to have a constant bad attitude.

On Christmas Eve 1968, Rolfe's father, Brian, had been beaten to death by his mother Lorraine's lover. At the time, Lorraine was expecting Craig, her fourth child. Her lover, John Kennedy, was later convicted of the murder and sent to prison for life. Lorraine was convicted of making false statements in an effort to impede his arrest and sent to prison for 18 months. It was while serving this sentence in Holloway Prison that Lorraine gave birth to Craig. It is no surprise, therefore, that he had an immense chip on his shoulder and that he had ended up living a chaotic criminal lifestyle.

As Rolfe was my new business partner's best friend, it was inevitable that I would learn a lot more about him and his sordid past. By the age of 16, I was told Rolfe had grown into a classic juvenile delinquent: at odds with everything that society had to offer and accumulating several minor criminal convictions along the way. He worked for a short time as a tyre fitter, then as a plasterer, but the only trade in which he ever excelled was the sale and distribution of drugs.

Rolfe met his partner, Donna Jagger, after her family had moved to the Basildon area. Keen to impress his attractive girlfriend, Rolfe began dealing drugs in nightclubs around Essex to fund a better lifestyle for them both. The relationship grew turbulent, but regardless of how much the couple fought and argued they remained hopelessly devoted to one another.

Rolfe was a devious man rather than an intelligent one, but it didn't take him long to realise that selling pills to nightclub revellers was never going to make him rich. If you wanted to make serious money, the quickest but most dangerous way was to order large amounts from suppliers and, once delivered, simply not pay them. Stupid or fearless – I'm not sure which – Rolfe stole from countless drug dealers and never once suffered any form of reprisal.

In the autumn of 1990, Rolfe and Donna's daughter, Georgie, was born. A few weeks later, Rolfe made a drugs sale that was to dictate the path the rest of his life was to follow. A man turned up at Rolfe's home, having been told by friends that he had good-quality cocaine for sale. As is the norm, a small test sample was given to the man to try.

'This is fucking good gear,' he said. 'Who did you get it off?'

Rolfe, high on his own supply, replied, 'Fuck knows! I ripped off some idiot in Southend.'

The pair fell about laughing and spent the day snorting the rest of the cocaine together. The man was Tony Tucker – Rolfe had finally found a kindred spirit.

Rolfe had developed a fairly serious cocaine problem, so hanging around with Tucker was useful because there was a constant supply of drugs, if not for free, being sold at a discounted price.

Shortly after Tucker's birthday party, Steve, Nathan and Thomkins began working at Club UK in Wandsworth, where Tucker ran the security. (The details of their appointment had been agreed at Tucker's birthday party.) For the exclusive right to sell drugs in Club UK, they paid Tucker £1,000 per weekend. On average, their return for Friday and Saturday nights was £12,000. The Bristol trio were happy, Tucker was happy and the revellers were happy. The drug dealers who had been ousted from Club UK, however, were seething.

On Christmas Eve 1993, Tucker's firm celebrated in style. My brother Michael and his wife came to a party we were attending at the Café de Paris in the West End of London. It was one of the most exclusive clubs in the UK at the time. There were queues of people outside, which we ignored as a matter of course. These events where the firm got together were extraordinary. Nobody connected to us paid to get in anywhere. Nobody paid for drink or drugs. Huge bags of cocaine, Special K and Ecstasy were made available to the firm and their associates. When you looked around the dark room, you were surrounded by 40 or more friends, all 'faces'. The music was so loud it lifted you; you were all one – we felt like we had total control. Those on the firm created an atmosphere that demanded respect from other villains. Straight people hardly noticed. On the surface, everyone was friendly, but there was this feeling of power and evil. Tucker felt it, too. Often he would look across the crowded room, clench his fists and smile knowingly. We were all immersed in something that could only ever end in bloodshed or death.

After the party, we went back to Steve and Nathan's flat in Denmark Court in Surrey Quays, an exclusive development in the South London Docklands. Strewn across the floor, spilling out of a carrier bag, lay more than £20,000, the proceeds of that weekend's drug dealing. They earned so much money they didn't know how to spend it or where to put it.

Around that time in London there was a little firm going around the clubs who used to look out for the dealers, follow them home and rob them of their proceeds. It was quite a lucrative operation because the victims couldn't go to the police. Steve and Nathan had been targeted by this gang while dealing in the Ministry of Sound. Somebody had knocked on the door while Steve was in the house alone. When Steve had answered, two men had pushed their way in, tied Steve up and threatened him with a knife. Steve refused to say where the money was, so one of the men cut him several times in the mouth, demanding to know where the cash was hidden. Eventually, when the men had become increasingly violent Steve, who genuinely feared for his life, handed over £4,000. The robbers had then left.

Steve was convinced he would be targeted again, so he paid me to protect him, Dave and Nathan. During their career in the drug world, the men from Bristol were to call on me many times for assistance.

Business in Basildon was far from booming and so the club owners decided that a change was needed. Out went the grand piano and in came framed gold discs, electric guitars, trumpets, American football jerseys, helmets and baseball bats (purely for decor). They converted

Strings into an American-themed venue and renamed it the Buzz bar.

The revamp had the desired effect and attracted a lot more custom. Along with the good came the bad. Opposite Raquels in the market square stood the Bullseye, the pub where Whidlake and Downes had been attacked by machete-wielding maniacs. The regulars rather inventively called themselves 'the Bullseye gang'. The most notorious member of this gang was a man in his 20s named Jason Draper.

Whenever I had cause to speak to Draper, he was polite, but when he was with his minions he did tend to act up for their benefit. When the Buzz bar opened, the Bullseye gang turned up for a drink. They were generally well behaved and so I let them remain on the basis that everybody deserves a chance.

In January 1994, there was a bomb scare on the Southend to London rail line. All trains were prevented from leaving Basildon, and passengers weren't allowed into the station, so within a very short period of time there was a large crowd hanging around the town centre. Rather than stand in the street on a miserable winter's night, a lot of people headed to the Buzz bar for a drink.

As soon as I arrived at work, I informed the manager that we would need additional door staff or there was going to be trouble. The penny-pinching manager disagreed and suggested that I was more than capable of resolving any incident that may arise. I wasn't happy about it, but he paid the invoice and I certainly wasn't going to get additional men in without paying them. When I walked back into the Buzz bar, I noticed that there was a group of about ten men from Romford. Seven or eight men from the Bullseye were eyeing them with menace.

By half past eight, the bar was completely packed, so much so it was difficult to move from one area to another. One of the men from the Bullseye sidled up to me and said, 'Look, Bernie, we don't want to cause trouble in here, but one of those geezers from Romford is giving it to us.'

'What do you mean, giving it?' I asked.

'Every time he walks past, he knocks into us, and it's going to go off in here in a minute,' he replied.

Rather than get into a debate about what might or might not happen, I said to him, 'I do not want any grief in here, so if you wish, I will ask the Romford lads to leave. You can then do what you want outside.'

I didn't get back anything that resembled an answer, so I made my way outside to get a cup of tea from a nearby burger van. I was followed outside by one of the Bullseye gang, who kept insisting that it was going to kick off and that a fat man had been mouthing off about using a CS gas dispenser.

I wasn't prepared to delve into the future; I had explained my position to the Bullseye gang and, as far as I was concerned, if they wished to maintain good relations with me they would accept my offer to have the men ejected.

I had bought my tea and was making my way back up the stairs to the Buzz bar when I heard a loud roar, glass being smashed and people screaming. I dropped my tea and ran into the bar, where I found a huge fight in progress. The Bullseye gang were hammering the lads from Romford, and others were throwing glasses, bottles and stools at random targets. True to his word, the fat man had let off the CS gas canister, which had sent those customers not involved in the melee running from the building, coughing and choking, with their eyes streaming. I tried pulling people apart, but the fight was spilling out onto the stairs. Several men were bleeding heavily; at least one lay unconscious.

I managed to bundle the Bullseye gang out of the doors and lock the men from Romford in the Buzz bar. As soon as the doors were secure, one of the men from Romford struck me in the face, so I began fighting with him. At that moment, the doors burst open and the Bullseye gang came flooding back in. The men from Romford then seemed to lose their will to fight – some jumped over the bar to escape, others fled out into the street. I grabbed the man that I was fighting in a bear hug and ran as fast as I could into a large pillar supporting the ceiling. I felt the man's breath leaving his body and when I stepped back and released him, he crumpled to the floor.

The Bullseye gang had by this time run out into the street, so I followed them. When I got downstairs, I found a man lying on the ground with blood gushing from a gaping wound near his eye. I ran over to him just as a convoy of police cars arrived on the scene. The wound was so large it was hard to tell if the man had been stabbed or glassed. I put him in the recovery position and wrapped my coat around his head to try and stop the flow of blood. An ambulance was summoned and the man was taken to hospital. I found out later that he had lost the sight in one of his eyes.

I didn't dwell on the incident because an equally violent incident occurred every week at the club. It was just the way things were at Raquels. The police appealed for witnesses, but in Basildon they might as well have been appealing for God to return to earth. Nobody in his or her right mind would give evidence against the Bullseye gang.

On 11 February, the Bullseye gang attempted to get into Raquels. I told them to fuck off because of their behaviour in the Buzz bar and a fight broke out. They backed away, then appeared with weapons they'd produced from their cars, which were parked nearby. As the door staff walked towards them, they started throwing bottles, bricks and pieces of wooden pallets they'd smashed. I ordered the door staff back into the club and closed the doors. The Bullseye gang must have sensed victory because they charged the doors, trying to smash them with an axe and iron bars. They then doused the doors in petrol and tried to burn them. I didn't fancy being incinerated, so I opened the doors and we ran outside.

Draper, the man the Bullseye mob looked up to, wasn't present, so they didn't have much heart. They dropped their weapons and ran. We gave chase and managed to catch two or three of them; one was beaten so badly he stopped breathing. When the police arrived, an ambulance was called and paramedics fought for some time to resuscitate the stricken combatant.

Several of the Bullseye gang made statements saying that I had repeatedly jumped on the man's chest and stamped on his throat. I was duly arrested, but as far as I was concerned it had been a clear case of self-defence. I had the usual coachload of witnesses from the club to verify the fact. I was released from custody the following day and no charges were ever brought against me. Fortunately, the man lived to tell the tale and so both sides walked away happy.

The format for nights out at Raquels had been the same for years: three hours of chart music and five slow dances at the end, interrupted at regular intervals by morons trying to fuck or fight each other. When a new manager named Mark Combes took over at the club, it was agreed that change was the way forward. At the time, rave music had swept across the country, so the idea was to have rave nights. There was no place for violence on the rave scene – all the kids were into the fashionable 'peace and happiness' thing. Raquels was now an ideal venue to stage such events. I had recruited what I considered to be a decent door team. I had men who were able to stand their ground if there was trouble, but they were certainly not bullies. Previously, we had endured regular visits from the local constabulary, but we rarely saw them now. On the face of it, the police could see a trouble-free, well-run club, so they diverted their attention elsewhere. The police had what they wanted, the customers were getting what they wanted and the firm was getting what it wanted. The lunatics had taken over the asylum.

When word got round about the proposed change in music at Raquels, the manager was approached by a promotions team from Southend who were very professional and very successful. They were hiring out a club in the Southend area at the time that couldn't hold enough people to fulfil the demand they had created, so a deal was struck and a date was set for them to begin putting raves on at Raquels.

The following day a man named Mark Murray and his partner 'Chemical Bob' came into the Buzz bar and asked to speak to me. They told me that they sold most of the drugs in the clubs around the Basildon and Southend area and they had heard that the promotions team from Southend were coming into Raquels. They asked if we could reach a financial agreement that would allow them to sell their wares exclusively in the club.

I rang Tucker and he asked me to tell them that they could have their deal. The 'rent' for operating in the club would depend on the amount of drugs they sold per night. If the club got busy because of the rave nights, then the deal would be adjusted accordingly, making the sale of drugs more lucrative for all involved. For now, both parties agreed to see how things went. It was going to be the door staff's job to ensure there was no trouble from other dealers and also that an early warning of any police presence would be given.

In March 1994, 20-year-old Kevin Jones collapsed and died in Club UK after taking Ecstasy he had purchased there. It didn't take long before Steve, Nathan and Thomkins were named as possible suppliers of the drug that had killed Kevin. Instead of raiding their homes and arresting them, the police mounted a surveillance operation in the hope that they could arrest and convict those at the top end of the drug chain.

On 6 May 1994, the police pounced and found 1,500 Ecstasy pills in a car parked beneath Steve and Nathan's flat. The car was not registered to either man. Police checks revealed it had, in fact, been reported stolen in Bristol some weeks earlier.

At the same time as the police swooped in London, Dave Thomkins was arrested at his home in Bath. Steve and Nathan were placed under arrest and refused bail, while Thomkins was interviewed and granted bail pending further inquiries.

As soon as Dave was released, he rang and told me what had happened. I said I would organise a 'proper' solicitor for Steven and Nathan and suggested that we should meet up for their appearance at Tower Bridge Magistrates' Court.

When I told Tucker about the arrests, he began shouting and screaming. He was worried that Steve and Nathan were going to grass on him for taking rent; I told him that there was absolutely no chance of that.

The following day, Dave and I met Nathan's girlfriend, who gave us £20,000 in cash. We took the money to Leman St police station in the City, pushed it over the counter and asked for our friends to be released. The officer at the desk was gobsmacked. He didn't know how he should proceed. Dave and I were kept waiting for hours whilst he checked with his superiors. We were taken into a room and asked about our identities and where the money had come from; we told the police a family friend had lent it to us.

In the end, the officer said he could not accept it and that bail would be granted only if it could be shown that the money was in an account prior to Steve and Nathan's arrest. After making several frantic phone calls, we found someone who was able to do the necessary and the following morning Steve and Nathan were freed on bail. No charges were ever brought against Dave.

At Steve and Nathan's trial, the jury could not reach a verdict, but they were acquitted at the re-trial and returned to live in the West Country. With Dave, Steve and Nathan out of the picture, Tucker needed to recruit a new gang of drug dealers for Club UK. He telephoned me and asked how Murray was performing at Raquels. I told him that he and his dealers were discreet, efficient and problem-free. Tucker then asked me to escort Murray over to his house for a meeting.

When we arrived, Tucker informed Murray that he wanted him to take over the sale of drugs in Club UK. Murray would have to buy all of his drug supply directly from Tucker and pay £1,200 rent each weekend, but in return, Tucker told Murray, he could earn in excess of £12,000 profit. Murray stuck out his hand without hesitation: the deal was struck.

For the introduction to Tucker, Murray said he would pay me £500 a week once he had started work at Club UK and I would have no further involvement. It was, as he said, a drink as a favour. It had been quite a lucrative ten-minute meeting.

In order to make Club UK pay, Murray would have to run a pretty slick operation. He would have to have enough dealers in the club to meet the demand in order to reap the rewards his predecessors had earned. But Murray found the going hard. He couldn't earn any money because he couldn't recruit enough dealers. He was selling approximately 500 Ecstasy pills a night, nowhere near enough to earn a profit. Needless to say, Tucker demanded his rent regardless.

By the time Murray had paid for his stock, there wasn't anything left. Each week he remained at Club UK, he was simply getting deeper and deeper in debt. He begged Tucker for more time to pay, which was initially granted, but he was never going to be given the time he needed. It was becoming increasingly clear to me that people in the drug trade were all operating on borrowed time. To be successful, a drug dealer has to make it known to as many people as possible that they have drugs for sale – it's no good them standing in a nightclub with 500 Ecstasy pills in their pocket and keeping the fact to themselves. But the more people you tell and the more pills you sell, the higher the chance of being apprehended

9

BANK HOLIDAY MADNESS

THE problems at the club with the Bullseye gang had festered rather than gone away completely, and the threats from Dunbar's friends and the man whose chest I had allegedly jumped on were becoming more frequent. When you work on the door of a pub or nightclub, you regularly get told that people are coming back to sort you out, to stab or shoot you. You have to take every threat seriously, even though 99 per cent of these threats are hollow; it's that 1 per cent who will genuinely try to harm or kill you. Those making the threats against me constantly mentioned the name Jason Draper. I wasn't concerned at the time because I had become quite friendly with him and we would often socialise together. On occasion, he would come into Raquels. He never caused any problems and I therefore didn't consider him a threat.

Make no mistake: Jason Draper was no fool. If riled, he could become extremely dangerous. After falling out with one man, Draper recruited a woman to go into his local pub and flirt with him. When the couple left the pub to hail a taxi to the woman's home, Draper was lying in wait. He temporarily paralysed the man after hacking his head with a machete.

One Friday evening, there was a mass brawl in the top bar at Raquels. The DJ called for security and when I arrived I found Draper beating up a man and offering to fight several others. I pulled him away from the very relieved and bloodied reveller and asked him to calm down. He was extremely irate, claiming the man deserved further punishment because he had assaulted his girlfriend. The manager insisted Draper leave. He wasn't happy about being ejected, but he did as I asked. People with reputations do not like being asked to leave a bar or club because they feel they've lost face, so I had a feeling this wouldn't be the end of the matter.

The following evening Draper returned to Raquels. I stopped him at the front door and explained that he was barred. He said he wanted to talk to me in private. We went outside into the street and he began to get angry, repeating that he had done no wrong because the man had assaulted his girlfriend. Right or wrong, he had been fighting in the club and therefore he was barred.

One of the other doormen came outside and asked me if everything was all right. Draper took exception to this. 'If everything wasn't, what the fuck would you do about it?' he shouted. The doorman laughed at Draper and said that if he had a problem with him, he would gladly sort it out. A slagging match ensued, but as the doorman walked towards Draper he backed off. As he did so, he threatened that he would be back.

'What's the point of going away if you're going to come back?' I shouted. 'Why don't we resolve this whilst you're here?' But he did not reply. I walked back to the club and thought no more about it.

Ten minutes later Draper walked into reception. He said that he was sorry and had got upset because the other doorman had intervened. I explained to him that the manager would not let him in the club regardless of any conversation that we might have and so his best bet would be to leave it for a few weeks until the dust settled.

The following weekend I went to the Gass nightclub in London's West End with Draper. He was very apologetic about the problems he had caused and we agreed that I would let him back into the club in a few weeks' time. I was making the same mistake Venables had made: I should have fucked Draper up when he put his first foot wrong, but I considered him a friend. I should have known better; you don't have friends when it involves your business.

The personal battles I regularly fought were intermingled with the never-ending grief that the firm's enterprises produced. During the same week that I had sorted matters out with Draper, I received a telephone call from Dave, Steve and Nathan. They told me they were having trouble with some doormen from Bristol who, seeing them wearing designer clothes and driving round in BMWs whilst claiming benefits, wanted to relieve them of some of their ill-gotten assets. I told them I would make a few phone calls and sort it out.

I rang the doormen and told them to leave it out otherwise they would be dealt with. I gave them the impression that the Bristol trio were working for a very heavy London-based firm. We knew the Bristol doormen's names and where to find them. They didn't have a clue who we were or where we were from, which put us in quite a powerful position. The doormen argued that Dave, Steve and Nathan were the cause of the trouble, but they conceded that it wasn't worth falling out over and the grief would now end.

The next morning, I got a frantic phone call from Steve and Nathan. They said they had been driving through Bath in their BMW when they had been flagged down. They were dragged from the car by two men, who informed them that they were taking the vehicle and keeping it. Steve and Nathan said they wanted their car back, but they were scared of the thieves. I told them that if I was to go down to Bath to recover a car, I would have to go firm-handed because I did not know who or what I would be up against. I asked them how many men I'd need and they said if I could muster ten, they would pay us £300 each. I asked for a contact number for the man who had taken the car and said that we would be down that evening. I told Steve and Nathan to stay out of the way until the car was retrieved.

The man holding the vehicle was called Billy Gillings. He had a reputation in the Bristol area as a hard man and had just come out of prison for robbing a security van. I rang Billy and asked him if he had the car. He got all shirty at first, so I told him to calm down and listen. I pointed out to Billy that I knew where he lived and he didn't even know my name. I was coming to Bath to recover the car whatever.

I had no particular loyalty to Steve and Nathan so I suggested we come to an agreement. 'Falling out over a BMW is hardly worth it,' I said. Billy agreed. I told him for recovering the car I was going to be paid £1,000 and he should meet me at Bath railway station and hand over the vehicle. I would then give him half the money. I told Billy that he would have to tell people that a group of ten men had confronted him and repossessed the car. We'd both be £500 better off and everyone would be happy. Billy laughed and agreed to meet me.

I rang Steve and Nathan and told them that there were ten of us travelling down to Bath in two cars. They had to ensure that they stayed out of the way until I called them. I drove to Bath on my own and met Billy as arranged. I confirmed the plot to him and said that I would meet him again in an hour's time, but first he would have to give me the car. He agreed.

I then drove to meet Steve and Nathan. I said there had been a bit of trouble with Billy and so the other people with me had driven out of Bath because they feared the police would be looking for them. I added that I was meeting them later, as they needed to be paid. I then gave Steve and Nathan the car and they gave me £3,000.

Dave, who had arrived with them, was ranting and raving. He said another man, named Steve Woods, had burgled his home. He had stolen a lot of electrical goods, then covered his children's bedroom floor and walls with excrement. He was under the impression that Woods was also going to be sorted out as part of the £3,000 payment. He claimed that Woods and Gillings were in on it together: Gillings had the car; Woods, he alleged, had carried out the burglary and given the goods to Gillings to sell.

I wasn't aware that Dave's home had been burgled, but I said I could resolve the issue for him if he wanted me to. I added that it wouldn't get sorted out that day; however, Dave was adamant that it had to be sorted immediately.

'Suit yourself. But you will have to do it on your own,' I said.

I shook hands with Steve and Nathan, jumped into a cab and went to meet Billy. I gave him his £500 and kept £2,500 for myself.

Later that night, I got a call from Dave. He told me he couldn't stand the thought of Woods robbing his home and defiling his children's bedroom and thinking he'd got away with it. I told him Woods hadn't, to which he replied, 'Too right he hasn't. I've just fucking shot him.' He then began ranting about what he had done.

After leaving me, he had gone home and picked up a shotgun. He had gone to Woods's house and before knocking on the door had put on a balaclava. Woods's girlfriend had answered. Dave pushed her aside and found Woods in the hallway. Dave fired and hit Woods in the upper thigh. He then ran over to Woods, who had collapsed on the floor, put the gun to his head and shouted, 'I want my fucking television back.' Woods's girlfriend was screaming. Dave levelled the gun at her head and told her to shut up. He then made good his escape. I told Dave it was all a bit over the top for the sake of a 14-inch Nicam television – but he obviously didn't think so.

This kind of behaviour was becoming the norm for more and more people in and around the firm. The shooting wasn't about a television; it was about front, nothing more and nothing less. Dave simply wanted people to know that you couldn't take liberties with him.

Now that Dave had calmed down, he didn't have a clue what he was going to do. It wasn't really my problem, but he was associated with the firm and you have to help your own. I suggested he hide the weapon, jump in a car and meet me in Basildon as soon as possible. I didn't know if Woods still had Dave's television or not. Either way, it didn't really matter: according to the tabloids, everyone who's sent to prison these days gets their own one anyway. I always try to find a positive, whatever the situation.

I could have done without Dave's problem at that particular time. The police in Basildon, although maintaining their distance, were keeping a very watchful eye on my activities. I wasn't going to be able to keep him at my house because the police often watched who came and went, so instead I rang the landlady of a pub in Basildon who owed me a favour. I had sorted out a bit of trouble for her when she had run a pub in Southend. I asked if she would put my friend up for the night. She was reluctant to help me at first, which is understandable – I had just told her Dave had attempted to murder somebody and she had never even met the man; the thought of spending the night alone with him must have been quite unnerving. However, she relented in the end.

The following day we contacted a few people in Bath to try and find out about Woods's condition. We learned that Dave had blasted a large hole in Woods's upper thigh. It was unlikely that he would ever be able to walk properly again. His life was not in danger, but the police were treating the shooting as an attempted murder.

We arranged for the gun to be picked up and disposed of, and for Dave to go and stay with people in Liverpool for a few days until the dust settled.

Meanwhile, a well-known Basildon villain named Wally Birch was acquitted of a variety of violent offences mid-trial after the judge had decided there was no evidence against him, so he decided to celebrate with his friends in Raquels. Wally was a decent guy who was more than welcome in the club, but unfortunately his party included Jason Draper. I let Wally and his friends into the club, but I had to stop Draper at the door; it had only been five days since he had agreed to stay away. He insisted that this was an exception, even though I explained that there were no exceptions to my decisions and he would have to come back in a few weeks, as agreed. He got angry and offered to fight me, so I went out into the street. As I advanced towards him, he walked away. So I just went back into the club.

I went upstairs and told a doorman named Liam to stand by the fire exit to ensure that nobody entered that way or left. The manager had asked me to ensure this because in previous weeks people had been opening the fire exits to let their friends in without paying. Liam wasn't what I considered to be a proper doorman; he was one of a minority whom you have to employ whilst running a door. They are there simply to guard fire exits, collect tickets and search the punters as they enter the club – tasks genuine doormen generally frown upon.

I went to have a drink with Wally at the bar. As we were chatting, I felt a sharp blow to the side of my head. I spun round to find Draper facing me. He struck me again. I pulled out my sheath knife and Draper rather wisely stepped back.

'You wouldn't use that on a friend, would you?' Draper shouted.

I threw it on the floor and said, 'I don't need it for a cunt like you.'

He raised his hand, as if to hit me, and I saw that he was clenching a knuckleduster. I tried to avoid the punch, but it smashed into the side of my face. The fight dissolved into little more than a stand-up grappling match because the bar was so packed with people. As we pulled one another to and fro, I kept thinking to myself that I should have stabbed him because he had used a weapon on me.

The DJ had alerted the other door staff that there was a fight at the top bar and they were making their way towards me. Draper must have realised this because he pushed me away and ran through the fire exit.

It pains me to admit it, but I have to give him that one; it wasn't an all-out victory for him, but it certainly felt like a defeat to me.

I couldn't work out how he had managed to get into the club and hit me without being seen. I asked the doormen how he got in and they told me that his girlfriend had walked past Liam and opened the fire exit. Draper had entered and Liam had been too frightened to say or do anything. I called Liam into the toilets and when he walked in I head-butted him. As he fell to the floor, I hit him a second time. He never worked at Raquels again.

The following day the whole town was poised for a return battle. Rumours and speculation were rife. Everyone knew that I would not let Draper get away with what he had done: the only way to maintain an effective door was to be seen to take action. Messages were coming from the Bullseye gang that Draper was going to kill me, but I chose to say nothing and bide my time.

Later that same week Dave rang me from Liverpool. He told me he had outstayed his welcome and had nowhere else to go. I had a friend in Edinburgh who would have put him up, but Dave wanted to come back to Basildon. I spoke to my landlady friend again and Dave returned.

The August bank holiday weekend fell over the 29th of the month. I knew Draper and the Bullseye gang would be out in force at one of the pubs in Basildon and so I asked various people to look out for them. I was driving back from London with Dave when I received the call I had been waiting for: Draper and four of the Bullseye gang were in the pub where Dave was staying. They were waving a gun about, saying that they were looking for me.

As I sped towards Basildon, I saw Tucker ahead of me in his black Porsche. I pulled up next to him and sounded my horn. He didn't even acknowledge me; I could see he was punching his steering wheel, then he accelerated away. It wasn't hard to work out that he was in a bad mood.

I drove after him and followed as he turned off the main road onto a roundabout. When we stopped at some traffic lights, he was going berserk, punching the steering wheel and screaming. He clearly didn't want to talk. I reckoned he'd be making himself unavailable that day.

By the time I arrived in Basildon, I had managed to contact 14 members of the firm, who had agreed to assist me in resolving the problem with the Bullseye gang. I rang the pub landlady to find out if Draper was still there, but she told me he had left to go to the Bull on London Road. The other members of the firm and I drove to the Bull and parked in a side road. I had a gun with me, and a machete. I was clear in my mind what I had to do. It was pointless beating Draper up – he would just bide his time and attack me at a later date; the only way to end the problem, as far as I could see, would be to cripple or kill him. At that moment, in my current state of mind, I wasn't particularly bothered which one it was. The other members of the firm were armed with coshes, truncheons, industrial ammonia, knuckledusters and knives. Dave said he was already going to prison for shooting Woods, so it wasn't going to make much difference if he shot somebody else: 'Give me the gun, Bernie, and I will walk in the pub and blast him,' he said. I told him I didn't want him going to prison for life for me, so I would sort it out. However, as Dave was not known locally, I asked him if he would go into the pub, walk up to Draper and squirt him in the eyes with ammonia, then push him through a set of double doors into the street outside, where he would be beaten and then left.

I told the other members of the firm that once Draper was on the floor, I wanted them to walk away: there was something I had to do. I had decided that I was going to shoot Draper through the head.

Dave walked up to the pub with a large bottle of industrial ammonia hidden in his jacket, but luck wasn't on our side. Since it was a bank holiday, there was security on the door (who weren't there normally). The Bull was full of families, and customers had to have a ticket to get in. Dave returned and explained the problem. I wasn't keen about going armed into a pub full of women and children, but everybody agreed that Draper and his gang needed to be sorted out now. So we walked up to the door and pushed past the doormen, who put up little resistance. Draper was standing directly in front of me as I entered the bar. He was having a drink with members of the Bullseye gang. They saw me, jumped over the bar and ran. Draper stood his ground. I pulled out the machete.

'What are you doing with that, mate?' Draper said.

'Fucking mate? Fucking mate?' I shouted, before I tried to slash him.

Dave then squirted Draper with the ammonia.

Just then, the publican shouted for help. Running blind through the pub, Draper was crashing into tables and chairs as we chased him. Unfortunately, the ammonia had hit several innocent bystanders and they too were screaming and running for assistance. I really wanted things to end; I had to catch Draper and shoot him. I couldn't let it go now.

Draper ran out of the pub and into the beer garden. People there began to scream and run as we chased him. The doormen were trying to prevent us from grabbing Draper by blocking our paths and so they too were assaulted. For a brief moment, Draper was snared. A large wooden truncheon was repeatedly brought down with force on his head. As I raised my machete, the doormen grabbed my arms and pushed me to one side. 'Leave it, Bernie. Fucking leave it! You will kill him!' they shouted.

Draper managed to break free and ran once more through the crowds. Blood was pouring from wounds to the top of his head. In desperation, he vaulted the bar, but not before I had struck him twice with the machine. As I raised the weapon a third time, the manager of the pub ran towards me with a lump of wood. I turned towards him; he begged me to put down the weapon and leave the pub. Meanwhile, Draper had managed to hide in the cellar.

The pub was in utter chaos. It was time to leave. There could be no debate about who had won this fight. As far as I was concerned, the matter was now closed. If the Bullseye gang wanted to take it further, they now knew what to expect. We never did hear from them again.

Now that my problem had been resolved, I decided to help Dave with his problem in Bath. Stupid is probably the best description for feeling the need to assist others with shit they've caused themselves, but that is my nature. It always has been. That's probably why I made such a lousy gangster. I was more than capable of inflicting as much pain and suffering on another man as any of my counterparts, but, unlike them, I was a sucker for a sob story.

It wasn't going to be easy sorting Dave's problem out because of the serious nature of the offence: trying to persuade a man who has been shot that the person who shot him was not all bad and didn't deserve to go to prison was going to take more than tact. Woods had a bit of form himself, so he knew the score and it meant our task was not impossible.

I rang Billy Gillings, the man who had taken Steve and Nathan's car, and asked him if he would mediate and arrange a meeting between Woods and myself. I said that if it made Woods feel safer, he could bring anyone he wanted.

Billy went to see him and he agreed to meet at Leigh Delamere motorway services near Bristol. Woods, who had just been discharged from hospital, insisted that his brother, who was nicknamed Noddy, should accompany him. A date was set and I went to the meeting on my own. We all sat down at one of the cafeteria tables. Noddy started getting a bit lippy about Dave, so I told him in no uncertain terms that we didn't have to sit and discuss it. I was offering him and his brother a way out. 'If you persist with your lip,' I said, 'you'll get taken out of the game like your brother. I suggest you go and get some tea for us both, while I discuss this with Steve.'

It was important to let him know who was in the driving seat. I told Woods that we didn't normally do deals with people who inform on one of our number to the police but because he had suffered over a rather trivial matter we were making an exception. We were prepared to offer him £20,000 not to make a statement against Dave.

Woods said he had already made a statement. I said he would be paid the money if he retracted it. Woods wanted half up front and half on completion, but I told him: 'Bollocks – our word is our bond. Do your part of the deal and you'll get your cash.' He agreed and we went our separate ways.

Of course, we didn't have any intention of giving him a penny – as soon as he retracted his statement, he was going to be told in no uncertain terms that he wasn't going to be compensated.

A member of the firm named Mark accompanied me to our next meeting. Gillings and Woods met us at an out-of-town location near Bristol. Billy came over to our car and I asked if Woods had retracted his statement; Billy said he wouldn't unless he got half of the money up front.

'Put Woods in your car and take him down the road,' I said. 'Then tell him to get out. Drive away and don't look back.'

Billy asked why. I told him that Woods was going to be shot.

Billy said he didn't want any part of it.

'OK. Tell Woods to get in our car because we want to discuss payment with him.'

Billy agreed, but he kept repeating he wanted no part of it.

When Woods approached me, I said, 'There's no problem. Get in the car.'

We drove away to a deserted lane. A gun was produced and Woods was told to get out because we didn't want any of his 'shit or blood' messing up our vehicle. Woods was laid on a grass bank. The gun was put to his head. He was terrified. He hadn't yet got over the shooting six weeks earlier. His whole body was shaking and he was weeping. He was told that the firm did not pay grasses. 'Now you are going to die.'

'I don't want any money, I just don't want any trouble,' he said.

'First, you break into our friend's house and rub shit over the walls. And now you come and demand £20,000. It doesn't work like that,' I said.

'I'll retract my statement and that will be the end of it,' he replied.

He was told that if he didn't, people would come back. The talking was over.

Woods went away and within three hours he had retracted his statement. We returned to Basildon and Dave contacted a solicitor. The solicitor said he would check to see if Woods had told us the truth. If Woods had, the solicitor would arrange for Dave to give himself up the following day. The solicitor was not aware that Woods had been threatened; he thought he had retracted his statement of his own free will.

The next day I took Dave to Barking station in East London and we said our goodbyes. He travelled to Bath and surrendered himself to the police.

Unfortunately, in our plan something we hadn't factored in was Steve Woods's wife. She had not retracted her statement, so Thomkins was charged with attempted murder, threats to kill and possessing a firearm with the intention of endangering life. He was remanded in custody to await trial.

A lot of our conversations around that time revolved around Dave Thomkins. Some liked him, some didn't. Once he was out of the picture, I was told that he had been talking about me behind my back. It was a hammer blow, really. I had done all I could to help him and yet he had been slagging me off to promote himself. I wasn't happy at all, but my world at the time was overflowing with such people. Men like Tucker and Rolfe would happily sit and socialise with so-called friends, but as soon as they left the table the verbal daggers would be drawn. It's just the way the drugs world is. There are no true friends; people are merely stepping stones on which others tread in their efforts to reach the top of the heap.

I contacted Woods via a third party and told him Dave's protection had been terminated. Woods and his friends could do as they wished.

I went to visit Dave in Horfield prison in Bristol with two friends who were going to see him. I told them I wanted to go in first – I would only be five minutes – so they waited outside while I went into the visiting room.

Dave held out his hand. 'All right, mate,' he said.

'You're no fucking mate of mine. You've been slagging me off,' I said to him.

A prison visiting room isn't the best place to settle one's differences, but at that moment I didn't really care. I went for Dave.

The prison officers were alerted and Dave ran over to where they were standing for protection. I just walked out of the visiting room and have not seen him since. It is a shame because I considered him a good friend. Why he did what he did to me, I will never know.

He was later sentenced to ten years' imprisonment for shooting Steve Woods.

10

ENTER THE HULK

ON Friday, 25 July 1994, Raquels opened its doors for its first house and garage night promoted by the team from Southend. The club was absolutely packed; this type of event was rare in a violent town like Basildon, where peroxide blondes, cheap drinks and drunks in ill-fitting suits were the accepted norm in clubs. We kept that type of customer out, so it turned out to be a really enjoyable night. There wasn't any trouble and the atmosphere was fantastic.

It's hard to describe what it was like in Raquels back in those days. You could feel the music, it was so loud. The walls physically shook and a steady stream of condensation ran down the ceiling and walls. It was hard to see anything because it was so dark, but there was a real feeling of unity among the revellers that you couldn't help but get sucked into. Along with the crowds and the house music, there soon came a demand for Ecstasy. Eager to please, Murray and Chemical Bob did not fail their customers and Raquels was hit by an avalanche of drugs. It was also a good time for me: the trouble-free nights meant that I could relax a little and the additional money I was paid by Murray came in very handy.

During the same month that Raquels started hosting rave nights, a man named Pat Tate was freed from prison after serving four and a half years of a six-year sentence for robbery. I had been made aware of Tate long before his release date; a teenage girl who regularly came into Raquels had told me during a conversation that her uncle was in prison and she often visited him. Over the following weeks and months, I asked her how her uncle was getting on, and would let her into the club for nothing or get her the occasional drink. Having been in prison myself, I know how much it means to have your loved ones 'on the outside' taken care of. After Tate was released, he came down to the club to thank me and introduce himself. He struck me as an extremely likeable person, so when he invited me to a party that was being held in Southend later that night, I readily accepted.

When I arrived, the likeable Pat Tate whom I had met just a few hours earlier had become a drugged-up, slurring zombie. His huge frame was propping up a wall in an alley that ran down the side of the house. He was sweating so much that vapour was steaming from his head. The cold night air was visibly cooling him down, but his mood was ablaze. He was rambling about people he wanted to sort out and other firms he wanted crushed. I had no idea who or what he was on about, but I remained with him – I was concerned he was going to collapse any minute. Eventually, I talked him into getting into my car and I dropped him off at an address in Leigh-on-Sea.

When I mentioned my evening with Tate to friends, it turned out that the Hulk, as he was known locally, was a legend within the Essex underworld. In December 1988, Tate had got into a dispute with some staff over his restaurant bill and had punched the cashier, taking £800 from the till as compensation. He was duly arrested for robbery, and found to be in possession of small amounts of cocaine, cannabis and speed for his personal use. Billericay Magistrates decided that Tate would see in the New Year within the confines of Chelmsford prison. However, he had made other plans.

Tate jumped over the side of the dock and made for the door, ploughing his way out of the court onto an awaiting motorcycle. Roadblocks, which were immediately set up, failed to trap him. His escape was so speedy, the police couldn't say what type of motorcycle it was, or whether he was alone or travelling as a passenger.

Tate surfaced in Spain a few days later. He had planned to work alongside Costa del crooks, smuggling cannabis from Morocco into mainland Europe. But, while Tate was initially welcomed with open arms by the expats, after a few weekends of witnessing Tate's drug-induced bad behaviour his potential partners began to avoid him. Likewise the Spanish authorities – who were prepared to suffer the presence of British fugitives – would not tolerate having local people terrorised by them, so eventually both the police and the British criminal fraternity in residence made it clear he was not welcome and would have to leave.

Unable to understand why others were not prepared to have fun and run amok, Tate went in search of amusement across the border in Gibraltar, where he was promptly arrested by British police officers.

Three days later, Tate had waved goodbye to his place of exile in the sun. He was deported to languish in a British prison cell. When Tate was eventually released, he met Tony Tucker and Craig Rolfe quite by chance in a cafe in Southend. Tate had gone there with a man named Shaun Miller, who happened to know Tucker and Rolfe. The men were introduced by Miller and Tucker immediately warmed to Tate. Weighing 18 stone and standing 6 ft 2 in. tall, Tate was the type of man Tucker would deem 'useful'. They agreed to meet for a drink that night and by closing time Tate was a fully fledged member of the firm. However, Tate's appointment was met with resentment by some.

Chris Wheatley, whom Tucker had latched onto as a 'close' friend, was soon dropped as if he didn't exist. Wheatley had been given control of the door at Club Art, one of the venues Tucker provided security for in Southend. Tucker also began to badmouth him to other doormen, casting doubt on his ability and sneering at the way he handled incidents in the club. I really liked Chris and couldn't understand why Tucker was behaving the way he was. There was no room for sentiment in the firm, though: Chris had fallen from grace and Pat Tate was to take his place.

Others who had no reason to dislike Tate felt their position was threatened. Few felt comfortable about his appointment because he was unpredictable and had an explosive temper. Tucker, on the other hand, was loving every minute of it. He enjoyed pitching people against one another and causing unrest; he always wanted to see who would come out on top.

The following evening Tucker arrived at Raquels with Tate and a man named 'Nipper', whose real name was Steve Ellis. A likeable man from Southend, Ellis was inoffensive and funny, and in time I got to know him well. Nipper had earned his nickname because of his lack of height and, rather foolishly, I thought such a small man was way out of his depth, immersing himself in the firm.

I could see Nipper felt uncomfortable in Tucker's company, so I warned him not to take any notice of anything Tucker told him and not to get too involved.

I led the trio through reception and up two flights of stairs to a dining area, where they wouldn't be disturbed. After introducing them to one of the bar staff, I said that anything they required would be on the house. It was a fantastic atmosphere in the club that night and everybody appeared to be having a good time. As the champagne flowed, a group of girls gathered around Tucker's table. Nipper began talking to one or two of them. A man in his 20s approached the girls and asked them if they were sorted for drugs. Tucker called him over.

'Have you got any gear for sale?' he asked.

'Sure, mate. What would you like?' the man replied.

Tucker grabbed him by the throat, slapped him hard across the face with his free hand and demanded he hand over all of his drugs.

'Fuck off! You can't do that to the guy,' Nipper said.

'He's nothing. I can do what I fucking want!' Tucker replied.

Before Nipper could say another word, Tucker had emptied the trembling man's pockets and was shouting at all of the girls to fuck off.

One of the barmaids activated the panic alarm and the DJ began calling over the PA system, 'Security to the dining area! Security to the dining area!' Myself and several other doormen arrived moments later, expecting trouble.

Tucker pointed to the young man he had robbed, alleging that he had been threatening people. Almost immediately the man was apprehended and ejected from the club via a fire exit. I had genuinely believed Tucker when he told me the man had been causing problems – I'm just pleased the guy didn't resist when we ejected him. When I found out the truth some years later, I felt sick. I realised I didn't know Tucker at all.

The attention-seeking, jealous and vindictive Tucker in the club that night was the real Tony Tucker; the muscle-bound man-mountain with the dodgy smile and equally dodgy haircut was little more than a fraud. It had taken me a while to see through the likes of Draper, Tucker and Thomkins, but thankfully my ignorance didn't result in me being injured or killed. Not everybody in Essex got away as lightly as I did.

One afternoon, Tucker, Tate and Nipper met up in a gym near Southend. Most of the doormen and bodybuilders around that area used to train at this particular premises. As soon as the trio met, Tate gave Tucker and Nipper energy drinks. After they had finished them, he fell about laughing, saying that they had been spiked with large amounts of the mind-bending drug LSD. 'Don't worry, I am loaded, too,' he said.

Nipper hadn't planned on spending his day hallucinating, thinking he was resident on fucking Mars, but as the drug took hold he began to see the funny side of Tate's prank.

Nipper was driving his white BMW 5.35 Alpina, Tucker his black Porsche, and Tate was behind the wheel of a brand new Porsche 928s he had acquired earlier that day. Tate was extremely proud of the car and the number plate he'd purchased for it: NO-928S. Banter about each car's performance turned into bravado and boasting, and before long the three vehicles were being raced around the streets of Southend. Tucker, Tate and Nipper were driving on the wrong side of the road and jumping red lights at more than 100 mph whilst high on drugs; it's surprising nobody was killed.

After defying death for nearly an hour, they screeched to a halt outside the 7-Eleven shop on Hamlet Court Road. They all went inside to buy drinks and, as they were doing so, Tate threw a bread roll at Nipper. He returned fire with a ten-inch birthday cake. Within seconds, all three were engaged in a full-scale food fight. The store manager shouted at them to stop and said he was going to call the police. Tate snatched the phone from the manager's hand, punched it until it smashed and advised the ashen-faced man never to mention the police again. Unbeknown to Tate, however, the manager had already alerted the police using a panic button and, as Tate continued to lecture the man about the pitfalls of involving them, they burst through the door.

Tate and Tucker remained tight-lipped and were allowed to leave, but Nipper was abusive and was therefore detained overnight. After nine hours in a police cell coming down from his acid trip, Nipper was interviewed by the arresting officer. It was all rather informal; he asked Nipper what he had been drinking to get into such a state. 'I think my drink may have been spiked,' Nipper lied. 'I became abusive because I thought you were going to arrest my mate, Tony Tucker.'

At the end of the interview, Nipper was also released without charge and warned about the dangers of leaving one's drink unattended in pubs and clubs. Nipper didn't realise it at the time, but he was walking further and further towards trouble with three drug-crazed psychotic lunatics. Like so many of the people who latched onto our firm back then, Nipper was oblivious to the fact that drugs had turned these men into Jekyll-and-Hyde characters. They would be smiling at you one moment, then discussing how to beat you or kill you for committing a small misdemeanour the next.

A few days later, Nipper's house phone rang. When he answered it, Donna Garwood, Tucker's 16-year-old mistress, asked him if he had seen Tucker. Nipper, as usual, could not give a straight answer, so he replied, in what he thought was a light-hearted tone, 'No, I've not seen him. He's probably at home giving his missus one up the arse.' As soon as Nipper had finished talking, Garwood slammed the phone down.

Early the next morning, Nipper was woken up to the sound of somebody hammering on his front door. Still half-asleep, he opened it to find Tucker, Rolfe and a man named Peter Cuthbert. Without saying a word, the three men walked into his home. When he asked them what they wanted, Tucker made the sign of a gun with his two fingers against his head. Nipper assumed that meant he had come to pick up the 2.2 revolver he was storing for him.

Nipper had been careful to wipe the gun clean of all fingerprints before hiding it in a cupboard, so rather than touch the gun himself Nipper simply showed Tucker where he had secreted it. As soon as Tucker picked up the weapon, however, he grabbed Nipper's throat with his left hand, lifted him off the floor and shoved the gun into his temple. Spitting phlegm, he began screaming, 'Fuck my missus up the arse, would you? Fuck my missus up the arse? You are going to die, you bastard. You are going to die!'

Tucker then shoved Nipper into his bedroom and threw him on the bed. Sitting astride Nipper, Tucker kept jabbing the barrel of the gun into his head and mouth and shouting obscenities. Nipper could tell by the froth around Tucker's mouth and the crazed look in his eyes that he was high on crack cocaine.

Tucker then suddenly stopped shouting.

He ordered Rolfe to search the house for jewellery and anything else of value. Then he returned his attention to Nipper, asking him if he would prefer to lose one of his hands or one of his feet, while producing a butcher's meat cleaver from inside his jacket. Nipper thought if Tucker was just going to sever one of his limbs, he would at least survive the ordeal, and would be able to exact his revenge. Nipper is left-handed, so he held out his right hand, closed his eyes and waited for the searing pain.

When Nipper had finished silently counting to ten, he realised that Tucker was not going to carry out his threat and opened his eyes. Tucker was standing over him; his eyes were bulging and he was grinning like a mad man. After snapping out of his trance-like state, Tucker put the meat cleaver back in his jacket, turned and walked away.

Nipper immediately jumped off the bed and began shouting,

'What the fuck have I done?' Cuthbert held Nipper back and repeatedly asked him to calm down, but he was incensed. He pushed Cuthbert out of the way and went after Tucker.

As he reached the front door, Tucker turned quickly, grabbed Nipper by the throat and lifted him off the floor. Slamming Nipper against a wall, he pulled out the meat cleaver and threatened to bury it in his head. Cuthbert grabbed Tucker's arm and pleaded with him to calm down. Fortunately for Nipper, Tucker released his grip and walked out of the door.

When Nipper's unwelcome guests had all left, he rang Tate to ask him what he was supposed to have done. Tate told Nipper that Tucker was having a bad day and that he shouldn't worry about it. Nipper couldn't work out if Tate was joking, or if he simply couldn't grasp the enormity of the liberty that Tucker had taken with him. Nipper thanked Tate for his words of wisdom and rang Tucker to ask if he could give him an explanation for his abhorrent behaviour. Tucker exploded into a rage and began screaming at Nipper, 'Have you sorted it?' When Nipper asked him what it was that he was supposed to sort out, he replied, 'You told Donna that I do my missus up the arse!' Before Nipper could explain that it was a comment made in jest, Tucker said that he was going to put him on his knees, make him apologise and then shoot him in the head.

'Go and fuck yourself up the arse, you mug,' Nipper replied, before ending the call.

Nipper has never claimed to be a hard man, but he is certainly nobody's fool either. Others may have been intimidated by Tucker and his firm, but Nipper wasn't going to forget what he'd had done to him, nor was he prepared to take any more of Tucker's shit.

Nipper left the flat immediately and purchased a combat knife. He then went in search of somebody who would sell him a gun. The first person he approached had an array of firearms for sale, but when Nipper mentioned he was intending to shoot Tony Tucker the man refused to sell him anything.

'I am not protecting that bastard. It would make my day if he got blown away. But I'm scared that he'll find out I've sold you a gun to shoot him with,' the arms dealer explained.

Nipper got much the same response from all of the people he approached in Essex; however, he did eventually find an arms dealer in South London who didn't know of Tucker.

He sold Nipper a bulletproof vest, and initially offered him a submachine gun. Nipper couldn't afford it, so settled for a pump-action shotgun and a 2.2 revolver.

When he returned to his flat, he was horrified to find that all of his clothing and most of his household goods had been stolen. Anything the thieves couldn't carry had been smashed, slashed or broken. Food and a substance that looked like excrement had been smeared all over the carpets and walls: his home had been destroyed. Nipper rang his girlfriend and advised her to avoid any contact with Tucker, Tate and Rolfe's girlfriends. He explained that he was in an extremely dangerous situation, and he assumed his adversaries would try to use his family and friends in their efforts to find and harm him.

After ringing his family and warning them that Tucker and his henchmen might come looking for him at their homes, Nipper rang Donna Garwood and asked her what she had said to her moronic boyfriend.

'I told him what you said about his missus because it was out of order,' she bragged. Garwood had clearly overlooked the fact that she was having a sordid affair with the partner of the woman she was pretending to be concerned about. Nipper gave Garwood specific instructions that involved sex and travel and put the phone down.

Having completed his rant, Nipper telephoned Tucker and asked if he was responsible for the carnage at his flat. Tucker didn't admit or deny responsibility, he just laughed at Nipper and said his possessions had been used to furnish a flat he had acquired for Garwood.

'You don't need your stuff anyway, Nipper, because I'm going to kill you,' Tucker said.

Nipper couldn't see the point in shouting about what he might or might not be prepared to do – he is the type of man who believes actions speak much louder than words – so he simply hung up. He went into his flat and hid in a small cupboard under the stairs that had a clear view of the front door. He'd decided that as soon as Tucker or anybody else walked into his home, he was going to open fire on them with the shotgun.

Nipper spent six hours crouched in the cupboard; he had to abandon his plan in the end because he was suffering from extreme cramp and lack of sleep. Still clutching his weapons, he went into his bedroom and lay down on what was left of his bed before falling into a deep sleep. He was awoken the following morning by the sound of his phone ringing. When he lifted the receiver and groaned hello,

Tate asked him how he was and apologised for Tucker's behaviour.

'Don't worry, Nipper, it's all sorted,' Tate said. 'We are going to Canning Town to sort out a bit of business and then we'll come around to see you at midday.'

Nipper told Tate that he would wait in for them and replaced the receiver. As soon as he had done so, he pulled on his bulletproof vest, grabbed his firearms and ran towards the cupboard under the stairs. At the last minute, he changed his mind and ran out of the back door and into the garden. As he left the garden and walked up an alleyway at the side of his flat, he heard the screech of tyres and car doors slamming. Nipper dashed behind a parked car in the street and checked that his weapons were loaded. He could see Tate's and Tucker's Porsches, which had been abandoned in the middle of the road, and he could hear his front door being kicked open. Nipper then heard Tate calling out his name, as he searched the flat, and Tucker was shouting out to Rolfe to look for Nipper in the back garden.

All three of them then met in the street, just yards from Nipper's hiding place, and began discussing their next move. When they eventually left, Nipper went back into the flat and found a note Tate had left for him. It read: 'Don't let me lose all respect for you, Nipper. I am trying to help you. Please get in touch.'

Nipper rang Tate and asked him how trying to kill him was ever going to help him. 'You kicked my fucking door in, you prick, I watched you. I was only going to kill Tucker before today, but now you're all going to die.'

Tate didn't answer and the line went dead.

Nipper ran out of the house and hid in an alleyway opposite his flat. Moments later Tucker's Porsche pulled up, and he and Rolfe got out and walked down the alley to the rear of Nipper's home. Nipper remained where he was, waiting for Tate to pull up in his vehicle, but after a few minutes he concluded that he must have gone home.

The hour had arrived for Tucker and Rolfe to die. Nipper had cut the barrel off his shotgun and tied a length of rope to the stock so that he could sling it over his shoulder and hide it under his jacket. As Nipper entered the alleyway, he practised opening his jacket and letting the shotgun fall before swinging it up from his hip into the firing position. Fuck knows where he'd seen the move, but it was extremely slick and effective. In Nipper's left hand, he clutched the 2.2 revolver, which was loaded and ready to fire.

As he reached the rear of his flat, he saw that Rolfe was in the process of stealing his motorbike leathers from the garden shed. Nipper could hear loud banging and thought Tucker must be in the shed, trying to break the padlock off his 750 Suzuki motorcycle, but the noise stopped as he approached. Nipper decided to hide behind a nearby garden gate and wait for the two intruders to step into the alleyway, where they would have little or no chance of escape.

As Tucker walked out of Nipper's garden with Rolfe immediately behind him, Nipper emerged from his hiding place with a weapon in each hand. Tucker was visibly shocked and could only utter, 'Nipper . . . Nipper, you cunt!'

'Fucking Nipper! Fucking Nipper!' Nipper shouted. 'Have some of this, you mug!'

Nipper pulled the trigger of the handgun whilst aiming at Tucker's head, but it failed to fire. Rolfe dropped the motorbike leathers and ran. Tucker, to Nipper's amazement, fell to the ground and began making a pathetic whimpering noise interspersed with pleas of 'No, no.'

Nipper pulled the trigger again, but the gun failed him once more.

Tucker realised that he had an opportunity to escape, got to his feet and ran. As he did so, Nipper pulled the trigger again and on this occasion the weapon fired. Nipper had no idea where the bullet went, but it failed to find the intended target. Nipper ran after Tucker and Rolfe and opened fire with the shotgun. They immediately vaulted a hedge and began running through people's gardens in an effort to escape their deranged attacker.

Nipper did manage to unleash two more shots, but he was chasing the duo as he did so and his aim was poor at best. As the duo disappeared from view, he knew that his problems were far from over; he would have to kill Tucker, Tate and Rolfe before they killed him.

I had been receiving regular rants from Tucker and Tate about events concerning Nipper and I knew that if they found him he would die. I liked Nipper and sympathised with his plight. If somebody had threatened my family, I too would have armed myself and attempted to execute them. My history of assisting the underdog didn't encourage me to bear arms on Nipper's behalf, but I couldn't stand by and leave a man to face a problem like this alone. So, that night I rang Nipper and offered my assistance. I told him that Tate and Rolfe had been to Raquels looking for him. Tate had told me that if Nipper turned up I was to let him in, ring Tate or Tucker, and keep Nipper there until they arrived.

'They're going to top you, Nipper. They're telling everybody that you grassed them up for an incident in a 7-Eleven store,' I warned. 'If you want somewhere to lie low, I have people up north you can go to. If you want to stay in Essex, I can try and talk to them.'

I offered to meet Nipper, but he told me in no uncertain terms that I was too close to 'those three bastards' to trust. With Tucker, Tate and Rolfe looking for him, Nipper was probably right to trust only his own instincts and the good Lord above.

The next day I was driving home from visiting a friend in prison when I heard on the radio that a man had been found dead in a ditch in Basildon. I didn't think too much about it at the time: dead men being found in ditches around Essex were hardly rare occurrences. When I got home, I telephoned Tucker, but, unusually, his number was unobtainable.

He was due to hold his birthday party at a snooker hall in Dagenham that Sunday and I had been invited. I wanted to know what time it started and if the firm was meeting up anywhere for a drink beforehand. At work that night, the doormen were telling me various stories about what was happening regarding Nipper Ellis. I was surprised to hear that even Nipper's father had been threatened. Tate, they said, was going berserk.

I decided I didn't fancy Tucker's party, which would probably entail listening to hours of what he and Tate were going to do to Nipper, so I rang Tucker's house and left a message on the answering machine saying I had fallen ill. I later learned that only 20 people turned up. Tucker's and Tate's behaviour was obviously being noticed by more people than just myself. The previous year there had probably been nearly 200 people at his party.

I could see the writing was on the wall for the firm, and for myself. The drugs and the violence were completely out of control. As soon as somebody put a foot wrong, their loyalty was questioned. Once their loyalty was in dispute, they were deemed an enemy. Once they were considered an enemy, they became the subject of a violent attack. We were all waiting for our personal tragedies to happen.

11

HAPPINESS IS A WARM GUN

ON 17 November 1994, Nipper Ellis spent the evening driving around looking for Tate, Tucker and Rolfe in their usual haunts, but they were nowhere to be seen. He drove past Rolfe's home in Chafford Hundred, but his vehicle was not on the drive; Tucker's car was also missing from outside his home. Nipper knew that if their cars were not there, then they, too, would be absent. He then drove over to Basildon to look for Tate. The sight of the black Porsche parked outside Tate's bungalow on Gordon Road sent his heart racing.

Nipper knew Tucker was due to celebrate his birthday at a snooker hall in Dagenham that night and imagined Tate would be at home getting ready. He hadn't put any planning into what he intended to do next, so he decided to just empty the gun he had in his hand into Tate as he stepped out of the front door.

While watching the bungalow, Nipper noticed a light being switched on in a bedroom, and he could see the silhouette of a slightly built woman moving across the room. When he realised that Tate's long-suffering girlfriend Sarah was in the bungalow, and no doubt her son Jordan was also present, he knew he'd have to abandon his last-minute plan to blow Tate away. It was highly likely that Sarah and Jordan would come through the door with Tate, and Nipper would not risk putting either of them in danger. Dejected, he started the engine of his car and roared off down the street.

Common sense would have told Nipper to keep on driving, but common sense had no place in our world: Nipper knew that if he allowed Tate to live, then he was going to die. It really was that simple. He felt he had no choice – he had to carry out his murderous plan.

Nipper had hidden a pump-action shotgun not too far away from Tate's home and, reasoning that he might need it, he made his way to the outskirts of Basildon, where he retrieved the weapon. Feeling more confident now, he convinced himself that he could end Tate's life and, in doing so, end his own personal misery.

Back in Basildon, he checked his weapons were loaded and secreted the guns in his jacket. He hadn't had time to obtain a balaclava, so instead he tore one of the sleeves from his jumper and, using a knife, cut two eyeholes in it, making himself a makeshift mask. If Sarah saw his face, she would have been able to help police identify him as Tate's killer.

Nipper scaled a fence and made his way down a steep railway embankment and onto the tracks. It was pitch black and he stumbled more than once as he made his way to the rear of Tate's home. Climbing the railway embankment, he eventually crashed through a thorn bush and landed in Tate's garden. Fearing he might have made too much noise, he ran towards the back door. The rear of the bungalow was lit up. The kitchen window was to Nipper's right, a bedroom window to his left; in the middle was the frosted-glass window belonging to the bathroom. Terrified by the very thought of the task in hand, Nipper had to keep telling himself that if he didn't kill Tate, Tate would kill him.

The bathroom light was on and Nipper could see Tate's huge silhouette moving about behind the frosted glass. After finding half a house brick, Nipper hurled it through the bathroom window, which exploded on impact. Standing less than three feet from the broken window, Nipper suddenly came face to face with Tate, who had peered out of the gaping hole made by the brick. Without saying a word, Nipper aimed the gun at Tate's face and squeezed the trigger. Tate called out 'No, no!' but his fears proved to be temporarily unfounded when the gun failed to fire. Realising he had been given a stay of execution, Tate turned to run, but Nipper leant through the broken window.

'Click' – the gun failed him a second time.

He pulled the trigger again. The sound of a deafening explosion filled his ears. The bullet found its target and Tate began to scream: 'Get the police, get the police! I've been shot.' Nipper had been in Tate's bungalow on many occasions in the past and so he was aware of the layout. As Tate fled from the bathroom, he turned right into the kitchen, so Nipper ran around to its side window and attempted to shoot him once more. Again, the gun failed to fire.

Tate was looking directly at Nipper. He continued to scream, begging Sarah to call the police. As Nipper pointed the gun at him once more, he ran out of the kitchen and headed towards the front of the property. Nipper assumed Tate was going to leave through the front door, so he stood facing it, legs apart in a firing position, waiting to blast him with the pump-action shotgun he'd taken from his coat.

Nipper could hear Tate shouting down a telephone, 'Police! Police! Get here fucking quick. I've been shot and the gunman is still outside.'

Nipper could have burst into the bungalow and finished Tate off, but he assumed Sarah was comforting him and therefore he would be putting her in danger. His only option was to save himself and leave the scene before the police arrived. He ran through the back garden again, clambered over the fence and hurled himself into the thorn bush. Half-running, half-falling, he made his way down the railway embankment and along the tracks into the darkness.

* * *

Tate's injuries were not life threatening. The bullet had struck his elbow, as he had raised it to shield his head, and had then travelled along his arm.

Before arriving at Basildon hospital, Tate made Tucker aware of the attack and he vowed to seek the bloodiest revenge possible. That night, Nipper's phone did not stop ringing, as he was bombarded with threats from the firm and warnings from well-wishers.

Nipper became so concerned not only for his safety but also that of his family that he decided to telephone the root cause of all his problems: Pat Tate.

Nobody knows what Tate's blood pressure was like before Nipper rang, but he was certainly in danger of suffering a heart attack by the time they had finished talking. The call started in a civil manner. Nipper reminded Tate how friendly they had once been, but when he suggested that drugs had destroyed his associate, Tate became incoherent.

'Shut up, you fucking idiot!' he screamed down the phone.

'I'm going to come up to that hospital and put one in your head,' Nipper said, before hanging up.

Tate was in no doubt Nipper would carry out his threat – the lump of lead in his arm bore testament to the fact that his word was his bond. Tate immediately rang Tucker and pleaded with him to bring a gun to the hospital for his protection. It wasn't the brightest idea Tate had ever had; the hospital staff were already tiring of him and his visitors taking illegal drugs and being unnecessarily loud. When a prostitute had been found giving oral sex to Tate, he had been moved to a private room off the general ward. The move had made matters even worse for the staff because Tate's guests ignored the official visiting times and partied well into the night. When I had visited Tate one afternoon, two topless teenage girls were lying on his bed and he was snorting cocaine. I wasn't impressed.

It was during this visit that I first met Darren Nicholls. Tate had befriended Nicholls and two other men, Mick Steele and Jack Whomes, whilst in prison. Nicholls promoted himself as a big player in the drugs world, but few took much notice of him.

He had been released shortly before Tate, on 17 May 1994, but despite ringing all of his 'friends' to announce his release, not one of them took him up on his request to give 'the big drug baron' a lift back to his home in Essex. Feeling humiliated and desperate, Nicholls phoned his fellow former inmate Jack Whomes and pleaded with him to give him a lift. Never one to refuse anybody in need, Jack agreed. When Jack asked Nicholls why none of his friends and family had met him out of prison, Nicholls told him that he hadn't informed them of his release because he wanted to surprise them. Jack didn't believe him, but said nothing, as he didn't wish to hurt his feelings.

When Nicholls heard on the grapevine that Tate had been shot, he thought it would be in his interest to contact him. In prison, Tate had been the man to arrange things. Nicholls was sure Tate would be able to help him expand his drug-dealing business by selling him cheaper stock and introducing him to more customers.

Nicholls rang Mick Steele and asked him if he had a contact number for Tate. Steele, rather foolishly, complied. When Nicholls finally got through to Tate, he learned he was in Basildon hospital. Tate sounded pleased to hear from him, so Nicholls arranged a visit the very next day. When I met Nicholls at Tate's bedside, he was carrying four bottles of lager, which he said were a 'well done for not being dead' present. Within a minute of being in Tate's company, Nicholls realised the man he had met in prison was no more.

One of the teenagers lying on Tate's bed was named Lisa, and Tate had asked Nicholls if he wanted her to perform oral sex for him. 'She's just here to give me a blowjob, so I don't have to trouble my missus when she comes to visit me,' Tate said. 'Lisa doesn't mind, she does it for a living. She's fucking good at it, too,' he laughed. To emphasise the power he had over this young girl, Tate started ordering her about, telling her to sort his pillows and sending her to fetch drinks.

When Lisa was out of the room, Tate began to ramble about setting up Nipper so that he could kill him. It was obvious to everybody present that Tate had been embarrassed that Nipper had not only stood up to him but had also fought back.

When Nipper had gone on the run, he had telephoned Tucker and left a message on his voicemail: 'Hey you, you cunt. This is Steve Ellis. I've fucking just shot Pat Tate and you're next. Now, fucking leave my family alone, you fucking wanker.'

When Tate heard about the message, he asked Tucker to telephone Nipper and say there was no need for any more violence. Tate, Tucker was to say, wanted Nipper to visit him in hospital so that they could resolve their differences.

Nipper was no fool; he sensed that he was being lured to his death and refused to go anywhere near Tate or Tucker. Tate's intention had been to blast Nipper in the head as he walked up to his bed with the gun Tucker had given him. The gun would then be taken away by another firm member and disposed of. Tate would then say a hit man had entered the hospital ward, executed Nipper and fled.

Nicholls, embarrassed and clearly out of his depth, was keen to change the subject and asked Tate if he could supply drugs to a friend of his. Tate, always one to relish the prospect of making money, began to reel off what and how much was available.

'I can get fucking truckloads. I can get the lot: Ecstasy, speed, cocaine, cannabis. Tell him, no matter how much he needs, I can get it. I'm the man.' I could see Nicholls was regretting visiting Tate, who made it clear he considered Nicholls 'small time'.

Tate was enjoying every minute of making Nicholls look like a fool. I could see Nicholls was seething with anger, but he knew he couldn't say anything because he didn't want to upset Tate or his friends, who were gathered around the bed. He eventually left, looking like a scolded child.

Within a couple of days, a nurse discovered Tate's gun while making up his bed. She contacted the police and Tate was arrested.

Because he was still on licence for his eight-year robbery sentence, he was automatically returned to prison for being in possession of a firearm, as this broke his parole conditions.

* * *

The weekend Tate was shot had been, by anybody's standards, an eventful one. But as dramatic as it was, the shooting paled into insignificance when compared to another incident that occurred involving the firm and a man from Basildon.

The first inkling I had that something else had gone terribly wrong was when a police officer rang my home and said that he wished to speak to me. I was the head of security at Raquels and I often had to attend dreary council meetings about incidents at the club that could affect its licence. The police would also attend these meetings, but the tone in the officer's voice left me in no doubt that this particular meeting was going to be about something very sinister. Initially, I was asked who might have shot Pat Tate, but I acted dumb and pretended I wasn't aware that he had been shot. I was then asked about the whereabouts of Craig Rolfe over the weekend because he had been linked with the murder of a local man. Again, I did my best to look apologetic when I told the officers I had no idea where Rolfe had been and certainly knew nothing about a murder. Accepting that their fishing expedition had been futile, the officers thanked me for my time and said that I was free to leave.

Once I had left the area, I rang Tucker and told him in the briefest of terms just what the police had been questioning me about. He asked me to meet him as soon as possible. Ten minutes later Tucker and I were sitting in a quiet corner of the Highwayman pub on the main Southend road just outside Basildon. I was aware who had shot Tate and why, so that incident was barely touched upon. However, Tucker explained in some detail how a friend of Rolfe named Kevin Whittaker had met his death.

According to Tucker, Whittaker thought he had recently turned a corner in his life. He had managed to kick his long-term cocaine habit and had secured employment, working for a man named Ronnie, laying crazy paving. His long-term girlfriend, Alison, was expecting their first child and Kevin was really excited about becoming a father; he had told his friends he was never going to touch cocaine again because he wanted to be a decent dad.

But then disaster struck. In April 1994, Ronnie sacked Kevin after an argument and Kevin found himself unemployed, with a baby due in a few weeks. Desperate for cash to support his new family, Kevin couldn't resist going back to his old ways. When he picked up the phone to call his friend Craig Rolfe, it was to be the biggest mistake of his short life.

Kevin was asked to act as a courier on a cannabis deal with a firm from Manchester. He agreed, but the deal went horribly wrong for him. It had been Kevin's job to travel to the north-west, pick up the drugs and bring them back to Basildon, but when Kevin arrived in Essex and handed them to Tucker, it was noted that there was one kilo missing. As Kevin was the courier, the missing drugs were down to him. Tucker wanted to know how he was going to pay.

Kevin knew what was coming. He tried his best to avoid Tucker, Tate and Rolfe. Towards the end of September 1994, he arrived out of the blue at his mother Joan's workplace, pleading with her to help him, as he was in serious trouble, though he refused to tell her exactly what was happening. Deeply concerned, Joan took Kevin home with her to explain things to his father. On 30 September, Kevin's father wrote a cheque out for £2,000 made payable to Russell Tate, Pat's younger brother. His parents gave him £500 in cash, as well.

When they returned from holiday three weeks later, they learned that Kevin and his girlfriend Alison had split up and he was slipping deeper and deeper into depression. Nobody knows if the separation from his girlfriend and son was the cause of his demise or if he had other problems on his mind. But everyone does agree that Kevin Whittaker was an extremely troubled man.

On Wednesday, 16 November, Kevin told a friend he was going out to meet someone. He left in a vehicle being driven by Craig Rolfe.

Rolfe had agreed to let Kevin get involved in another drug deal to help him get back on his feet. A drug dealer had approached Rolfe and asked him to supply 25 kilos of cannabis for £60,000. Rolfe, unable to come up with such a large amount of cannabis at short notice, stalled the potential buyer and frantically rang around everyone he knew, buying their stock in the hope he could supply the 25 kilos. Kevin heard about Rolfe's dilemma and knew where he could get his hands on a substantial amount of cannabis on short-term credit. And not only could he get the drugs on credit, he could also get them at a discounted rate if he bought in bulk. He thought it was his chance to make some quick, easy and much-needed money. Kevin had worked out he could make at least £5,000, but Rolfe convinced him he could earn more if he acted as a courier for the deal. Foolishly, Kevin agreed.

When he met the dealer to purchase the drugs, the cash was taken from him but no drugs were handed over. Kevin had been ripped off once more.

Tucker and Rolfe had turned up for the meeting with Kevin in Tate's cream-coloured BMW. As soon as Kevin joined Tucker in the back seat of the car, he had demanded the money back from the deal. Terrified, and with nowhere to run, Kevin blamed the drug dealer for the loss; Tucker and Rolfe said they would take him to the man to confront him.

Tucker and Rolfe were getting increasingly annoyed as they headed down the A127 towards Romford. It was dawning on them that they weren't going to get their money. Tucker was grabbing Kevin by the throat and threatening him: 'Thieve our gear, would you? If you like drugs that much, have some more of ours.' Tucker then began injecting him with cocaine and Special K.

Kevin tried in vain to resist. Fearing he was going to die, he became more and more terrified. He sobbed and pleaded with Tucker and Rolfe to let him go, but they were just laughing. Kevin was injected three times with massive doses of drugs and started to drift in and out of consciousness. Rolfe turned off the road, then pulled over and ordered Kevin to get out of the car. He got no response. Tucker and Rolfe knew Kevin was dead. They pulled him out of the car and put him into a ditch face down, surrounded by a few fly-tipped bags of rubbish.

Tucker insisted that they had not intended to harm Whittaker, but he didn't show any remorse over the incident; in fact, he was extremely annoyed that Whittaker's death was now going to cause him and Rolfe 'untold trouble'.

'The mug tried to have me over and now I have to face being scrutinised by the Old Bill. Can you fucking believe it?' Tucker ranted.

However inconvenienced Tucker and Rolfe were going to be, they were never going to have to face the trauma Kevin's parents were forced to endure.

Nearly 30 hours after Kevin left home, his parents' worst fears were realised. Two detectives knocked on their door and asked them to attend the mortuary at Basildon hospital to assist with the identification of their son.

The police began interviewing Kevin's friends and family to piece together his whereabouts in the hours leading up to his death. A few days later Craig Rolfe was arrested and taken to Basildon police station, where he made a statement. Rolfe's girlfriend Donna told police that she was with him at the time of Kevin's death. Donna said they had stayed in together watching a video. Nothing out of the ordinary had happened, it was just a quiet evening in. The police investigation soon ground to an unsatisfactory halt.

In January 1995, an inquest was held at Chelmsford Coroner's Court. Detective Inspector Peter Hamilton told the court that the police had investigated the possibility that Kevin had been murdered because of a drug deal that had gone wrong, but there had been no hard evidence to support this. The file, he said, had now been closed.

The court also heard evidence from Craig Rolfe, who turned up for the hearing with Tucker in tow. Rolfe repeated what he had said in his statement. The coroner, Dr Malcolm Weir, had no choice but to accept what the police had to say about Kevin's death. Depressed after the split with his girlfriend and the loss of his job, Kevin had started to inject hard drugs and had accidentally overdosed.

An open verdict was recorded, but those of us in the firm knew the truth: Tucker and Rolfe had murdered Kevin Whittaker. Getting away with murder was going to give Tucker and Rolfe the drug-fuelled belief that they were untouchable. They were dangerous before Kevin's murder, but they had now become monsters.

12

IMPORTING TROUBLE

AS well as experiencing the stress and strains of police scrutiny over the murder of Kevin Whittaker, Craig Rolfe was experiencing stressful times at home. For Donna Jagger, Rolfe's partner, the murder of Kevin Whittaker was too much to bear on top of his drug habit and drug dealing, so she and her daughter Georgia moved out of their home. Rolfe was devastated and vowed to change his ways.

Donna returned after about three weeks and Rolfe tried hard to stick to his promise. Most weekends he went out and Donna guessed that he took small amounts of cocaine and used Ecstasy, but it was not on the same scale as previously. It seemed the couple had reached a happy medium.

With Tate in prison and Rolfe off the scene, normality began to return to life within the firm. Perhaps 'normality' is the wrong word to describe debt collection, punishment beatings, robbery and the supply of controlled drugs, but that was 'normality' to its members. Conflict with other gangs or individuals was minimal and rarely descended into guns being used; when Tate had been at large, every incident had been settled with the threat of guns or murder.

One Thursday evening on the way into work, I received a call from an Essex villain named Nicky, who told me he needed a driver to take an articulated lorry to a warehouse in Liverpool. Nicky told me that two brothers from Dagenham had been stealing lorries loaded with different goods and one had contained 30 tonnes of coffee granules. Nicky said his associate, a notorious face in the East End named Danny Woolard, had tried selling the lorry load of coffee but hadn't had much luck. Woolard's partner had found two likely buyers, who had agreed to pay £30,000 for the load, but they needed three weeks to get the money together.

Woolard and his partner had paid the brothers from Dagenham £15,000 for the coffee and had parked the trailer on a farm in Essex.

Unfortunately, the buyers backed out and the trailer was left standing on the farm for weeks. One day, a villain from South London phoned Woolard and asked him if he would be interested in buying 30 tonnes of coffee for £60,000; Woolard asked him if he would like to buy the same quantity of coffee for £30,000, but the man said it wasn't possible to get a load of coffee that cheap. Woolard assured him it was; although he didn't quite own the 30 tonnes of coffee, he was willing to sell it at that price. The man agreed to buy the coffee on condition that it was delivered to a warehouse in Kirkby, Liverpool, by 1 p.m. on the Friday. Woolard said it would be there, but added, 'Once that coffee is in Liverpool, you own it.' The man, who I later learned was Great Train Robber Buster Edwards, agreed.

I do not have a licence to drive articulated lorries, but I told Nicky I would do the job regardless. I drove to a farm near Basildon, met Nicky and together we went to Manor Park in East London to pick up a lorry to pull the 40 foot-trailer up to Liverpool. It was a D-registered MAN, a right old banger, which belonged to Terry Edwards, brother of Buster.

The trailer had been parked on the farm for so long it had sunk into the mud and the brakes had seized on it. We therefore had great difficulty getting it onto the road. I finally set off for Liverpool at about 10 p.m. I was to meet four or five men at a bonded warehouse at five o'clock the following morning. Although I had never driven an articulated lorry, it wasn't too difficult. There was no traffic about, and once on the motorway it was just a case of pointing it in the right direction and putting my foot down.

It was when I reached the National Exhibition Centre turn-off in Birmingham that my problems began. Within seconds, the temperature gauge went from normal to red, and the lorry ground to a halt. I wasn't happy. I was sitting with a sure prison sentence, unable to go anywhere. However, rather than abandon ship I thought I would wait on the side of the motorway until the engine cooled a bit. I was panicking; I thought that every car that approached was a police car. Buster had obviously not put as much thought into this job as the Great Train Robbery.

Eventually, the lorry started again, and I drove it up the slip road and off the motorway. I tried ringing Woolard but couldn't get hold of him. I thought I would sit it out until it got light, then I could have a look and see if I could rectify the problem myself.

The following morning I tried in vain to repair the vehicle. I couldn't reach anyone by telephone, so I rang a local mechanic, who came out and finally got the lorry restarted at 3 p.m. that afternoon. It cost me more than £300 of my own money. I then set off for Liverpool.

The lorry started to play up again. On hills it was reduced to crawling speed. I couldn't believe that the police hadn't pulled me.

At 5.30 p.m., I eventually got into Kirkby. The warehouse had closed and the men I met up there said they had spoken to security at the warehouse and we would be able to park the vehicle in a compound until Monday.

'There's no way I am staying here until Monday, waiting for this warehouse to open,' I said. 'I'm going to unhitch the trailer, leave it here and get myself back to Essex.'

The men weren't too happy, but I wasn't giving them a choice.

I set off at about 8 p.m. When I reached Birmingham again, the lorry broke down. I called the same mechanic out. He cleaned the fuel system and once more I set off. Where the M1 and the M6 intersect, the vehicle broke down again. It was now the early hours of Saturday morning; I had been going since Thursday. I wasn't amused. I was £500 down, tired and pissed off. I thought 'Fuck this,' and telephoned Woolard. I made it clear I was fucked off with the job and told him exactly where the lorry was, then I got out and hitch-hiked back to Essex. My money was never reimbursed and I was never paid anything for the journey. I was unhappy, to say the least.

That same day, the police found the trailer laden with coffee in Liverpool. All of the men waiting with it were arrested. It had been my job to deliver it to Liverpool and I thought, under the circumstances, I had done well to get it there. When I had dropped the trailer off in the compound, I had simply driven out and away. The number plate on the trailer, which matched the number plate on the lorry, had been left on. The lorry was immediately reported stolen. Woolard made some frantic calls and managed to arrange for the broken-down lorry to be towed back to the East End, where it was cut up and disposed of. Once Woolard was happy he could not be implicated in the job, he telephoned Buster Edwards.

'I made it clear once the coffee arrived in Liverpool, you owned it,' he said. 'I don't expect you to pay the full £30,000, but the load has cost me about £17,000. Just give me £8,500 and we'll both lose a bit.'

Buster agreed, but told Woolard he didn't have any money.

'Buster, don't worry,' Woolard said, 'just give it to me when you have it.'

The next morning Buster Edwards was found by his brother Terry hanging from a metal beam in a lock-up shed near his flower stall at Waterloo station. An article in the *Sunday Mirror* stated that it was the fear of going back to prison that drove Buster to hang himself.

In his book, *We Dared*, Woolard blames me for causing Buster to commit suicide. He claims he gave me £250 for diesel, which I failed to put in the lorry. This, he says, caused it to break down and that, in turn, caused the job to go horribly wrong. Only I was on the motorway that night, only I know the lorry overheated. I knew Buster Edwards. At the time of his death, he was in debt over another lorry load of goods that had fallen into the hands of the police. Buster was hoping the money from the load of coffee was going to enable him to pay that debt. When that job went wrong too, he decided to take his own life rather than face his debtors or a possible prison sentence. I fail to see how that is my fault. A professional firm would have supplied a reliable vehicle, which would have arrived in Liverpool with time to spare and without any problems. Woolard and I have since become friends and agree to disagree about events in the past.

* * *

On 31 October 1995, Pat Tate was released from Whitemoor prison. Without him and Rolfe around, trade had been very good at Raquels. Tucker's drug dealers had capitalised on the trouble-free environment and he had done very well out of it. So much so, in fact, that Tucker had been able to purchase Brynmount Lodge, a luxury hacienda-style bungalow on the outskirts of Basildon, with stables and stunning views of the countryside.

To celebrate the success of the club, the promoters held a party at the Cumberland Hotel in Southend and we were all invited. It was an excellent night. Tucker, Tate and Rolfe were there. I could see from the excited look on Rolfe's face that his promises to stop using drugs and stop dealing were about to come to an end. He idolised

Tate and if his hero asked him to do something, I just knew that he would do it.

The boys were back in town.

Everybody at the party was talking about an article that had appeared in the local papers. Half a million pounds' worth of cannabis had been found in a farmer's pond near a village called Rettendon. It was believed that the 336 pounds of cannabis, which was wrapped in 53 different plastic parcels about the size of video tapes, had been dropped from a low-flying aircraft. Instead of the drugs landing in the field, they had landed in the pond and the dealers were unable to find them. A farmer named Yan Haustrup had found one parcel while cutting the hedges; he didn't know what it was and threw it on a fire. He said he then found another piece near the pond and contacted the police. Divers recovered the haul.

Tucker and Tate were saying what a fucking idiot the man was to throw it on the fire and then hand over £500,000 worth of drugs to the police. Tate thought it was worth looking to see if any of the shipment had been missed. He asked me to get in the car with him and go straight to Rettendon, but I declined; I knew it was the drugs talking. Rettendon village consisted of a roundabout, a church, a post office and probably 50 or so houses. There wasn't anything else there. We were hardly going to scour the fields after the police had crawled all over it. But Tate kept on about the drugs. He couldn't believe that someone could be that honest and hand over anything of that much value to the police. Tucker said he was going to find out whom the drugs belonged to; he didn't like the idea of people trading on his manor if he wasn't getting a slice of the profit. He also knew that, as the drugs had been lost, there would be a replacement shipment arriving soon.

Within a short time of arriving at the party, Tate's excessive drug-taking had left him out of his mind. He was boasting about the prostitution business he was going to build across London and the South-East. He said he was also going to flood clubs and pubs with drugs he was going to import from abroad. Rival firms that dared to threaten us would be crushed. Anybody who could be bothered to listen to him must have thought he was on the way to the top of the criminal heap; the reality was he was on his way back to prison or an early grave.

Word soon reached Tucker that the drugs that had been found in the lake at Rettendon had been destined for a heavy firm from

Canning Town in East London. Tucker and Tate approached the people concerned and told them they were interested in purchasing any future shipments. The Canning Town firm told Tucker and Tate that they were due to receive a replacement drop soon and they would keep them informed so a deal could be struck when the shipment arrived. Tucker and Tate had a better idea: they were going to steal the drugs.

Tucker and Tate telephoned me and we met in the car park outside the Accident and Emergency entrance at Basildon hospital, a place we often met. They said they wanted me to act as a back-up driver on a robbery that they were intending to pull off soon. They had arranged to intercept a large shipment of drugs. They had done this type of thing many times before but, they said, this was different. This was the big one.

Before Tucker and Tate's suicidal dive into excessive drug use, they had been my friends. The drugs had turned their brains into porridge and they were oblivious to any danger. Tate was driving on Tucker with his constant talk of riches. I warned Tucker to be careful, but as usual he just laughed and turned my advice into ridicule.

'Nobody can fucking touch us,' he boasted. 'This is money for nothing.'

'That may well be the case,' I replied, 'but I can't do it because the police are watching me. I've got to keep my head down.'

Tucker looked at Tate, rolled his eyes and the pair walked off. As I watched them swagger away across the car park, I knew our firm was reaching the end of its reign. Tucker and Tate would either get locked up for murdering somebody or they would get murdered themselves. Robbery, drugs and murder were all they ever talked about.

Whilst Tate had been in prison, he had been given the details of some very useful contacts in Holland. Rather than take a pittance every weekend from the likes of Murray, Tate said the way forward was to import drugs from abroad and go into the wholesale business, supplying firms he knew in Birmingham, London and Leeds. Most of the people he approached to assist him in this venture made their excuses and declined, but one person in particular was extremely enthusiastic. Darren Nicholls needed money, Darren Nicholls wanted to be a somebody, Darren Nicholls was desperate to be associated with his hero, big Pat Tate. The one thing both men lacked when they decided to join forces was money. Tate had a solution; he approached Tucker and Rolfe, some shady car dealers, villains and dodgy businessmen and asked them to put up the cash. He assured them that, however much they invested, they would get a good return within ten days.

One evening Tate telephoned me and asked me what I was up to. I had nothing planned and told him so.

'Give me a lift, Bernie,' he said. 'I've not got a motor at the moment and I need to go over the bridge to see a mate.' Over the bridge was a reference to the QE2 Bridge, which separates Essex from Kent.

'Look, Pat,' I replied, 'I don't mind giving you a lift, but I need to be back at a reasonable hour, is that agreed?'

Half an hour later Tate and I were driving down the A13 towards the M25, which we would join and then cross over to Kent via 'the bridge'.

'Where are we going then, Pat?' I asked.

'Near Brands Hatch racetrack. My mate lives there,' he replied. Tate didn't elaborate, so I knew he didn't wish to discuss his 'mate'.

We spent the 40-minute journey talking about Raquels and the various characters who went there. We laughed together about some of them and for a short time the old Tate everyone had spoken so warmly about was back.

When we crossed the bridge, we continued along the M25 until we reached the A20 exit. Tate told me to leave the motorway and head for West Kingsdown. After about ten minutes, Tate pointed to a pub coming up on our right and told me, 'We have to meet him in here.'

We sat in the corner of the lounge, Tate with an orange juice and me with a Coke. Tate began laughing, saying, 'I bet that barmaid thinks we are a couple of queers sitting here alone, sipping soft drinks.'

Every few minutes, Tate would get up and look out of the window and into the car park. 'He's fucking late,' he kept repeating. 'But he will get here.' It sounded to me like Tate wasn't sure if his friend would turn up, so I reminded him I wanted to be back in Essex at a reasonable time. After half an hour, I said, 'Look, Pat, he isn't going to show. Can we call it a day?'

'He will, he will,' Tate insisted. 'There's no way he'll let me down.'

Ten minutes later, Tate's friend walked into the pub. I recognised him immediately – it was one of Britain's most infamous villains, Kenny Noye. Tate had expected Noye to sit down with us and have a drink, but he made it clear that he did not intend to hang around. He took a canvas satchel out of his coat and handed it to Tate.

'You'll find it's all there, Pat,' he said. 'Gotta go, catch you later.' With that, Noye turned and walked out of the door.

I could see Tate felt let down. When we got into the car to drive home, Tate was unusually silent. I asked him if everything was OK and he replied, 'Yes, sure, I just don't like people who think they can treat me like a mug. That geezer's invested a bit of money in my business; he can fuck himself if he thinks he's getting it back.'

And that was that: Tate never mentioned the man or the meeting again.

Darren Nicholls had no such influence over people and had no affluent friends, so his contribution to the operation was to travel to Holland and physically purchase the drugs, then use what he called his 'suicide jockeys' to bring them into the country. These were the people, obviously desperate for money, who were prepared to drive cars laden with drugs from the Continent to England for between £6,000 and £8,000 a trip. The risk lay only with the 'jockeys'. Nicholls assured Tate that two out of three cars would get through customs without being caught – more than enough profit to cover the occasional loss. Tate didn't care how many got caught because he wasn't even risking his own money; he felt he couldn't lose.

Tate, Tucker, Rolfe and the consortium managed to raise £124,000. On 6 November, this sum was given to Nicholls in a holdall. He and one of his sidekicks then left for Harwich to catch the ferry. When they arrived at Harwich, Nicholls got right into his role. He insisted that he would purchase the tickets, that he would carry the bag of cash through customs and that his 'mate' would have to keep a discreet distance from him at all times. Nicholls did not realise that all he was doing was leaving a paper trail of evidence with his name stamped all over it. Nicholls really thought he had arrived in the big time; he told his mate to remain in their cabin with the money whilst he spent the journey in the bar and the casino, where he lost all of the spare cash he had.

When they arrived in Holland, Nicholls carried the cash through Dutch customs and booked the train tickets, again in his own name. But upon arrival in Amsterdam, his bravado began to falter. He had no idea if he was going to be robbed or even murdered by the Dutch drug dealers he was about to meet, so he told his friend it was his turn to carry the bag. Nicholls made his way to a bar called Stones

Cafe, where he had been told he could purchase 'grass', a type of cannabis. The dealer, a man named Harris, explained that there was no 'grass' available, but he could supply him with cannabis resin. Harris switched on the television and searched Teletext for the current exchange rate. He then tapped figures into his calculator before informing Nicholls he could sell him the resin at £1,125 per kilo, roughly half of what it would sell for in England. Nicholls stuck out his hand: the deal was done.

Harris, Nicholls and his friend took a taxi over to Eurocar, where Nicholls had pre-booked a vehicle. Nicholls completed the necessary paperwork and handed over his credit card. When the assistant swiped it through the machine, it was declined. Harris knew at this point he was dealing with a fool. Embarrassed, Nicholls asked Harris if he could use his phone. The three men went back to the bar, where Nicholls telephoned his bank, the TSB in Braintree. Nicholls was told that he had exceeded his £250 limit and they were not prepared to extend it. He was advised to contact somebody in England who could go into a TSB bank for him and deposit further funds. Nicholls then telephoned his wife Sandra, who spent an hour running around trying to borrow money from people. Eventually, she managed to get £300, which she took to the bank and paid in. Harris called another cab and the three men went over to the Eurocar depot. As the taxi drove off, Nicholls realised he had left his bags in the boot, so he had to run after the vehicle, waving his arms and shouting until it stopped. Harris was beginning to regret the moment he had set eyes on Nicholls; he certainly wasn't the type of man he wanted to do business with.

Nicholls eventually hired the car and was told by Harris to park round the corner from the bar to await delivery of the drugs. Ten minutes later, Harris and another man appeared carrying large cardboard boxes. There were five in total and these were placed in the boot. Nicholls drove away and met up with the 'suicide jockeys', who were going to bring the drugs to England. On this occasion there were two: one vehicle was loaded with two boxes, the other vehicle carried three. Nicholls' friend was ordered to travel back with the driver whose car carried the three boxes, to ensure the haul was safe.

His work over, Nicholls drove back into the centre of Amsterdam and returned the hire car. He then booked into the Delta hotel before returning to Stones Cafe, where he drank himself into a stupor.

Harris, a man who had dealt with heavyweight drug dealers for years, was no longer concerned about Nicholls. He had ensured Nicholls wouldn't be dealing drugs for much longer, and there would be no comeback on him.

Back in Basildon, Tate was prematurely celebrating the success of his first major drug importation. The £124,000 he had given to Nicholls was going to be turned into almost £250,000 overnight. If he could do a drugs run twice a month, he would be a millionaire by Christmas. If anybody who had given Tate money (except for Tucker and Rolfe) honestly believed they were going to get it back, they were mistaken. It just wasn't the done thing in Tate's world. Even Noye – a man few, if any, would mess with – was due to lose his investment.

Since he had no car of his own, Tate had borrowed Tucker's black Porsche. He had arranged to take a young girl named Lizzie Fletcher out clubbing in Southend as part of his celebration party. Throughout the day Tate had been taking large amounts of cocaine, Ecstasy and Special K. High on drugs, and high on the thought of being rich, the inevitable happened. Tate misjudged a mini roundabout and transformed Tucker's gleaming Porsche into a heap of twisted scrap.

In the early hours of the morning, Tucker was woken by his house phone ringing. 'This better be good,' he told the caller, without even asking who it was.

'It's me: Pat,' said Tate. 'I'm sorry to have to tell you this, but I've totalled your fucking motor. Don't worry, though, Tone. I will pay for it.'

Tucker remained silent.

'To top it all, I've been nicked,' Tate explained. 'They think I stole your car.' Tate, still out of his mind on drugs, began to laugh uncontrollably. 'They are also going to do me for no insurance and driving under the influence. You couldn't come and give me a lift home, could you, Tone?'

Tucker put the phone down and rang Craig Rolfe. 'That silly bastard Tate has wrote my car off,' Tucker ranted. 'He was showing off to some silly little tart. I need you to go down to Southend police station and pick him up.'

Tucker didn't give Rolfe time to reply: he slammed the phone down and rolled over in his bed.

Rolfe roused his girlfriend Donna and informed her that they had to go to Southend to pick Tate up. When the couple arrived at the police station and secured Tate's release, they were both surprised by his demeanour. They had expected him to be remorseful about Tucker's car and grateful that they had got up in the middle of the night to help him out, but they couldn't have been more wrong. As soon as Tate got into the car, he wanted to know if Rolfe had any cocaine or Ecstasy on him. When Rolfe said he didn't, Tate insisted they go round to a dealer's house to get some. Donna objected, and said that she and Rolfe were going straight home. Tate exploded into a fit of rage. He began punching the dashboard and screaming that he was going to have a good time regardless of what they wanted.

Then almost immediately he seemed to calm down. He began telling Donna that he had loads of big drug deals in place and he was going to make Rolfe rich. Donna just looked at Tate and nodded.

The following morning Tucker got out of bed in a foul mood. He immediately telephoned a man who had been paid to fit a kitchen at his home. 'Get around here now, Jeff,' Tucker screamed down the phone. 'There's a problem with this fucking kitchen you fitted!' The man, who knew Tucker well, assured him that any problem would be rectified without charge, there was no need to be aggressive, he would come straight away. When Jeff arrived, Tucker grabbed him by the throat and dragged him through the house into the kitchen. See this, see fucking that, Tucker shouted, as he pointed to minor faults: 'I've fucking told you to fix them and you keep mugging me off. You treat me like some sort of fucking dog, now I'll treat you like a dog until you learn some manners.'

Jeff was slapped and punched, then dragged out to the back of the house, where Tucker's Alsatian dogs were kept in a kennel. Tucker opened the kennel door and shoved Jeff inside. 'Stay in there with the fucking dogs until I decide you can come out.' Jeff lay whimpering next to two Alsatians; he was covered in their urine and faeces, but he did not dare move until Tucker released him the following day.

When Tate got out of bed, he went to see his old friend, ex-Metropolitan policeman Barry Dorman. The pair had met in the mid-'70s at various car auctions which are held around London and Essex. Dorman had left the police service by this time and subsidised his income by buying and selling second-hand cars. Tate, despite his age, 19 or 20 years old at that time, owned his own car front on Southend's London Road. The pair met regularly through their business and soon became friends.

In 1984, Dorman was involved in a very serious car accident and as a result of his injuries he had to give up his full-time job. The following year, as he made a slow recovery, Tate urged Dorman to go into the second-hand car trade full-time. Through Tate, Dorman managed to acquire a rented forecourt. It was here that Tate arrived, asking his old friend for a favour. He told Dorman that he had crashed Tucker's Porsche and it had been extensively damaged. 'Could you get it fixed up for me, please, Barry?' Tate asked. 'He is a really good friend and I've given him the hump.'

Dorman agreed and the vehicle was brought to Dorman's business premises. His daughter spent a lot of time trying to locate cheap second-hand spares for the repair and Dorman also arranged for quotes to carry out the body work. As a result of the repairs that needed to be done on the Porsche, Dorman began to have virtually day-to-day contact with either Tate or Tucker, or both. The majority of the time they were together and were accompanied by Rolfe.

At that time, Dorman had a blue Range Rover 3.5 Vogue S.E. on his forecourt, as he had recently taken the vehicle in as part exchange. As Tucker was now without a vehicle, he and Tate showed interest in purchasing the Range Rover, which Dorman had priced at £10,995. After some negotiation, Dorman agreed to sell it to them for £9,800. Dorman knew that neither Tate nor Tucker would be able to get finance on the vehicle. When he pointed this out, Tucker said that his friend would be buying it on his behalf. Dorman, therefore, agreed to accept a £2,000 deposit and Tucker's friend, Peter Cuthbert, soon arrived to provide sufficient details for him to complete the finance agreement. They then took the keys from Dorman and drove the vehicle away from his forecourt. Little did they know they had just invested in the perfect vehicle to carry out their own murders.

If Tate had not crashed Tucker's Porsche, they would still have been driving around in it three or four weeks later. A Porsche would never have made it down the potholed farm track where they were to meet their deaths.

That same morning Nicholls was waking from his drunken slumber at the Delta hotel. He made his way to central station and caught a train to the ferry terminal. Upon arrival, he booked a cabin, but he spent most of the journey losing even more money on the roulette wheel in the casino. When the ship docked in Harwich, Nicholls purchased some duty-free lager for himself and several boxes of cigarettes for his wife. He then made his way to his car and drove home.

Nicholls and the drugs had made it safely back to England. All

Tucker, Tate and Rolfe had to do now was distribute them to the dealers and wait for the money to come rolling in. It seemed nothing could possibly go wrong now.

Rolfe had been involved with a drug dealer from North London named Gary for about five years. When the cannabis from Amsterdam arrived in the country, Rolfe immediately contacted him and agreed to sell him £10,000 worth of the load. No money would change hands; Rolfe was going to give the drugs to Gary on credit and collect the cash when they had been sold.

Nicholls was also waiting for the money from the cannabis to start rolling in. He had supplied numerous dealers, who had been waiting for the consignment to arrive. Within a few hours, all the drugs Nicholls had were gone. Pleased with himself that things had eventually worked out after several mishaps in Amsterdam, Nicholls sat back and prepared himself for a long, hard drinking session in his local pub. Within minutes of the celebration starting, however, his phone began to ring.

Elsewhere in Essex, Rolfe had begun to receive an unusually high number of phone calls. When his partner asked him what was the matter, Rolfe told her his dealers were saying that the cannabis was of a poor quality. Donna could hear people shouting down the phone and could see that Rolfe was getting very aggravated.

Eventually, Rolfe told Donna that all of the cannabis was being returned because it was rubbish. Nicholls was being told the same thing, although he initially refused to believe it. He accused the dealers of trying to rip him off. Nicholls began to get aggressive with the callers, but they were equally vocal: they were adamant Nicholls had sold them shit.

Nicholls finally realised that nobody was trying to rip him off and agreed to look into it for them. The celebrations were put on hold.

When he sat back to think about the numerous mishaps in Amsterdam, and Harris's attitude towards him, Nicholls came to the conclusion that Harris, annoyed about his lack of professionalism, must have loaded the boxes with dud cannabis. If so, his and the firm's troubles were just beginning.

* * *

Shortly before Nicholls' trip to Amsterdam, the police had raided

Club UK in Wandsworth. The whole operation was televised. There were more than 1,000 revellers in the venue at the time. Mark Murray's dealers had thrown all of their pills and powders on the floor in order to escape arrest and as a result Murray had lost a total of 800 pills – pills that he had not yet paid for. Already heavily in debt to an impatient Tucker, to Murray prison would have seemed like a salvation. There are no financial advisers in the drug world, and there are certainly no overdraft facilities. Tucker wanted his money, and he wanted it immediately.

He arrived at my house with Rolfe, demanding to know where Murray was. I wasn't sure but guessed he would be at home, and so we all got into a car and went round to his flat. Murray's girlfriend answered the door, but Rolfe just pushed past her. The girl looked terrified. He asked where Murray was, but she claimed she didn't know.

Rolfe asked if Murray had taken his phone with him. She said no, he had left it in the flat, so Rolfe switched it on and started making calls. Tucker was sitting on the settee with me. He was laughing at Rolfe's antics.

He pointed at the television and asked Murray's girlfriend if she was watching whatever programme was on. When she said no, he ripped the plug from the wall, wrapped it round the television and told Rolfe to go and load it and the stereo in the car. He then told Murray's girlfriend she was coming with us, too.

The girl was very frightened. She said Mark would be home soon, but Tucker just glared at her and said, 'Don't worry about that! Just get in the car.' We all drove round to another friend's house. Fortunately, if he'd ever had a reason, Tucker forgot why he had taken Murray's girlfriend around to somebody else's house – I think it was to ensure she didn't forewarn Murray that he was looking for him. Whatever, tired of waiting, we all went home, leaving her there.

That night Tucker and Rolfe returned to Murray's flat and this time he was home. Tucker pulled out a huge Bowie knife and grabbed Murray by the neck, pressing the blade to his throat. 'I want my money,' he said. 'And for every week you owe me, you pay £500 on top. If I don't get it, you're dead.'

Murray, terrified that Tucker was more than likely to carry out his threat, and equally concerned that his debt now carried interest, contacted everybody he knew, asking for financial assistance. When people learned that Tucker was Murray's creditor, they didn't want to know. In desperation, he turned to a man he had recently met on the Essex club circuit: John Rollinson.

Rollinson was a small-time drug dealer who worked during the day as a hairdresser. I had met him once or twice when he had visited Raquels with Murray. To me, he was a mature, scruffy, short and overweight individual. He gave himself the rather grand title of 'Gaffer' by night, when he peddled drugs and sat in the quieter pubs telling anybody who would listen that he was not just a face in the Essex underworld but 'the most dangerous man in the country'. It was Rollinson, or Gaffer, who came to Murray's aid, although he didn't have the capital to settle his debt in full. Gaffer scraped together £2,000 for Murray, a generous amount by most hairdressers' standards.

Murray, who still feared Tucker was going to damage him – or worse – asked me to arrange a meeting with him at Raquels, so he could pay him the cash and ask for the interest agreement to be dropped. At the meeting, which was held upstairs in the diner, Murray pleaded with Tucker; he'd only been able to raise £2,000 and needed more time.

'I'll have what I owe you soon,' he said. 'If you don't let me carry on, I won't be able to get the money to pay you.' Tucker reluctantly agreed and dropped the interest clause, but he told Murray that he must purchase all of his drug supply from him at an inflated rate so that his debt could be paid off sooner rather than later. Unfortunately for Murray, there was another 'but' . . . Tucker had recently acquired a batch of Ecstasy pills named Apples, because they had an apple motif imprinted on them. Tucker said they were extremely strong and that people who had taken them had complained of headaches. 'The dealers can't get rid of them once everyone knows what they're like,' he said, 'so sell what you can.'

Tucker then took the £2,000 that Gaffer had given to Murray and handed the Apple Ecstasy pills to him. Breathing a sigh of relief as Tucker strode off, Murray felt safe for the moment. He was back in business. Soon, those extra-strong pills would be in the hands of his dealers, being distributed in Raquels. Soon, he thought, his troubles would be over.

The following Friday night I was standing at the bar in Raquels, talking to Tucker and Rolfe, and the assistant manager. While we were chatting, one of the barmaids telephoned him and asked him to come and see her, as she had a problem. Tucker and I were asked to accompany him to resolve whatever problem there was. We went to the bar near the main dance-floor area. The barmaid told us that she knew a girl in the club was underage, so had refused to serve her, but now the girl was getting stroppy. We called the girl over. She looked distressed, and I asked her if she had any identification, so that she could prove her age.

'I haven't. My purse has been stolen,' she said.

'I'm sorry,' I replied, 'but if you don't have ID, then you'll have to leave. The barmaid says she knows you and that you are underage.'

The girl became very irate. 'I've had my purse stolen! I showed you my ID on the way in! Why are you asking for it now?'

'You may appear to be 18, but the barmaid says you are not,' I said. 'So, you must show your ID or leave.'

'I've had my purse stolen! There's £300 in it! My dad's a policeman. I'm going to get him and you'll all be in trouble.'

'Look, any story you tell me, I've already heard,' I replied. 'If you haven't any ID, you will have to leave.'

'My dad's a policeman,' the girl repeated. 'I've had my purse stolen!'

'I'm sorry, you will have to leave,' I told her again. 'If your dad is a policeman, he will understand that if you haven't got ID, we cannot let you remain here.'

Eventually, she left. To be honest, I couldn't have cared less if the girl was 17 or 18; I have always judged people by the way they behave. Most of the 17-year-old girls who came into the club were trying to act older than they were anyway, so were well behaved. It was the 30-year-old men who behaved like 12 year olds I objected to. If the barmaid hadn't said anything, I certainly wouldn't have asked the girl to leave.

At closing time, I was putting the chains on the fire doors and waiting for the staff to leave before going home myself when I heard shouting. I thought somebody was being attacked, so went to see what the problem was. At the front door, I found the barmaid who had told me the girl was underage. She told me she had just fought with the girl she had pointed out to me; she said the girl had waited outside the club to have it out with her. I told the barmaid she had better wait inside until the girl had gone. Half an hour later, when I was satisfied the incident was over, I went home and thought no more about it. It was some time later before I found out the truth.

Somebody who had objected to the way the girl had been treated told me that the barmaid had stolen the girl's purse from the toilets. The girl knew that the barmaid had her purse and had demanded that she return it immediately. The barmaid had then telephoned the assistant manager to say that the girl was underage so that we would eject her and the accusations would cease. Leah Betts, the girl who had had her purse stolen, was rightfully upset. She had waited outside the club after being ejected and had been assaulted after confronting the barmaid. As a result of this incident, Leah was barred from Raquels.

On Friday, 10 November, it was business as usual in the club. Ecstasy, cocaine and amphetamines were being sold discreetly near the top bar. Murray was selling the drugs himself that night because of his financial problems.

A nervous teenager sidled up to Murray and asked him if he could score. Murray nodded. The teenager, a friend of Leah Betts, held the folded notes in his hand; Murray the Ecstasy pills in his. They pretended to shake hands. Murray took the money, the teenager the pills. In this moment, Leah Betts's fate was sealed.

The deal would end her life and would change that of a lot of others. Unfortunately for Leah, the drugs were the pills with the apple motif, which had come from Tucker.

The following night, in her father's home, against the advice of her closest friend, who had been given a warning about the strength of these particular pills, Leah took one, thinking it was going to give her the best night of her short life.

13

THE LAST SUPPER

MONDAY mornings: don't you just fucking hate them? To many, they mean crawling out of bed for an unrewarding job after a weekend on the piss. To me, Mondays were when two very different worlds would collide and I would find myself in the epicentre of the shit that followed.

Working as a doorman at weekends, I would leave for work just after my children returned home from school on Friday evenings and would rarely see them again before they were preparing to depart for school on the Monday morning. Physically and mentally exhausted after my last shift, I would leave the peace and tranquillity of my car and walk into chaos: shrieking kids and a partner who never tired of telling me that if I didn't give up working in nightclubs, she would give me up. Hands up, she was right; I was everything she alleged and some. I can't argue that my lifestyle was hardly a blueprint for family bliss.

Debra, at the time my long-suffering partner and the mother of our two wonderful children, yearned for normality, whatever that may have been. I, on the other hand, couldn't handle the thought of semi-detached suburbia, two weeks' holiday a year in Spain, the latest offering from the Ford motor company on the drive and a piece of toast from the one you love most each morning as you head off for your dreary 9-to-5 job. Our differences led to inevitable rows, so I would dread every Monday morning, when I would return home.

I wanted more: I wanted to have everything my shit upbringing and non-education had supposedly deemed me unable to own or be. In order to fulfil my dream, I chose to live a nightmare existence, beating drunks, drug dealers and various other forms of pond life up and down the dance floors and streets of London and Essex.

Monday, 13 November didn't feel any different from any other Monday, but my life and the lives of several others would be changed forever that day. After the mandatory argument with Debra, I dropped our children off at school and went to fill up my car with petrol at the Tesco store in Pitsea, on the outskirts of Basildon. I was tired as usual and thinking about Christmas, of all things. I always look forward to Christmas – not because I immerse myself in the 'Yo fucking Ho' atmosphere, but because it signals the end of yet another year.

For me, the previous 12 months had been horrendous. I'd suffered enough grief to last me a lifetime: police raids, internal feuds within the firm, and I was on bail for possessing firearms. During one police raid, an extremely vigilant officer had discovered a handgun that had been secreted in the ceiling of my kitchen. It couldn't get any worse, surely.

Post-Christmas, things just had to get better. A brand new year, a brand new beginning: aims, hopes and dreams aplenty. Then again, resolutions are usually forgotten by the end of January, and the dreams soon join the diet, which is always postponed until tomorrow.

As I walked to the garage kiosk, I glanced at the news-stand. Every paper had a picture of a young girl on its front page. Her eyes were closed, her mouth slack, agape; tubes had been inserted into her mouth and nose. I picked up a tabloid out of curiosity and paid for the petrol. Looking at the photograph, I couldn't help but think what a terrible waste of a young life it was. I had three children and I couldn't begin to imagine what this stricken girl's parents were going through.

As I turned the page, my heart sank. In fact, it hit the floor, bounced back up and lodged in the back of my throat. A picture of Raquels leapt out at me. The accompanying text said that an 18-year-old girl named Leah Betts was on a life-support machine after taking an Ecstasy pill that had been purchased in Raquels. I knew this incident was going to cause my associates and myself serious grief. When I got home, I sat on the stairs and put my head in my hands.

I wasn't sure what to do, but I knew I had to do something; it was more than a possibility that the police would want to talk to me, along with Murray, Tucker, Tate, Rolfe and all of the other members of the firm. After much thought, I decided to ring Murray, but his phone was unobtainable. I tried ringing Tucker, Tate and Rolfe, but like Murray they had obviously heard the news and gone to ground.

The first person to call me was a drugs squad officer from Essex Police HQ in Chelmsford. He asked if I was aware of the stricken teenager. I said that I was. He told me that Leah was going to die, but the hospital had agreed to keep her on the life-support machine until every avenue of hope had been exhausted. One of those avenues was obtaining a pill from the same batch of pills that Leah had taken, so that it could be analysed. Once its ingredients were known, doctors could possibly help her.

At this time, everybody was under the impression that the pills were contaminated, which I found hard to believe. Drug dealers want customers to return to them; it wouldn't happen if people thought they were selling poison.

The officer suggested we meet, but I told him I was unable to do so, as I was out of town. The following day the flat where Tucker's teenage mistress lived was raided. It was owned by Pat Tate. A quantity of amphetamine was found – not a lot, just a bit of personal – but the fact that the police had raided Tate's property spoke volumes to me. The police were clearly on to the firm; it was only a matter of time before all of our homes were raided.

Our reign at Raquels had won us few friends: everyone who bore a grudge was on the phone to the police or Crimestoppers. True or false information, it did not really matter; people knew it would cause me or the firm shit.

Despite the problems we were now all undoubtedly going to be facing, Tate continued to rampage through Essex, drawing unwanted attention to everyone connected to the firm. Tate was desperately trying to locate Darren Nicholls over the dud cannabis. He was still seething with rage and swearing bloody revenge.

When I finally managed to speak to Tucker about Leah Betts collapsing and Raquels being named as the source for the Ecstasy that she had taken, he made it quite clear that he wanted his name kept out of any police inquiry. He said he'd got the hump over Donna Garwood being arrested for the amphetamine that had been found at the flat. Garwood had claimed a doorman from Raquels had grassed her up, even though at that time the police had not spoken to any doormen.

The pressure was getting to Tucker: if he was arrested over the Betts incident, he knew he would be ruined. He could see his empire crumbling and he was panicking. A menace fuelled by paranoia was growing. Everyone was putting his or her back against the wall and somebody else's name in the frame.

Wednesday, 15 November was the first night that the Buzz bar had been open since Leah had collapsed. As usual, Gavin and I were working. We arrived at approximately 8.30 p.m. There was an eerie atmosphere to the place. It was as if everyone had their eyes on us, looking for a reaction. What made it even more surreal was that the Buzz bar had four television screens. Every time the news was broadcast, images of Leah lying in her hospital bed were displayed on all four screens. There we were, in this dark room full of revellers, some under the influence of drugs, some not, with images of Leah looking down on us: she was dying because of what had gone on in that very building. It felt strange – very strange and unnerving.

There were the usual fools asking Gavin and me our opinions about Leah and who had supplied her. A couple of undercover reporters were present, trying to purchase drugs. They were so obvious: long raincoats; short, tidy hair; middle-class accents. They were asking everybody if they 'could score'. I asked them to leave and, wisely, they complied.

I was really pleased to get home from work that night. As I climbed the stairs to go to bed, the house phone rang. It was a man I knew from the club. He wanted to know if I had a problem with somebody called Steve Packman. I had never heard of Packman.

'Assure him that I haven't,' I replied.

'Is it all right if I give him your number?' the man asked.

I told him that it was and went to bed, thinking that was the end of the matter. Ten minutes later, the house phone rang again. I got out of bed, rather reluctantly, picked up the handset and sat on the stairs.

'This is Steve Packman,' said a voice.

'I'm sorry, I don't know you,' I replied.

'I'm on police bail for supplying Ecstasy to Leah Betts.'

'What has that got to do with me?' I asked.

Packman claimed that he had been told that Tucker's firm were looking for him because of all the problems the Leah Betts incident had caused them. I reassured him that until I had received the call just a few minutes earlier, I had never heard of him. 'Don't believe whatever you're being told. We don't have a problem with you,' I said.

Packman did not appear to believe me; he sounded very nervous and asked if we could meet so that he could explain himself. 'Can you come out now and meet?' he asked me.

'Look, mate, it's nearly midnight. I've just got in from work. I'm not getting out of bed to meet you so that I can listen to something that doesn't concern me. Ring me tomorrow and, if you wish, I will meet you,' I told him.

I didn't have a very good night's sleep. The call played on my mind, and the more I thought about it, the more I convinced myself that somebody was trying to set me up.

Debra and I were due to move home the following day. We had purchased a beautiful property in Mayland, near Maldon in Essex. Just a hundred yards from the sea, the house was located down a remote track and was surrounded by woodland – a far cry from the Alcatraz estate in Basildon where we had once lived. We both hoped it would be a new beginning, away from the madness we had endured over the last decade.

Debra drove over to Mayland early in the morning to wait for the removal lorry and I took our children to school. I turned on the car radio and on the nine o'clock news heard that Leah had lost her fight for life. Even though I had known two or three days prior to the event that Leah was going to die, I still felt saddened, particularly when I heard her family being interviewed. When I arrived in Mayland, Debra was standing at the front door. 'Have you heard?' she asked. I replied that I had. Debra had been very upset by what had happened to Leah. She had no idea of the firm's involvement and I couldn't bring myself to tell her.

Tucker rang me around lunchtime. He was shouting and screaming about the effect the police inquiries were having on his drug-dealing activities. 'I want this fucking sorted and I want it sorted today,' he ranted. Now Leah had died, he said that the shit was really going to hit the fan. 'I've got enough to fucking worry about without the police breathing down my neck or sniffing around anybody I know.'

I told Tucker about the call I had received from Packman and explained that if the police charged him, it should bring about an end to their inquiries. Tucker wasn't convinced.

The world's media had descended on Essex. Reporters were making their own enquiries and were learning more from people who were prepared to sell their stories than the police were learning from their informants.

'If Packman is on bail for supplying Leah, he's the one who deserves to be in the spotlight, not us,' Tucker said. 'He's already in the frame, so it's not grassing. Just make sure everybody knows who he is and they'll leave us alone.' I wasn't sure how we were going to achieve that, but I knew it certainly wasn't going to be easy.

Later that morning Packman rang me and we arranged to meet the following day. I telephoned Gary Jones, the reporter that I'd known for several years. He was aware that people had been arrested and bailed for supplying Leah, but he was not aware of their identities. He was very keen to find out who they were. I told him about Steve Packman and, although I didn't know at that stage where our meeting was to take place, said that I would ring him as soon as I found out. When Packman rang me again, I suggested we meet on a garage forecourt in Basildon town centre. I chose the garage as a meeting place because, as I said, I was afraid Packman, or somebody else, might have been trying to set me up. In addition, the garage forecourt was always busy and was monitored by CCTV, so Packman wouldn't be able to say he had been threatened.

I rang Gary and informed him of the details of the meeting. He was keen to expose Packman as the man who had been arrested for supplying Leah, but he had reservations about my information. How did I know Packman was on bail for the offence, and how did I know the man I was meeting was Packman, he asked. To allay his concerns, it was agreed that I would record my conversation with Packman and a photographer would secretly snap him.

Packman arrived at the garage at 6 p.m. We shook hands and he immediately asked if I had a problem with him. I assured him I hadn't. He told me that he was friends with Leah and another girl named Sarah Cargill. They had been planning Leah's forthcoming 18th birthday party, which was to have been held at her father's home. Leah was looking forward to becoming an adult, as she hadn't had the happiest of childhoods. Her parents had separated after her father, Paul, had begun a relationship with his current partner, Janet, who was married to one of his friends. Paul was a police officer and his friend was a colleague based at the same police station. When Leah's mother, Dorothy, learned of her husband's infidelity, she filed for divorce, citing adultery as the cause. Dorothy left the family home with Leah, who was then just three years old. Eventually, Dorothy met a man named Chris and they set up home together in Basildon. On 1 September 1992, Dorothy collapsed and died. She was just 45 years old. Leah, who had just turned 14, was naturally devastated. It was only after Dorothy died that Leah's father became involved in his daughter's upbringing.

Leah chose not to live with her father, remaining in Basildon with her stepfather, but she did begin to visit him regularly and formed a relationship with her new family. Leah attended Basildon college and worked in the Allders department store opposite Raquels. For months, she had been telling her friends in class and her workmates what a great party she was going to throw for her 18th.

Whilst planning the celebrations, her father and stepmother agreed that she could hold the party in their home, but they insisted that alcohol would be banned because some of the guests would be underage. They also stipulated that they would remain at the premises to keep an eye on things. One can only imagine how Leah felt as she contemplated celebrating her 18th birthday with lemonade, whilst being watched by her father and stepmother. Foolishly, she decided to circumvent the draconian restrictions and enjoy herself regardless by taking Ecstasy.

Like thousands of other teenagers at that time, Leah had experimented with drugs before, so she was confident taking one pill would not do her any harm. She had been barred from Raquels, so was unable to obtain Ecstasy directly from the dealers in the club.

Initially, she approached a friend named Louise Yexley to obtain them on her behalf, but she had been unable to do so. Yexley said that she would ask her boyfriend, Steve Smith, and his friend, Stephen Packman, if they would get them, as they regularly went to Raquels on Friday nights. Both men had agreed.

Packman said that Smith made 'amateurish efforts' to obtain the pills whilst they were at the club, but the dealers hadn't trusted him. Packman alleged Smith had told him that if a dealer approached him in the club, he should notify Smith immediately. Packman then said that whilst he was standing at the top bar, a man asked him if he 'was sorted'. He described this man as wearing a blue Schott bomber jacket with curly shoulder-length hair. It sounded just like Mark Murray, to me. Packman said he returned to Steve Smith, who gave him the money. He told me he then bought the pills, which were passed down the chain of friends to Leah. Later, in court, he said he only told me this because he was so frightened of Tucker and me.

I told Packman that he had nothing to fear; he hadn't directly caused us any problems, it was just one of those regrettable things.

We shook hands and he walked off into the night. I approached the reporters who had been photographing Packman from a van nearby. Nothing untoward had been said about Tucker, me or the firm. The press now had a photograph of the man who was on bail for the offence, and who would ultimately be photographed when he turned up at court.

As soon as the photograph was published, the spotlight on Tucker and our firm would be switched off. The club management would also be happy, as it was now evident that Leah had not been in the club. I was happy because it was all over, or so it seemed.

I gave the recording of my conversation with Packman to Gary Jones and walked away. I wasn't offered any money for the story and I didn't receive any. Whatever happened regarding the Leah Betts inquiry, common sense told me that the management would want to show that there had been changes (i.e. changes in security). Matters were coming to a head. Without telling me, Tucker had already consulted a solicitor about the Betts case, despite the fact he hadn't been questioned. Murray had disappeared off the face of the earth. It was plain to see it was now every man for himself. Common sense told me we had reached the end of our reign.

The next time I went into work, it was very quiet, as I recall it. I didn't do anything at all that night, work-wise. I just sat at the bar and had a drink. I'd had enough of the place. I hated it, loathed it. About 11 o'clock, I thought, 'Fuck this, I'm going.' I went over to Maurice, a doorman from Bristol, and said, 'I want you to be head doorman. I'm going.' He looked rather puzzled, but thanked me. We shook hands and I went up to the office.

'I'm leaving,' I told the manager.

'What's the problem?' he asked.

'There ain't no problem. I'm leaving. See you later,' I said and walked out.

I had no idea how I was going to support my wife and children from that popint on, but I did not care. My leaving had to be a total departure, no occasional acquaintances from memory lane. The firm, the violence, the police, the grief: it all meant nothing now. It was a thing of the past. Or so I thought.

The night I walked out on Raquels, I decided I would celebrate, so I drove over to a club in Southend called Ad-Lib. The promoters who hired Raquels out on a Friday also hired out Ad-Lib. I walked in the door and down a flight of three or four steps; Tucker and Tate were standing at the bar with two girls. Tate smiled and put his arms around me. He patted my back and said, 'It's great to see you, Bernie. How are you?' Tucker grunted something; he looked as if he had the hump.

'What's the matter?' I asked him.

He shook hands with me and said, 'Nothing.' Then he added, 'Can I have a word?'

We went out of earshot of the others and he told me that one of the doormen had informed on his mistress.

Donna Garwood was constantly causing problems. In Raquels, she would say to me that such and such a man was giving her grief, such and such a man was staring at her. Tucker had insisted, she said, that if she had a problem, I had to throw out the person who had upset her.

'What's the matter with her this time?' I said to Tucker.

He got annoyed, saying that one of the doormen had grassed her up because she had been in Tate's flat when the police had found a small quantity of amphetamine.

'That's bollocks! The police haven't even spoken to any doormen,' I said. He told me another doorman had confirmed it. 'Well, who's this other doorman, then?' I asked. 'We'll go and see him.'

'I've got to go now,' he replied.

'Fair enough,' I said. 'Ring me and we'll discuss what has been said.' Then he walked out of the door. Tate turned round and put his arm on my shoulder again.

'Don't worry about him,' he said. 'He's under a lot of pressure and has just got the hump.'

We shook hands and Tate left to join Tucker. I waited a minute and thought, 'I'm not having this, I am going to clear this bollocks up.' I went outside and found them sitting in their recently acquired blue Range Rover. I leant against the driver's door and said to Tucker, 'I'm telling you, no doorman's grassed Donna up. Someone's just saying it to cause trouble. And as for this doorman, who confirmed it? Why don't we go round and see him tomorrow, and if you think he's lying, we'll bash him?'

'Fair enough,' Tucker replied, 'we'll fucking bash him.'

Tate slammed the vehicle into gear and they roared off down the street.

I don't know why I said what I'd said. I had just decided to walk out of Raquels. I had told myself I wanted nothing more to do with the firm's shit. I suppose the habit of the past five years was proving hard to break. The conversation had put me in a lousy mood. I was sick of bloody wannabes trying to get in on the act and causing trouble.

The following morning, I rang Tucker, but as usual he wasn't in or wasn't answering his phone, so I sent him a fax telling him I had quit Raquels the night before and Maurice was taking over. The fax read: 'There are no problems, it's safe, it's sorted.'

The following day, Monday, 20 November, Tucker rang me. I wasn't in, so he left a message on my answering machine. He was being abusive and threatening. He said I couldn't just walk out of Raquels; he wanted an explanation. 'I'm going to fucking do you,' he said.

My problems are my own: nothing would have made me involve Debra and our children. But I knew what might happen: I didn't need to ask Nipper Ellis, Kevin Whittaker or their families. When my children came out of school, I booked them and Debra into a hotel just outside Basildon, near a village called Rettendon. They were to remain there until the issue with Tucker had been resolved.

I was still owed a week's money by Tucker, as we were paid in arrears at Raquels, so I rang the door staff and told them I would be turning up on Friday to collect it. One of the doormen said, 'You had better ring me before you come, as I've heard Tucker has got the hump.' I told him I didn't care, but I didn't want to involve him and the other doormen, so I agreed. Always cautious, I armed myself. I put a huge combat knife in the back of my trousers, a bottle of squirt in my pocket and went down to Basildon town centre to collect my money. Two doormen, Maurice and Gavin, met me near Raquels and advised me not to go round to the club.

'Tucker's there now with Tate, Rolfe and a few other people we haven't seen before,' Gavin said. 'Tucker's told me that he's holding your money and if you want it, you should get it yourself. But I wouldn't advise it – he's firmed up. I'll give you my wages and get yours off Tucker. You can go round if you really want to. You know I'm with you. But I wouldn't advise it.'

I agreed. Gavin gave me his money and went back to the club. When he arrived, Tucker asked him if he had seen me. 'I know he's your mate, but we've got a problem with him,' he said.

'I have seen him,' Gavin replied, 'and I've given him my wages, as you've got his. Now, I need you to pay me.'

Tucker hesitated, apologised and gave Gavin his money. As far as I was concerned, that was the end of the matter. Everyone was happy. I was out of Raquels and out of that way of life. There was no need for anyone to continue with a vendetta.

The following night, Saturday, 25 November, I was told that Tate and Rolfe went into the Buzz bar allegedly looking for me. I don't know what Tate's problem was. He and I had always got on well. I suppose, as with Nipper, because Tucker had the hump with somebody, he felt that he had to follow suit. It was always the way with these fucking morons.

Gavin was in the Buzz bar and Tate asked him if he had seen me. 'Tell Bernie he can't hide forever,' he added. 'And when we see him, we're going to take lumps out of him.'

'He's my mate. I don't pass on messages like that,' Gavin replied.

Tate should have learned from his experience with Nipper that you shouldn't go around making threats. If he was looking for me, he knew where I lived. And I was hardly going to try and hide forever. Nor was I going to give him forever to find me. I had no idea why Rolfe was involving himself either; he had nothing to do with Raquels or my arrangement with Tucker. Regardless, if they wished to go around threatening people, they had to expect a response. Fucking mugs.

The following morning I rang Tucker about the threats he had been making, along with Tate and Rolfe. 'I hear you want to speak to me,' I said.

'Why didn't you tell me you were leaving Raquels when I saw you in Southend?' he asked.

'I'd had enough of everything,' I explained. 'I admit I was wrong not to discuss it with you, but I just wanted to walk away. I told the manager Maurice was taking my place, the door is safe. You've not lost out. It's still your door. In fact, you have complete control now, instead of going down the middle with me.'

'But people are talking,' he said.

'I don't give a fuck about people,' I replied. 'I'm out of it.'

Tucker said, 'I don't believe you,' then the line went dead. I assumed he'd switched his mobile phone off.

On 5 December, I was contacted by a detective. He told me they had received information that Tucker and Tate were telling people that they were planning to shoot me and these threats were being taken seriously by Essex police. People within the firm had said an attack on me would be carried out very soon. The officer also told me that Detective Chief Inspector Brian Storey wanted to talk to me about the Leah Betts inquiry. I told him I'd moved away from Basildon and didn't need any of that shit.

However, it was impressed upon me that I had no safe quarter. If I wanted to move away and start a new life, I should do what he asked. Matters needed clearing up; it would be an informal chat, then I could go off and begin my new life, no strings attached. He also asked if Debra would be willing to talk. 'She has nothing she can tell you,' I said. 'She knows nothing.' The detective said that every doorman would be spoken to, so it was in my interest to get it over and done with.

I eventually agreed that Debra and I would both attend South Woodham Ferrers police station the following day at 2 p.m. I insisted that it be an informal chat rather than any type of official interview, otherwise I would have to bring a solicitor. The detective agreed.

That night Tate, who had only been out of prison for six weeks, was up to his old tricks. He was at home with one of his many mistresses, Lizzie Fletcher, who called the London Pizza Company in Wickford and asked for a pizza with different toppings on different sections. Roger Ryall, the manager, told Lizzie that they didn't do that type of pizza. Tate grabbed the phone and started swearing at him. The manager said later, 'I wasn't going to take that, so I said, "Get rid of that attitude and I will send you a pizza."' He obviously didn't realise the type of man he was talking to.

Tate became more irate and slammed the phone down. Half an hour later he turned up at the pizza shop, picked up the till and hurled it across the room at the manager. Fearing for his life, the manager backed out of the office and pushed the panic button, which was linked directly to the police. That was Ryall's second mistake of the evening.

Tate, fearing arrest and a return to prison, over-reacted. He punched Ryall in the face, grabbed him by the hair and smashed his head into a glass plate on the draining board. Tate told him not to call the police or he would come back, smash the place up and hurt his staff. However, the panic button had already been activated. Officers arrived just after Tate left.

When Tate's call was traced to his home, and the police told Ryall who he was, Ryall decided not to press charges. Only Tate could turn ordering a pizza into an orgy of violence.

The next day Debra and I drove to South Woodham Ferrers police station. We were met at the door by four detectives. Two wished to speak to Debra. DI Storey and another detective wanted to speak to me. Debra knew nothing about events surrounding Leah Betts's death and therefore couldn't say anything of relevance, so I said I had no objection to her being questioned. However, as far as I was concerned, if, as they had said, this was an informal chat, then I would only be prepared to talk to DI Storey on his own.

DI Storey made it clear to me that he was well aware of the firm's involvement in just about everything. He also knew what he could prove and, despite knowing the facts, what was impossible to prove. Murray had been arrested and questioned, but nobody was going to give evidence against him. I could see his task was painful, but he knew at that time the only people he could realistically prosecute were the friends of Leah whom he believed had purchased the drugs in Raquels.

He knew Tucker and Tate had threatened to shoot me and, as these were serious people, he knew it wasn't an idle threat.

He asked me if I would make a statement about the night Leah Betts's pill had been purchased in Raquels. Storey added that there was always the possibility that if I refused, I might be subpoenaed to court, although he made it clear he wasn't offering me an ultimatum, he was just being honest with me.

I told him I understood my position. I couldn't put my family at risk for things I had done, but I wouldn't rule out the possibility of doing what he'd asked. I would give it some serious thought, discuss it with my family and speak to him again in a couple of weeks. I wanted matters with Tucker and Tate sorted out first.

DI Storey warned me that I should be careful of Tucker, Tate and their minions. I thanked him and reassured him that their threats were certainly not being ignored. Our conversation had lasted until four o'clock. When I walked out of the police station, Debra was waiting for me. She said they had only kept her for half an hour and had asked about trivial matters, facts they would have already known.

Debra and I drove to her mother's home, as she had been looking after our children. The snow that had been falling since lunchtime was now quite heavy. It was perhaps three or four inches deep. We arrived at Debra's mother's home 20 minutes later and stayed for a cup of tea. We then drove to Wickford, where we had something to eat, before heading towards the Rettendon turnpike, the main roundabout on the A130. It was half-six. The traffic was heavy and it was a miserable night. The snow was still falling and it was by now pitch black. Ironically, at around the same time, Tucker, Tate and Rolfe were travelling along the very same road. Fifteen minutes earlier they had picked up a friend who they believed was going to take them to a field at the end of a remote farm track where a plane was due to land. This plane, they had been told, was going to be carrying more than £1 million worth of cocaine and they intended to steal it. But there was no cocaine and there was no plane: Tucker, Tate and Rolfe were being lured to their deaths by former associates who had been ripped off and repeatedly bullied and threatened.

The Range Rover lurched from side to side as it made its way slowly down the farm track. The occupants laughed and warned Rolfe to watch where he was going. At 6.45 p.m., Tate's mobile phone rang. It was his partner Sarah. She wanted to apologise for a row they had had earlier. Tate couldn't have been more polite, saying, 'Oh, don't worry. I'm sorry for going mad and everything else.' Before Sarah could answer, Tate said, 'Listen, I can't talk at the moment, I'm with people. Give me a call tomorrow and we'll sort it all out.' Sarah said goodbye and the line went dead. Tate had hung up. He never did get the chance to sort it all out.

The 'people' Tate had mentioned to Sarah were sitting alongside him in the rear of the Range Rover. One of their co-conspirators was waiting patiently nearby, eager for the prey to fall into the deadly trap that had been set. When the vehicle reached a locked five-bar gate, the sign facing it and its occupants read:

> *Countryside premium scheme. Farming operations must still take place; so please take special care to avoid injury. The use of guns or any other activity, which disturbs people or wildlife, are not allowed on this land.*
>
> *Enjoy your visit.*

Nobody was going to take any notice of it.

The time now was approximately ten to seven. Rolfe's girlfriend Donna, Tucker's girlfriend Anna and Tate's date for the night, Clare, would have been glancing at their watches, as they put on their make-up and their finest threads. They would have been thinking that the boys would be home soon to take them out to dinner. This was to be no ordinary dinner; they were all going out to celebrate becoming millionaires. Tucker, Tate and Rolfe had bragged about their 'big deal' for weeks. Their minds mangled by drugs, their common sense blinded by greed, they genuinely believed that night was the night they were going to become rich. Fucking idiots.

As eight o'clock drew nearer, their anxious dinner dates began to ring them. A message left on Tucker's answering machine said, 'Hello, babe, give us a ring and let me know how you're getting on. I'm all ready now. Bye.' The calls were in vain; dinner was going to be ruined. The boys were going to be late. Very late.

When the Range Rover had pulled up in front of the locked gate, the man sitting next to Tate in the rear of the car got out, claiming he had a key to open it. As soon as the rear door had opened, the man who had been lying in wait emerged from the bushes with a pump-action shotgun in each hand. The vehicle's interior light had come on, ensuring those sitting inside the car couldn't see what was going on outside, because it was pitch black. The man clutching the shotguns handed one of the weapons to his accomplice before leaning through the open rear door of the Range Rover. He shot Rolfe in the back of the head. The hot lead shot blasted a hole five centimetres in diameter just behind the ear before exiting between his nose and eye, which was left hanging down on his cheek. Rolfe's facial skeleton was destroyed completely, causing his features to collapse. The shotgun barrel had been so close to Rolfe's head that the explosion caused burns to his neck and the seat headrest.

As Tucker flinched with the noise of the explosion, the gunman pointed his weapon at him and fired. The shot punched a 6.5 cm hole in his lower jaw before exiting through the left side of his mouth. His jaw and teeth were totally destroyed and pellets were later found lodged in his tongue.

In the rear of the vehicle, Tate, having witnessed the slaughter, began to scream. He pleaded with the killers to spare his life. The gunman showed no mercy and blasted Tate in the chest rather than the head.

Tate had been the catalyst in all the trouble that had been caused, so it seems it was deemed essential that he should witness the gruesome murder of his friends before he too was executed.

The gunmen had to work quickly because the shot had broken Tate's sixth and ninth ribs and lacerated his liver. He was alive but the amount of blood pouring from the six-centimetre hole in his chest indicated that he would not be for much longer. Tucker's injuries, although terrible, had not damaged any vital organs and he had begun to groan loudly, so the gunman shot him once more in the face. The pellets tore a 4.2 cm hole in his head, just in front of the right ear. The right side of his brain was totally destroyed, killing him instantly.

Having incapacitated the occupants of the vehicle, the gunman turned to his accomplice and invited him to shoot them. Stepping forward, the trembling man pointed a shotgun at the back of Rolfe's head, closed his eyes and squeezed the trigger. The blast ripped a gaping hole in Rolfe's neck, which left his back teeth and lower jaw exposed. Turning his weapon on Tate, who was by now curled up in the foetal position and sobbing uncontrollably, the gunman mocked the man that he had grown to hate before opening fire. Tate ducked instinctively before the trigger was pulled, resulting in the shot causing an 8.5 cm graze across the top of his head before smashing the passenger door window. The gunman who had initially opened fire on the men walked around to the broken window and began taunting Tate. 'Fucking hard man, look at you now! Stop crying like a baby and take what's coming to you like a man.' Before Tate could reply, the gunman shot him in the back of the head just behind the left ear. This shot caused Tate's skull to splinter, resulting in extensive destruction of his brain. His work almost done, the gunman opened the front passenger door of the Range Rover, pressed the barrel of the shotgun against the base of Tucker's head and fired. The force of the detonation snapped his neck and destroyed the lower part of his skull. It was so powerful it blew bone fragments out through his scalp, leaving a hole the size of a man's fist just above his ear.

When the weapons fell silent, the gun smoke cleared to reveal the carnage. Rolfe, Tucker and Tate lay dead. Flesh, bone and brain tissue were sprayed throughout the car. Blood poured from their wounds. It was a horrific scene.

Their task complete, the gunmen surveyed their handiwork before closing the doors of the vehicle and calmly walking away.

14

JUDGMENT DAYS

I had an appointment with my solicitor in London the following morning. I travelled on the train, as I didn't fancy battling through traffic in the snow. At about eleven o'clock, I rang home to see if there were any messages on the answering machine. There was one, from a detective, asking me to contact him as soon as I got his message. It sounded urgent.

I rang him from a phone box in King's Cross station.

'We've found a Range Rover with three bodies inside,' he said. 'They've all been shot through the head. We think it's your mates.'

'What do you mean?' I asked.

'Do you recognise this registration: F424 NPE? I'm sure it's them.' He told me he had seen them in the car before.

'I don't know what you're talking about,' I said. 'Tell me what's happened.' I was confused.

He repeated that they had found a Range Rover. He believed Tucker, Tate and Rolfe were inside, but they had not been formally identified at that stage.

'Are they dead?' I asked.

'They're very dead,' he replied.

The policeman asked where I was, but I didn't answer. I said I would ring him later and put the phone down. I rang Tucker's mobile. It rang and rang and rang. He wasn't going to answer. Unbeknown to me at that time, his mobile was still in his hand. The police had not yet removed it from the body. Nor had they taken the body from the Range Rover.

I rang home. Debra must have still been at the hotel, so I left a message, telling her not to answer the phone if it rang and to stay away from the house, as 'those three' had been found murdered.

I walked around London in a daze. I really couldn't believe what I had just heard. I even began to wonder if I had actually had the conversation.

Debra didn't get my message until much later. She went to pick up the children at 3.30 p.m. at their school, where she was met by two detectives. One asked her if she was my partner, and when she replied yes, he said, 'You and the children better come with me.' They were put in an unmarked car. Nothing was said in front of the children, but Debra was told what had happened. The police feared a revenge attack might be carried out on my family or me, so they were going to take Debra and our children into protective custody until I had been located. The police – and others – obviously thought that I was somehow connected to or responsible for the murders.

The police had also driven past my house to see if I was there and had found the front door wide open. This caused them further concern, so they radioed the officer in charge of the case. The area around my house was immediately cordoned off.

Debra could not explain why the front door was open. She rang the house and recovered the messages from the answering machine. I had told her to meet me at a railway station in Essex – it is in a rural area and wouldn't be busy at that time of night. I said I would be there at about 8.30. When I got off the train, there was no sign of Debra. The platform was deserted. I walked to a phone box just outside the station and rang her mother to see if she was there. A loud tap on the window of the phone box made me jump. I looked out and saw a detective standing there with Debra.

'You can guess what the problem is, Bernie,' said the detective. 'I hope you're not involved in this.' I asked him what had happened.

When he confirmed that it was definitely Tucker, Tate and Rolfe who had been found shot through the head in the Range Rover, I felt numb with shock. He told Debra to get into a car with his colleague and I was told to get into the back of another vehicle. Two detectives were already sitting in the front. The car sped off and the detective said to me again, 'I hope you're not involved in this, Bernie.'

'I'm not, I'm not. I'm telling you, I'm not,' I said. 'We fell out. What we fell out over didn't warrant that. If you're thinking I'm involved, then you've got it wrong.'

'A lot of people think it's you,' he said. 'You fell out with them. They threatened to shoot you. You didn't appear to take the threat seriously. The next thing, they all turn up dead. What else are we meant to think?'

As he was talking, I could hear the other detective telling somebody on the radio that they'd 'got O'Mahoney'. He was asking what he should do with me.

The voice on the other end of the radio said, 'Bring him into Wickford nick.' Then almost immediately, he asked if I was being cooperative. When the detective said I was, he was told he could take me home.

I was asked if I had left the front door of my home wide open. I said no. He suggested we both went in together, as there was a possibility that someone was waiting for me in the house. He was armed, but I said I would go in first. He wasn't going to argue.

I went in and called round all the rooms, but nobody was there. The door wasn't damaged. She had never done it in her life, but I guessed Debra must not have closed it properly when she left.

The detective told me not only did the police think I was involved in the murders, but also members of the firm believed I had played a part. I kept telling him I wasn't involved. I said I was willing to go to a police station right then. 'You can interview me or do what you want,' I said, 'but I am not involved in their deaths.'

So he put me in the car, left Debra in the house with the other detectives and drove me down the road. He stopped approximately a mile from my home and then asked me who could have killed Tucker, Tate and Rolfe. Darren Nicholls immediately sprang to mind. He certainly had a motive – but so had I. And the syndicate, and the countless people they had robbed and those they were planning to rob. In fact, nearly everyone they had ever met had a motive. I told the police I had no idea; I was the last person who was going to help them find the killers of my tormentors.

'Your best bet is to go home and keep your head down,' he said. 'We'll be in touch.'

They left me in my house with Debra and the children. I still couldn't believe it. The murders were the main story on the news – a reminder that I had not dreamt the events of that day.

I don't drink that often, only when I'm on a downer, but that night I sat down and drank till I could drink no more. I rang two members of the firm: both put the phone down on me. This couldn't be happening. I thought all of the shit concerning Raquels and the firm was behind me. I couldn't sleep, so I sat in the lounge gazing out of the window at the darkness. Every face, every horror committed and witnessed came to visit me that night.

The following morning I drove over to Rettendon and stopped near a phone box at Rettendon turnpike, which overlooks the countryside. Everywhere was covered with a blanket of snow. I looked out across the fields and thought about my friends. The men who died were not the same people as I had first met. The drug culture had turned them into unreasonable men. Drugs were giving them courage to do things any rational man would never have considered doing. Wannabes were boosting their egos, reinforcing the belief they couldn't be touched. The rewards cemented the notion that they were right.

I drove down the lane to the spot where they had met their deaths. To this day, I can't believe they were so easily led to such a place. It is a long, unmade road, barely passable in a car. At the dead end is the gate where they died. I leant against the gate and again I was filled with sadness, thinking about them. They were, after all, human beings with families.

My feelings of sadness soon passed – I resented my emotion, because the day before they met their deaths, those three bastards had been planning to murder me.

* * *

On 25 January, I met DI Storey, who wanted me to make a statement in relation to the Leah Betts incident. He informed me that reporter Gary Jones, who had taken possession of the tape recording of Packman, had handed it over to the police. Tucker, Tate and Rolfe were dead, I had walked out of Raquels, the firm was no more: why wouldn't I do as he asked?

DI Storey could see that I was struggling with the very thought of assisting him, so he told me to go away and think about it for a little while longer before making my final decision. For two or three days, I wrestled with my conscience, but I knew what I had to do. The nightmare had to end sometime. I realised that if I wanted to shed the criminal make-up I had worn for so long, the only decision I could make, which would not allow me to change my mind, was to agree to cooperate with his request. I contacted him and we arranged to meet at Maldon police station.

I will never forget sitting in that room, which overlooked a quaint row of shops. Below, people were going about their everyday business and I was sitting there, watching them, while I talked about the deaths of young people. I was sitting astride two worlds. But I knew which one I wanted to inhabit. I made the statement. I believed that the door to my previous life had closed firmly behind me.

The police bent over backwards to help me from there on in. Personal security alarms were given to my family, electronic panic buttons were fitted in the house and armed police were briefed to attend if any of the devices were activated.

The Leah Betts case had to have an end result; the whole of the country was talking about it. Even the Prime Minister had commented on the case in the House of Commons. I was going to be the principal witness against Leah's teenage friend. It was obscene, like asking Hitler to sit on the jury of a war crimes trial, but they needed their pound of flesh. They needed their 'result', and they thought I was the key to that result. I had to be looked after just in case I didn't turn up at court, for whatever reason.

On Friday, 1 March, I was asked to attend South Woodham Ferrers police station, where the Rettendon murder inquiry team was based. Two detectives led me through the back to an interview room. In the corridor outside was a storeroom, and on the door a sign read: 'Risk of health hazard: Rettendon exhibits'. In that cupboard, behind that door, were my former friends' clothing and personal effects, no doubt soaked in their blood. I don't know if I had been deliberately shown it for effect or if it was a mere coincidence, but it made the horror story real.

When the detectives sat me down, they asked me about my military career, adding that the gunman had executed the trio with ruthless efficiency. 'Someone who knew what they were doing, Bernie. An ex-military man, perhaps?' I said I knew what it looked like, but I had not murdered anybody. I was told that I had to understand that a lot of people believed I was involved. 'Even if you didn't pull the trigger, Bernie, you had good reason to see the back of those boys. They were threatening to shoot you. Maybe it was a case of you or them? You could have done it out of fear.' All the time they were 'chatting' to me, I was aware of one of the detectives who kept his gaze fixed firmly on me, as if he was looking for a telltale eye-flicker of guilt. When they had finished their 'chat', which had lasted for an hour and three-quarters, they said they would need to see me again. They gave me their names and numbers on a piece of paper – 'Just in case you remember anything, Bernie' – and told me to go.

The detectives couldn't resist a parting shot. 'Keep your head down, Bernie. You know, some people think you had a hand in this, and they aren't happy.' It wasn't a threat; I knew as well as they did it was a fact. Whether they actually cared about my well-being was another matter.

When I got outside, I felt the urge to run, to get away from this bloody mess. I thought the detectives would be watching me from the police station windows, though, so I walked around the corner before racing to the nearby gymnasium car park where I had left my car. I felt stupid. I felt hunted by the police and hunted by the people who, according to the police, were plotting my murder.

* * *

On Monday, 13 May 1996, Darren Nicholls and a friend named Colin Bridge were stopped in their vehicles by Essex police. Bridge had been at the wheel of a transit van and Nicholls was following close behind in a Jaguar. As soon as Nicholls stepped out of his car, the officers snatched his mobile phone from him and handcuffed his hands behind his back. As he looked up the road, Nicholls could see Bridge, who was also handcuffed, being put in a police van.

'Do you know why you have been stopped?' asked one of the officers.

Nicholls said nothing; he just shook his head.

'Where have you come from?' asked the officer.

'Colchester,' Nicholls replied.

'Well, there have been a number of burglaries in Colchester and you've been stopped today because we would like to search your van in connection with those burglaries.'

Nicholls nodded. 'OK, fair enough,' he said, 'but everything in that van is mine. Colin is just driving it for me. He has nothing to do with anything. It's all down to me.'

The back of the van was empty except for a toolbox, so it didn't take the officers long to locate the ten kilos of cannabis that Nicholls had hidden within it.

'What are these, then?' asked the officer.

'They look like chocolate bars to me,' replied Nicholls. 'What do you think they are?'

A huge grin broke out on the officer's face. 'I think they're drugs and you're under arrest.'

At 11.26 p.m., Darren Nicholls was interviewed by DC Winstone about the importation of cannabis, but he gave 'no comment' replies to all of the questions that were asked. At the end of the nine-minute interview, DC Winstone said, 'I don't intend to say any more about the possession with intent to supply at the moment. The time by my watch is now 23.35 hours and you're now going to be arrested for being involved in the murder of Pat Tate, Craig Rolfe and Tony Tucker. Do you wish to make any comment on the fact you've now been arrested for those murders?'

After a slight pause, Nicholls replied, 'No comment.'

The following day, as the extent of the evidence against him began to be revealed, Nicholls realised he was in a hopeless position, but he still refused to comment when each question was asked. In addition to the ferry booking records and CCTV footage concerning the importation of cannabis, the police had access to his telephone records, which proved his phone was in the Rettendon area at the relevant time on the night of the murders. But they knew Nicholls had not acted alone.

Nicholls was in an impossible situation, regarding the evidence against him, so they decided to offer him a lifeline. If Nicholls could tell them who had murdered Tate, Tucker and Rolfe, and tell them about the drug importations that he had been involved in, he and his family could disappear into the witness protection programme. This would give him and his family a new identity and a new home in a new area – a completely fresh start in life. Nicholls didn't hesitate; he implicated his former cellmates Mick Steele and Jack Whomes.

On Thursday, 20 June 1996, two detectives, whose job it was to escort me to court for the committal proceedings concerning Packman and his co-accused Smith, picked me up from my home. I felt exhausted because I had been unable to sleep and had sat on the end of my bed throughout the night, wrestling with my thoughts. I had made the agreed statement about my meeting with Packman, but I knew that it was the day in court that mattered. If I didn't turn up, the case would collapse and I could face a term of imprisonment for ignoring a witness order. It almost seemed worth it. It would solve many of my problems and I would be back on side with my associates. I had looked in at my sleeping children. I had to do what was right for them, despite the fact that doing right felt so wrong.

I walked out to meet my escort. I wasn't stupid – they were not there for my protection, they were there simply to ensure that I turned up at court. On the journey to Southend Magistrates Court, the detectives indulged in idle chat, most of it about Tucker, Tate and Rolfe. One of the detectives had been present at Broomfield hospital in Chelmsford when the three had been laid out in the morgue, awaiting an autopsy. He told me that Tucker and Rolfe had been grotesquely disfigured. 'Big fucking geezers, weren't they, Bernie? Their heads were a right mess,' he said. I wanted him to shut up, to not make conversation with me. I didn't even want to hear him speak. The thought of suddenly becoming friendly with the police made my stomach churn. It wasn't the men – I have known a few decent police officers – it was their authority, the way it was administered, and my own personal experiences of their prejudice that filled me with loathing.

When we arrived at Southend, I was driven to the back entrance of the police station. I was told they didn't want the press getting anywhere near me. 'Let's keep it low-key, Bernie,' one of them said.

Once inside I was led through a maze of corridors, the detectives flashing their warrant cards to get numerous locked doors opened. We passed through the custody area and eventually entered the court building. We climbed a dozen narrow wooden steps and emerged in the dock of the court. The proceedings had not yet started, so the court was empty. I looked across from my more familiar position – the dock – to the witness stand. I was going to have to stand on that platform and publicly assist those I had spent my life resenting. I was once more in turmoil. If I walked out now, I would be condemned as the man who brought about the collapse of the Leah Betts case; Leah, a girl who in death had become a national icon in the war against the evil drug trade. The media would have a field day speculating as to why I would rather face imprisonment than searching questions. The bitter finger of suspicion would once more be levelled at me. I could face prison, I could endure the press and the gossip, but should my family have to? They shouldn't have to endure anything; they had done nothing. Family, to me, always come first, second and last.

The detectives must have sensed my inner anguish, as they suddenly announced that we were leaving the court to go to another room where tea was being made. I laughed out loud, but did not tell them why. I was thinking of my mother, God rest her soul. Whatever the crisis, however dire the situation, she would always offer to make tea.

At ten o'clock, I was called in to court. Packman looked sheepishly around the room, eager to avoid eye contact with me. Only he and I know the truth about what really happened between us. I had nothing to lose and I genuinely hoped that he would be acquitted.

Once I had been seen to fulfil my promise, neither the police nor the media could criticise me. Old-style committals are no longer part of the judicial process. Back in 1996, they were, in effect, dress rehearsals for a Crown Court trial. The magistrates would listen to the evidence and the witnesses under cross-examination and decide whether the matter should proceed to a full trial with a jury. I was in the witness box for an hour and three-quarters and, at the end of it, the magistrates decided that the case would go to trial.

I felt dirty leaving the court, but the police were jubilant. It was a real kick in the teeth when they actually thanked me. I couldn't wait to get home. When the police dropped me off, they wished me luck before disappearing down the drive. I wondered if they would be slagging me off and laughing. Paranoid? I doubt it.

On Monday, 9 December 1996, the Betts trial finally opened at Norwich Crown Court. The first day was taken up with legal arguments that did not concern me, but I was told to prepare myself to be called as a witness the following day. I spent that night like a caged animal, unable to sit still or think straight. I paced up and down the house, trying to talk myself in and then out of facing my forthcoming ordeal. The police had telephoned twice during the evening and asked if I was OK. That was their story, anyway. I knew that they were ringing to see if I had left town.

I was also treated to the sight of a patrolling police car, which drove up and down the deserted lane outside my home. It must have been the only time in their history that the police have bothered to patrol that road. Barely a mile long, there is nothing there apart from a solitary house, fields, woodland and the sea.

My escorts arrived for me at eight o'clock the following morning. Two detectives in an unmarked van pulled up outside my house and told me to climb in the back and make myself comfortable. It was a two-hour drive to Norwich, so I was happy to comply. They had planned my arrival and departure at the court well. When we arrived at the outskirts of Norwich city centre, I was told to lie down in the back of the van. A coat was then put over me. The van drove into the court car park, avoiding the awaiting photographers and television crews. After passing through a security barrier, we arrived at the rear of the building. The police checked every path that we had to take before ushering me through a heavy wooden door. Once inside, a detective held the sleeve of my shirt as we made our way through the cell area, along various corridors and then finally up a flight of steps into the dock of an empty court. We then walked out into a waiting area, where I saw Packman with his mother and father. I looked at him and he quickly looked away. I was then shown into a small room and told to wait there. I was relieved to be alone – I hated having the police around me. They made me feel inadequate and weak. I neither wanted nor needed their protection. I'd rather have gone out to sit amongst the people outside the room but was told that I could not be seen talking to or even making eye contact with anybody. A glance or a glare could be interpreted as a threat. I sat in the room, reading a newspaper.

An elderly man entered and announced he was from the court service. He gave me a questionnaire to fill in and began to describe the court procedure, telling me where I would stand, where the judge would sit and advising me that I should speak clearly and directly at the jury. I didn't have the heart to tell him to fuck off. He obviously got pleasure out of being so important. To pass the time, I filled out the questionnaire, giving him a glowing report in the comments column. I imagined his next staff meeting, his fellow volunteers patting him on the back because of the bullshit I had written. It was my first time in court, I wrote, and the court volunteer had allayed all of my fears with his professional manner. How could I ever repay him? Clown – I had probably spent more time in the back of police vehicles than he had spent in court.

The door opened and I was told that I was wanted. As I entered the court, I noticed a few familiar faces in the public gallery. They were expectant, visibly excited: will he, won't he? The press gallery was packed. Packman sat alone in the dock, wearing a grey suit and tie, his long hair in a ponytail.

Paul and Janet Betts sat in the front row of the public gallery, approximately three feet from the witness stand. As I approached, the stand beckoned like an electric chair. I stood in position and gripped the handrail. I was handed God's good book and asked to swear an oath on it – a pointless exercise for most in this God-less day and age – but book or no book, I had no reason to lie.

Packman's barrister, John Cooper, QC, wasted no time in dispensing with the kid gloves. From the outset, he portrayed me as an extremely violent man with serious criminal connections. He told the jury that I was Tony Tucker's right-hand man, not directly involved in the importation of drugs but most certainly 'a man who dealt with rival criminals on Tucker's behalf and secured the clubs where the drugs were sold'. Packman admitted that he had met me and that it was he who had confessed on tape to supplying Leah Betts with Ecstasy; however, it was alleged that I had threatened Packman, saying I would burn his house down and break his legs if he implicated the firm. It was suggested that I was putting pressure on him to confess in order to save myself and Tucker. I told the court that wasn't the case: 'Packman is not an evil drug dealer, he's just a kid caught up in this mess. Mark Murray supplied the pill that killed Leah Betts. I'm sick of that scumbag sitting it out in Spain while others rot in prison because of him. He killed Leah Betts and I have no doubt he will have the blood of others on his hands.'

A steady stream of excited journalists filed out of the court, trying to reach a phone so that they could notify their editors of the dramatic allegation concerning Murray. I could almost feel the atmosphere behind me: Paul and Janet Betts and DI Storey appeared relieved that the true story was at last being made public.

I was cross-examined for the whole afternoon, and when it was all over the police escorted me back to my room of solitude. Alone again at last, I felt a great sense of relief. I just wanted to get out of there and go home, so that I could get on with my life.

Nothing happened for ten or fifteen minutes, then suddenly I was off in a rush between two detectives. I was taken outside and told to lie in the back of the van once more. A blanket was thrown over me. When Paul and Janet Betts emerged from the court, the press pack surrounded them; at the same time, the van drove out of the court and I slipped away unnoticed into the evening traffic.

I sat at home the following day, waiting for news of the trial. Packman had given evidence, saying that he was totally paranoid when he had met me. 'I said what I thought he wanted to hear because I feared for my safety,' he'd said. His friend, Steve Smith, told the court he was 'more frightened of me than he was of Mike Tyson'. I have no idea why Smith said such a thing because, to my knowledge, we had never even met.

The final witnesses gave their evidence on Friday, 13 December. The jury were told that they wouldn't be sent out to deliberate until Monday, as it was too late in the evening to begin. The weekend dragged on like no weekend before or since.

It was as if I was being deliberately tormented because as soon as my ordeal appeared to have reached a conclusion, an unexpected delay would arise. On the Monday morning, the jury retired to consider their verdict. Later that evening they informed the judge that they were unable to agree. He sent them to a hotel for the night, but after deliberating throughout the following day they were still unable to reach a verdict and the jury was discharged. I was absolutely devastated. I knew the prosecution would not throw in the towel. I would have to go through the whole thing again. It meant 1997 was yet another year that I was going to be wishing away.

The second Leah Betts trial got under way at Norwich Crown Court on Monday, 24 February 1997. It was far more low-key, as the media had milked the story dry. The entire country was suffering from 'Ecstasy fatigue'. I was called to give evidence on the second day. Once inside the court building, I refused to wait in the solitary waiting room – I was sick of being hidden away – so I sat amongst the others waiting to go into court. Friends of Smith and Packman moved away or averted their gaze. Only Packman's mother gave me a look filled with contempt. I didn't care – I admire honesty.

John Cooper, QC, awaited me in court. At the previous trial, he had done his job well, making me lose my temper, allowing the jury to see just how explosive I could be. Fortunately, on this occasion, the judge, Mr Justice Wright, was having none of it and refused to allow Mr Cooper to draw on my association with other criminals. This left Mr Cooper with very little ammunition to use against me. The whole point of cross-examining me was to portray me as a violent criminal so that the jury would understand why Packman had apparently been so frightened of me that he would have said anything I wished to hear.

Within a short time, I was discharged from the court. The prosecution decided that I would no longer be required. I savoured those words. They had entered my life like a runaway train, fucked up my head with worry, and now they were saying, 'We've finished with you. Goodbye.' At the outset, the police had talked about assisting me to move, even arranging a new identity for me, but I had declined. I had made my decision to attend court and would stand by it. I wasn't going to pretend it hadn't happened or deny who I was for anybody. We all make mistakes.

When the police dropped me off, they thanked me and wished me well. I had got to know them quite well during the time we had spent together. One had problems paying his mortgage; both had a resentful admiration for some of the more colourful, less serious criminals in Essex. I could not thank them, but I did wish them well.

On Friday, 28 February, the Leah Betts trial ended and the jury retired to consider its verdict. Once more they could not agree. Mr Justice Wright formally found Packman not guilty after the jury foreman said that there was no realistic chance of reaching a majority verdict in the case. Smith, who had pleaded guilty, was given a two-year conditional discharge. I was pleased for both Packman and Smith. My evidence had not harmed anybody but Mark Murray. He didn't give a fuck about me, Tucker or anybody else. After Leah had collapsed, he just upped and went without even giving me a warning phone call. I felt no sense of loyalty towards him whatsoever.

Later that year, in September, the Rettendon murder trial opened in court No. 2 at the Old Bailey in London. After four long months of evidence, the jury were asked to consider their verdict. In his summing up, the Honourable Mr Justice Anthony Hidden told them that they should treat the evidence of Darren Nicholls with 'great caution'.

'I need hardly stress the importance of Nicholls's evidence. So much hinges on what he said. Nicholls is a convicted criminal who was engaged in drug abuse and the importation of drugs into this country. You must bear in mind it was in his own interest to become a prosecution witness.'

The jury deliberated for four and a half days, and on Tuesday, 20 January 1998, Micky Steele and Jack Whomes were found guilty of importing cannabis and of murdering Craig Rolfe, Tony Tucker and Pat Tate. When they heard the verdict, Whomes and Steele looked at each other and shrugged their shoulders in disbelief before turning to look at the judge.

'There is no other sentence I can pass on you for these horrifying murders of which you have been convicted than that of life imprisonment,' Mr Justice Hidden told the pair. 'There is little that can be said usefully about either of you at this stage. You two were responsible in my view for taking away the lives of these three victims in a summary way. You lured them to a quiet farm track and executed them. They had crossed your path and you showed them no mercy. There is about these killings a hard and ruthless edge, which can only horrify and stagger the non-criminal mind. You are extremely dangerous men and you have not the slightest compunction for resorting to extreme violence when you thought it was necessary.'

Mick Steele and Jack Whomes were both told that they would have to serve a minimum of 15 years' imprisonment.

On Friday, 13 November 1998, Darren Nicholls appeared at Woolwich Crown Court to be sentenced for the importation of cannabis. Judge Hidden said, 'I have no doubt that without the evidence provided by this man, a terrible crime would never have been solved and two killers would still be walking the streets. In return, Mr Nicholls will undoubtedly have to spend the rest of his life in fear. I have no hesitation in awarding him full credit for the assistance he provided both police and customs in this matter.' Judge Hidden then sentenced Nicholls to 15 months' imprisonment, though he walked free because the time he had spent in custody prior to the Rettendon trial more than covered the sentence.

You will find no trace of Darren Nicholls now. His birth certificate and marriage licence have been deleted. His national insurance number has been withdrawn; his passport details destroyed. All his bank and building society accounts have been closed down, along with all his old store cards and hire-purchase loans. His driver details have been erased from the computer at Swansea and he no longer appears on any electoral roll. Even his criminal record is no more. Every way of tracking him down has been blocked.

Like Nicholls, the Essex Boys firm is thankfully no more. We came, we saw, we conquered. But in the end, boy, did we all lose.

15

DOCTOR MY EYES

ALTHOUGH we appeared to be emerging from the fog of the events of 1995, the strain on my family was proving too much. Paul Betts had appeared on television, calling me a 'bastard' and saying I was responsible for the death of his daughter, Leah. He based his allegations on the fact that I had admitted to turning a blind eye to drug dealing in Raquels. The publicity his allegation created resulted in older children telling my children that their father was a murderer. How can you tell your tearful son or daughter to ignore such a groundless allegation? What can you possibly say when they ask if it's true?

In an effort to stop these ridiculous claims, I wrote an open letter to Paul Betts, which was printed in the press. I urged him to confront me on live TV, so we could debate who was really responsible for his daughter's death. Unsurprisingly, he declined.

It was becoming apparent to me that staying with my children was causing them to be unfairly tarnished. They were suffering for something none of us had done. Paul Betts's vile allegations were causing the children so much upset that Debra suggested we should part for their sakes. I wasn't going to argue. After matters concerning the Taylor sisters, then the death of Leah Betts and the murders at Rettendon, I felt Debra's love for me had probably died, been cremated and the ashes scattered far and wide. I told her we had to look at the situation in a cold, clinical manner and do what was best for the children, not what suited us. Our tried-and-tested love affair ended with a knowing smile, as she agreed.

We sold our home in Mayland, Debra moved to a property near her mother and I returned to Basildon. I did not arrive in the best of moods. I was in turmoil over my family and I was tired of being blamed for causing the death of a girl who had been foolish enough to take drugs. I felt Paul Betts's allegation was ridiculous: you wouldn't blame a pub landlord for getting you convicted of drunk-driving, would you? We all have choices in life and we all have to take responsibility for our own actions.

I was equally sick of hearing about people who were supposed to want to kill me, and I was tired of being advised where I should or should not go. So many people appeared to have fucking opinions on me, yet few knew me and none had ever had any dealings with me. If people didn't like me living in Basildon, that was a matter for them, not me. I had been driven out of one home; I was not going to be driven out of another.

I started drinking in my old haunts. Most people I met droned on and on about the murders of Tucker, Tate and Rolfe, as few in the town believed the men convicted of the murders were guilty. Nobody said they had a problem with me personally, and several had nothing but good memories of the trouble-free rave nights I had been instrumental in creating at Raquels. The club had since closed down – the door team that had replaced ours were unable to control the local villains, who had swarmed back there. These days it is a snooker hall.

A few months after moving back to Basildon, I bumped into a girl named Emma Turner, who I had first met at Raquels. Emma and I had always got on well and we began to see each other quite regularly. Before too long, I gave up the flat I was renting and moved in with her. Since my catalogue of court appearances had ended, I had returned to work in the haulage trade, driving a tipper lorry. Within a short period of time, I was promoted to a managerial position and offered a post in Peterborough, Cambridgeshire. I didn't want to move away from my children, as being able to see them regularly had lessened the trauma of being separated from them, so instead I chose to drive to Peterborough each day, leaving the house at 4.30 a.m. and returning at 8 p.m. Earning an honest living was a real strain and the returns were hardly endearing, but I was happy and had peace of mind – something money cannot buy.

About this time the small-time drug dealer who had bankrolled Mark Murray after the police raid at Club UK in South London had been telling people in Essex he was looking for me. John Rollinson – Gaffer – was apparently unhappy that I had named Murray as a drug dealer during the Leah Betts trial. Rollinson might have been well advised to keep quiet about the fact he had financed the batch of drugs that had led to Leah's death, but he wasn't the brightest of people. He was the type who tried to make himself seem important by having views and opinions on villains others looked up to. Only the gullible and naive took any notice of the likes of Rollinson. It was a good friend of his who had told me that he had been bad-mouthing me, but I wasn't too concerned; I had never done anything wrong to Rollinson, so I reasoned he had no right to have a grievance with me.

'It's Gaffer trying to include his name in a high-profile case,' I told his friend. 'You know what he's like, the mug just wants to appear important.'

One evening, Emma and I went for a drink at the Festival Leisure Park in Basildon. It is a large entertainment complex comprising bars, nightclubs, a bowling alley, cinema and fast-food restaurants. Some of the more witty locals refer to it as 'Bas Vegas'. We had a drink in a couple of the bars and ended up in a nightclub called Jumping Jacks. When we entered the club, a small, thin, drug-ravished man started shouting at me. 'Fucking cunt,' he was yelling. He threw his baseball cap on the floor and repeatedly spat, each time repeating, 'Cunt! Fucking cunt!' I assumed he was either mentally challenged or suffering from some sort of embarrassing disorder, so I thought it best to ignore him. Emma, not used to witnessing such alarming behaviour, clutched my arm and asked me who he was.

It was only when he started shouting about 'grassing Mark Murray up' that I took a closer look and realised it was Gaffer. I hadn't seen him since I had worked at Raquels and he had lost a lot of weight. He looked gaunt, no doubt the result of a low-life existence, popping pills and feeding a cocaine habit. When you are out with your partner for a drink, you don't really relish the thought of rolling round the floor with a drunk or loud-mouthed druggie. I apologised to Emma and told her we would have a drink at the other end of the bar, but if Gaffer continued to be abusive or offered violence, then I would have to give him a clip around the ear.

Gaffer was in the company of another man who was also glaring at me and so their actions were twice as despicable. What sort of people start trouble with a man when he is out with his partner having a drink? Gaffer and his sidekick saw themselves as the type of so-called 'gangster' who follows a criminal code; so much for showing women respect. Throughout the evening, Gaffer glared down the bar at me, tipping his hat like some amusing clown.

'Come on,' I said to Emma. 'I've had enough of this. Let's go.'

As I walked past Gaffer, the gutless coward squirted me in the eyes with ammonia. I was temporarily blinded, so Emma opened the door for me and I stepped outside. Gaffer had been telling everybody in Essex that he was after me; now that I was temporarily blinded and standing in front of him, he had the best chance he was ever going to get to do me. He and his friend followed me outside, which frightened Emma, so I turned and confronted them. I knew Gaffer wasn't capable of fighting, so I was expecting him to pull out a weapon. To his friend's credit, he stepped back, making it obvious he wanted no part in any trouble. As Gaffer advanced, I grabbed his head and shoved him backwards. I was not the slightest bit concerned about what he might have tried to do, or what he might have tried to do it with, because I had a double-bladed 12-inch combat knife down the back of my trousers. If he got within striking distance of me with a weapon, I was more than prepared to bury the knife deep into his chest or head.

When I'd shoved him backwards, his cap had fallen off. As he approached me again, I could see in his eyes that he was unsure of himself. He pulled out a Jif lemon container and, lunging forward, squirted me once more in the eyes with ammonia. The red mist rose. At that moment, I wanted to end his miserable and pointless life. I pulled out the knife and raised it. He saw the blade, screamed like a hysterical woman and ran back into the club.

What the fuck am I doing? I thought. How did I end up getting involved with this fool? I could end up serving a life sentence because some little nobody has chosen to attack me.

A bouncer came out and told me the police had been called. 'You're on CCTV as well, Bernie,' he said. 'You had better make yourself scarce.'

Emma and I tried to get in a taxi, but the driver refused to take us home and the other taxis in the rank drove away empty. I could see Gaffer hiding in the club foyer behind the bouncers, so I knew he wouldn't be troubling me again that night. Emma and I didn't live too far from the leisure park, so we decided to walk home. We'd made our way across the car park to the main road when two police cars pulled up. My mind was racing; I had a certain prison sentence tucked down the back of my trousers and I didn't fancy being locked up over a loser like Gaffer.

'The knife, the knife, how the fuck can I explain away the knife?' I was asking myself. I knew everybody had seen it and I knew the CCTV had recorded me brandishing it, so I knew it was pointless denying its existence. There was only one thing for it, I thought: I was going to have to come up with a false but credible story.

I pulled out the knife and approached the police officers. 'It's OK, officers,' I said. 'I've got the knife.'

'Drop the weapon, drop the weapon!' they shouted.

I laughed and told them it was OK. 'It's not my weapon. I took it off a lunatic,' I said, then threw the knife on the floor.

One of the police officers forced my hands behind my back and slapped a pair of handcuffs on. 'You're under arrest for possessing an offensive weapon,' he said.

I asked the police to make sure Emma got home all right and they said they would. They then put me in the back of the car and took me to Basildon police station, where I was locked up for the night.

At 3 p.m. the following day, a detective came to my cell to take me to the interview room. I had a rough idea of what I was going to say, but I was unaware of how much evidence the police had on me. I decided I would wait to hear what the detective was going to allege before telling my story. The officer interviewing me told me a member of staff at the club had called the police after a man had run inside screaming that I was brandishing a knife outside the premises. He told me they had seized the CCTV footage and it clearly showed me lunging at this man with a large combat knife. I asked the officer if they had the video footage from inside the club and he said he hadn't, as the recorder inside had not been working. As soon as he said that, I knew I was home and dry. I told him he only had half the story, in that case.

'What do you mean?' he asked.

'That man attacked me inside the club, sprayed me with ammonia and pulled out a knife when we started to struggle,' I replied. 'When he tried to stab me, I took the knife off him and, fearing for my safety, went outside. The man followed me and was asking me to give him back the knife. I didn't want to, as I thought he was going to stab me, so I refused. When he came towards me, I pushed him away, but then he attacked me with a Jif lemon container full of ammonia. Having been temporarily blinded, I feared for my safety. I pulled out his knife, which I had secreted down the back of my trousers, and he ran away screaming. I had pulled out his knife purely to defend

227

myself. When he ran back into the club, I didn't run inside after him, as the danger had passed. No taxis would take Emma and me home, so we walked across the car park. I saw a police car and immediately handed the knife to an officer, who arrested me. If you ask the arresting officers, they will tell you I said, "It's OK, I've got the knife. I took it off a lunatic."'

'But that's not what other people are saying,' the interviewing officer said. 'They're saying it's your knife.'

'Well, you had better get these people to make statements, because it's not my knife, it belongs to the man who attacked me,' I said.

The detective said he had spoken to Gaffer and he did not want to make a statement.

I told the detective that Gaffer didn't want to make a statement because he had the knife in the first place and he was the one who attacked me. The officer insisted he had other witnesses and therefore I would be charged.

'Fair enough,' I said. 'Fucking charge me.'

Clearly riled, the officer replied, 'OK.' The charge was that 'without lawful authority or reasonable excuse', I had with me in a public place an offensive weapon, namely a knife. He also alleged that I had 'used or threatened unlawful violence towards another' and my conduct was such as would cause 'a person of reasonable firmness present at the scene to fear for his personal safety'. When he said this, I started laughing. 'How can you call a person reasonable when they are trying to blind you with ammonia?'

The officer just looked at me. 'Those are the charges,' he said. 'Have you anything to say?'

I did not reply, but the officer wrote on the charge sheet that I had said, 'Guilty.'

Fortunately for me, the interview was also being recorded on tape. I decided to say nothing about his 'error' because I knew I would be able to use it against the police when the case was heard in court. I was bailed to appear at Basildon Magistrates Court and then released.

It's hard to explain how depressing an incident like this can be. You go out for a drink with your partner and you end up being locked up for the best part of 24 hours. After your release, you spend the next few months agonising over whether or not you will receive a prison sentence. And for what? For some drug-pedalling peasant who took it upon himself to try and blind you with ammonia in the presence of your girlfriend. His motive? You had assisted the police, who then locked you up and charged you for resisting his attack. Your attacker, meanwhile, walks free. It's absolutely sickening. I can fully understand why some people end up serving life sentences for murdering this type of subhuman.

The law tells you to turn the other cheek and walk away, but what is the point of walking away when low-lifes stab you in the back, cut you, maim you or try to blind you? It's pointless walking away. I should have left him lying in the gutter, where he belonged.

Once more, the never-ending trauma of going back and forth to court became part of my life. The uncertainty of my future, and the pressure of preparing for yet another trial, left me marking time in complete misery.

I had written to the Crown Prosecution Service after the first two court hearings concerning the knife incident with Gaffer and asked them to drop the charges, as there was little or no evidence to disprove my version of events and only a little to support theirs, but they refused. Changing tack, I made a lot of the fact the detective had falsely recorded my reply to the charge, a point that would prove extremely embarrassing for Essex Police should it be aired in open court. Eventually, after a lot of haggling and mind-numbing games, both of the charges were dropped.

I had expanded the haulage business I managed in Cambridgeshire considerably and it was now taking up more and more of my time. My working day was growing longer and this was affecting my relationship with Emma. Her mother had recently been killed in a tragic accident and Emma was feeling isolated and lonely when I wasn't there. The answer was staring me in the face: I had to leave Essex if I was ever going to move on from the dreadful events of 1995.

Emma and I decided to rent a flat in Stanground, Peterborough. It's hard to describe how I felt. It was as if the troubles of the world had been lifted from my shoulders. For the first time in years, I felt free – that is, until one evening when a local man with a reputation recognised me from a newspaper article.

'Fucking *Essex Boys*?' he said, spraying phlegm as he spoke. Drunk, 'Johnny' went out of his way to goad me into fighting him. 'Tossers, mate,' he rambled on. 'Who the fuck do you think you are?' I consider it uncouth to brawl in front of your girlfriend or wife, so I did my best to ignore him. Eventually, his insults became too much and I escorted Emma out of the pub.

As we walked home, Emma was quiet. I am in no doubt that she could sense what was coming because I was physically shaking with temper. After she went to bed, I sat in the lounge watching the clock. By half-eleven, I knew the pub would have been cleared and perhaps drunken Johnny would be filling his drunken big mouth with a kebab on the way home. That would add 15 or 20 minutes to his journey. By one o'clock, I was pretty confident he would be tucked up in bed.

At 1 a.m., I left home with a bread knife tucked into the waistband of my trousers and headed for Johnny's house. I don't know why the locals feared him; he had served five years' imprisonment for stabbing his former girlfriend, but apart from that all he did was get drunk and shout abuse at people. Scumbag.

Psyching myself up for the job in hand, I checked the knife was secure, opened the garden gate and prepared to launch myself at Johnny's front door. 1, 2, 3, Go! I raced through the gate and down the path, before leaping into the air and kicking open the front door. Landing in the hallway, I grabbed my knife and ran upstairs. I entered the first bedroom I reached, turned on the light and prepared to attack Johnny in his bed. The room was empty. As I turned and ran out, I encountered a man dressed in his pyjamas on the landing. 'What the fuck do you think you're doing?' he shouted.

'Where's Johnny? Where's fucking Johnny?' I replied.

Looking puzzled, the man pulled hard on his pyjama bottoms' cord to stop them from falling down and said, 'Johnny? Johnny doesn't live here. He lives next door.'

Without saying another word, I ran downstairs and kicked open a second front door. Johnny had obviously been awakened by the fracas at his neighbour's home because I met him as he was walking, bleary eyed, down the stairs.

As soon as he saw me, he screamed and tried to run back up to his room, but I caught him before he reached the landing. After pummelling his face with my fists, I held the bread knife to his throat.

'Apologise, you maggot. Apologise or fucking die,' I said.

'I'm sorry, I'm sorry, I was drunk,' Johnny whimpered.

Having made my point, I left and went home.

The blade had cut Johnny's neck, so I was expecting the police to arrest me that day, but they never came. I am told that Johnny paid for the damage to his neighbour's door. He never troubled me again.

* * *

Over the years, I'd often wondered what had happened to my father. No one had seen him or heard anything of him since he'd left my mother's house in August 1976. Sometimes I fantasised about tracking him down. I suppose I'd have liked to ask him why he'd treated us so badly. I suppose, too, on occasion, I'd have liked a chance to kick his head in. But most of the time I tried to forget him and pretend I didn't care what had become of him. However, my mother, who wanted some sort of closure on his disappearance, kept prodding me to try to find out.

Every now and again I'd contact the police's missing persons bureau and the Salvation Army, always without success, then on a whim in 2001 – the 25th anniversary of his disappearance – I asked journalist Gary Jones to see if he could locate him. I stayed on the line as Jones tapped my father's details into his computer. Within five minutes, he said he'd found him. My father was dead. He'd died four years earlier of natural causes. His last address, according to Jones, was in a tower block opposite the cricket ground in Edgbaston, Birmingham.

I was in a pub in London's King's Cross when Jones told me, for which I was grateful, because I needed a drink. My father was dead. And all along he'd been living just down the road from the home he'd left. I abandoned my plans and headed to Birmingham. I had an irrepressible urge to see where my father had spent his last years.

On the journey, I experienced a whole spectrum of feelings, including sadness, but mostly shock and rage. I felt cheated. I could never now fulfil that fantasy of confronting him.

It was strange, and a little spooky, to stand outside my father's front door. It was on the tenth floor of a municipal block of flats. I knocked, but no one answered, so I went next door. An elderly West Indian man, wearing an 'Old Man River' trilby hat, opened his door cautiously. I explained who I was and asked if he'd known my father. He said he had. They'd even been mates. He said my father had lived for years in an attic flat above a shop round the corner. The flat in the tower block had belonged to the old woman who'd owned the shop.

She'd become ill and my father, who'd become good friends with her, moved in to her flat to keep her company. It wasn't a romantic relationship; they were merely companions. She'd died and my father had stayed on in the flat, living alone. He and the West Indian man used to go for a drink on Sundays to a pub round the corner.

One Sunday, they'd had their lunchtime drink and were heading home. My father, a heavy smoker, had coughed most of the way along the street. They'd said goodbye at their doors. The man said he used to see my father, or hear him coughing, most days, so when he'd neither seen him nor heard him by the following Tuesday, he called the police. They broke down the door and found my father dead in bed. He had been buried in a cemetery a few miles away.

I asked if my father had ever spoken about his family and the West Indian man said he had. Apparently, he'd occasionally mentioned he'd been married and had children, although he hadn't gone into detail. I thanked the man for his time and left.

That night I found myself standing outside the cemetery with my brother Michael. The gates had been locked for the night. Earlier that day I'd rung the council and had been given my father's plot number. Michael and I clambered over the big iron railings. Within a few minutes, we were standing in front of my father's last resting place.

Neither flowers nor headstone nor name decorated the plot. There was only a number. I broke down and cried. So did Michael. We both felt devastated. In the past, I'd genuinely hated my father, but as I stood there over his grave I realised I actually felt sorry for him. I'd spent so much time hating him I hadn't realised his own hatred and anger stemmed from the fact that he'd never received much love or affection in his tormented life. He'd been buried in a pauper's grave, which an Irish Catholic charity had supplied and paid for.

The next day I broke the news to my mother. She took it very badly. Over the following days, we spoke together about my father in a way that brought me a bit closer to him and made me understand better why he'd become such a vicious bastard. My mother told me things she'd never told me before. She said in Ireland during the 1930s my father's unmarried mother had become pregnant after sleeping with a married man. After abuse from locals, she had become so ashamed and scared that she went to the 'county home' (otherwise known as 'the workhouse') to give birth. She abandoned my father there – and disappeared. She was never seen or heard of again.

My father was at first brought up in the county home, where he was subjected to extreme cruelty and violence. His health and state of mind suffered badly. Eventually, his grandmother took him out and reared him herself. He worshipped her but grew to hate people because he'd been deprived of affection from anyone other than his grandmother. My mother said he'd been a good singer, so much so that he was known in pubs and clubs as 'Danny Boy' after his favourite song. The song in its original form had been an Irish republican anthem. He'd especially enjoyed singing it at the Royal British Legion Club in Codsall. He'd laugh to himself because he knew the clapping audience hadn't understood the significance of the song's anti-British words.

When my mother lay desperately ill in hospital after the birth of Michael, she'd confided in a consultant about my father's violence. The consultant had suggested that in my father's mind he wasn't beating us, he was beating his own mother. He thought my father hated the fact that we had a mother who loved us.

Our conversation was a bit like the final scene in Hitchcock's *Psycho*, where the psychiatrist gives an explanation of why the now straitjacketed lunatic murdered all those people and kept his mother's mummified body in the cellar. I phoned my oldest brother, Jerry, at his home in Brazil to break the news. He didn't say much. A few months after our phone call, he came to England. I took him to the cemetery, but he didn't want to go anywhere near our father's last resting place. In fact, he hadn't even wanted to get out of the car. Eventually, I persuaded him to come with me. We walked together towards the grave, but he stopped about ten yards away and refused to go any further. I could feel his anger. Afterwards we went for a drink in a pub near the huge Rover car plant. Neither of us said much. Jerry's eyes welled up with tears and we both started to cry. I went to the toilet, composed myself and went back to sit with him.

And that was it. We didn't mention our father again. We talked about work, our mother's health and the weather. Then, two hours after we'd met, he was gone.

Some years earlier I'd stolen a blank headstone, which I'd stored in my garage. I'd intended it for use on my own grave. Living the life I've led, a stolen headstone over my grave struck me as fitting and perversely amusing. But I decided to use it for my father's grave instead. I had it engraved with the words 'Patrick "Danny Boy"

O'Mahoney. Rest in Peace.' Despite my father's having treated our family like shit, I had done all I could for him in death and that would be that, as far as I was concerned. Sorting out the dead was so much easier than dealing with the living.

16

TILL DEATH DO US PART

AFTER renting for almost two years, Emma and I purchased a house in a Lincolnshire village called Market Deeping. It was only five miles from Peterborough city centre, where we both worked, so on the face of it the location was ideal. Described on a tourist board website as one of the prettiest villages in the county, it seemed the perfect place for Emma and I to start our new life together. Market Deeping borders the banks of the River Welland as it meanders between Lincolnshire and Cambridgeshire. The neat, quiet streets are lined with stone-built homes, some pre-dating the seventeenth century. This quaint village has a long history of habitation going back to prehistoric times. The land is low-lying and in the distant past it was frequently flooded by the sea, as waters rose and receded with each Ice Age. It's a land upon which roamed such animals as the mammoth elephant and woolly rhinoceros.

Little had changed from those prehistoric times when Emma and I arrived there in the spring of 2002. The locals viewed us 'outsiders' as creatures from another planet who, it seemed, threatened their very existence. 'Go back to where you came from,' one bitter old lady remarked to Emma. 'We don't want people from outside the village buying up our homes.'

After just a few short weeks in such a hostile atmosphere, the inevitable happened. A loudmouth expressed his opinions about Emma and me a little too loudly in a public house and a fight broke out. In the melee that followed, a man named Turton was hit with a glass, causing severe neck injuries, and another person suffered superficial injuries after being struck by fragments of flying glass. I was arrested and charged with two counts of wounding with intent.

Under legislation that had only recently been passed by the

government, anyone aged 18 or over on or after 1 October 1997 who was convicted of a second serious violent offence would have a mandatory life sentence imposed upon them. I had previously served two prison sentences for wounding and if convicted of these fresh offences would have a total of four wounding convictions, double the required amount for a life sentence.

It didn't mean I would have to spend the rest of my life in prison if convicted, but after completing a lengthy prison sentence I would be on licence for the remainder of my days and be monitored by the Probation Service. If those keeping an eye on me decided I wasn't living the kind of lifestyle they approved of, I could be returned to prison at any time. Whichever way I looked at it, a conviction had to be avoided at all costs. To make matters worse – if indeed they could be made worse – Emma and I had set a date to be married.

My trial date for the two wounding offences happened to fall one week to the day before what was supposed to be the happiest day of our lives. Emma was distraught. How could we invite guests, book a venue and plan a honeymoon if there was no guarantee I was even going to be there, she reasoned. I did my best to reassure her that everything would turn out fine, but after considering the evidence against me, even I began to doubt I could secure a not guilty verdict.

Lincolnshire Police had appealed for witnesses to the incident in the local newspaper and one man had come forward, who said he had seen everything. After giving an almost photographic description of me, the witness went on to say how he had seen the victim stagger backwards after having a glass smashed in his neck. I put on a brave face for Emma, but deep down I was convinced that I was now doomed.

The trial took place at Lincoln Crown Court; the victim, his girlfriend and another man all said that they were in no doubt I was the man who had wielded the glass that night. Two bouncers who had been working in the pub were not so sure; they agreed I had been involved in the fight, but neither could remember me picking up a glass. The court fell silent as the man who had contacted the police after they had appealed for witnesses took to the stand. The prosecution took him through his statement line by line. He was positive that the guilty party was wearing a white shirt and black trousers, the man was in his mid-40s, had receding hair and was heavily built. As the fighting factions were pulled apart by the door staff, the witness said he saw this man pick up a glass and stab the victim in the neck. Members of the jury gazed at me in utter contempt – until my barrister began to cross-examine the man. He then took the witness through his statement a second time and at the end of it he pointed to me and asked if I was the man he had seen wield a glass that night.

'Definitely not,' replied the witness. 'I remember seeing him on the opposite side of the room.'

The court erupted, as my friends and family began to cheer. The prosecution and the police looked devastated. They couldn't call their own witness a liar and should have taken steps to check his evidence before calling him to court. Simply because my description matched that of the assailant did not mean that it was me. An identification parade should have taken place if they were relying so heavily on identification evidence.

The judge directed the jury to find me not guilty and ordered my immediate release. As I looked towards my friends and family, I saw Emma sitting at the back of the court weeping tears of joy.

Our wedding could now go ahead as planned. It was to be another of my many new beginnings – my umpteenth new start.

I decided to have my stag night in Dublin. Around 20 of us flew there to celebrate the passing of my bachelor status. One of our group got very drunk and began pinching women's bottoms. I've never liked that sort of disrespectful behaviour, so I asked him to refrain from doing it in my company. He refused to comply with my polite request, and called me an arsehole into the bargain. Shortly afterwards the bottom-pincher was found lying in the street, unconscious with severe head injuries. Doctors at the hospital diagnosed a fractured skull and two blood clots on the brain. They placed him in intensive care when he failed to regain consciousness. The Irish police arrested 16 of the men in my stag party and told them the injured man might die. He underwent emergency surgery to remove the blood clots from his brain and spent the next six days fighting for his life. His family flew out from England to be at his bedside. Everyone feared he might be brain damaged, even if he pulled through.

The day before my wedding I was informed that he had regained consciousness and would be discharged from hospital shortly, though not in time to attend the wedding, which in any case he might well have opted to avoid. He didn't appear to have suffered any permanent brain damage, which was a relief to his family and friends.

The wedding went ahead as planned on 16 July 2004 at Peterborough

Cathedral. We spent our honeymoon in Cancun, Mexico, which is one of those beachside paradises most people can only dream about: miles and miles of pure white sand, overlooking the Gulf of Mexico. I am eternally grateful that Emma and I were able to go to such a beautiful place on our honeymoon. When we returned from Mexico, we both did our best to settle into some sort of normal existence. My children, Vinney and Karis, came to live with Emma and me, and so our house soon became a home. Then, just 19 weeks after our wedding day, tragedy struck.

Thursday, 2 December 2004 started off as a pretty unremarkable day. Around ten days earlier, Emma had fallen ill, with flu-like symptoms. She was normally one of those annoyingly healthy people, so her illness left me a little surprised and, I suppose, a little worried. I asked her not to go to work, but she insisted she wasn't sick enough to stay at home. She also wanted to work overtime to earn a bit extra for Christmas.

She worked hard, and late, all that week. The symptoms didn't seem to get any worse, though they didn't disappear either. On the Saturday night, we attended a wild party, a real mad one. On Sunday, we stayed in bed to recover. On Monday, we both got up and went to work. At home later that evening, Emma told me she felt really ill. We agreed she wouldn't go to work the next day.

In the morning, she didn't seem that bad. We even made love. Afterwards, we laughed about possible excuses I could give when I rang in sick for her. In the past, I hadn't always conveyed accurately the details we'd agreed. On one occasion – after she'd instructed me to say she had a bad cold – I'd rung her work with the excuse that she was stranded 100 miles away. I'd said that after visiting her sister Siobhan in Basildon she'd gone to drive home only to discover that someone had stolen her car's wheels. I neglected to tell Emma I'd altered the story slightly. Sitting at her work desk next day, with fake cough and theatrical sniffles, she'd been stumped by her boss asking sympathetically if the police had found her wheels.

I jokingly called her a skiver as I made up the bed before leaving home. I left fruit juice, books, magazines and the television remote control at her fingertips. At 9 a.m., I rang in sick for her. At ten, I phoned home. She said she felt awful, so I rang the doctor's surgery, which stood almost on our doorstep. Thanks to a cancellation, the doctor could see her in just over an hour. I phoned Emma to tell her to walk the 30 paces to the doctor's. In a weak voice, she replied she couldn't make the appointment because she couldn't get out of bed. I was so alarmed, I left work immediately and headed home.

The doctor agreed to come to Emma. I sat on the edge of the bed, holding her hand and talking to her, until he arrived. Then I left the room and waited downstairs till he'd finished. He diagnosed 'inflamed lungs' and prescribed anti-inflammatories and antibiotics. I went straight across the road to the chemist, who told me to bin the prescription because I could buy the same medication more cheaply off the shelf. I brought the tablets back to Emma, who started taking them. She seemed to pep up a bit, so I returned to work for a few hours. When I got home later that day, Emma told me she felt worse. She looked pale and poorly. I wanted to take her to hospital, but she thought I was overreacting. She insisted she didn't feel bad enough to merit a trip to casualty. I'll never forget her words: 'Stop worrying, Bernie. It's only a cold.'

On Wednesday morning, I said I wanted to stay at home with her, but she ordered me to go to work, insisting she'd survive without me. I spoke to her on the phone during the day. When I got back late that afternoon, she asked me, as she often did, to lie in bed with her and Brumble, her beloved teddy bear and almost inseparable companion. She loved watching TV in bed, snuggled up with me and Brumble rather than sitting in front of the screen downstairs. That Wednesday night, we hardly slept at all. She kept saying how awful she felt. I sat up in bed most of the night, holding her hand and stroking her hair. At five in the morning, I kissed her goodbye and told her I'd finish work early to be with her. 'Don't be long, Bernie,' she said.

During the day, I rang home to check on her condition. She said she felt a bit better and we talked about poxy curtains. At four, I finished work and went home to find her sitting on the sofa in the front room downstairs. She looked strange. She seemed scared, like she'd seen a ghost. I asked if she was all right. 'I love you, Bernie,' she said. I knew then that something was desperately wrong.

She seemed to know it, too. 'I love you, Bernie,' she said again, then added, 'Help me.'

'Don't fuck about, woman,' I said. 'You're scaring me.'

She laughed, which came as a relief, but then she repeated the words: 'I love you, Bernie.' I sat next to her with my arm around her, holding one of her hands. My son Vinney popped his head round the door to ask if everything was all right.

Over the next few hours, Emma's condition deteriorated rapidly. I wanted to make her a cup of tea, but every time I tried to leave the room, she would beg me to stay. I made another attempt to get to the kitchen; she said then what I later realised had been her last words: 'Please don't leave me, Bernie. Stay here with me. Don't go now. I love you, Bernie.' Her pleading tone filled me with fear. I guessed something dreadful might be about to happen – and I felt powerless to stop it.

I picked her up in my arms, like you'd pick up a child, and held her, trying to reassure her. Suddenly, her eyes rolled in her head. Gripped by a desperate panic, I laid her down gently, then rang the doctor's surgery and implored them to send someone immediately.

By now, Vinney had joined us in the front room. I put the phone down and again held Emma in my arms. All of a sudden, she leant forward. Her upper body stiffened, as if she were having a convulsion or even a heart attack. She seemed to stop breathing. Sick with shock and fear, I rang 999 and told the operator my wife had stopped breathing, though I could still feel a pulse in her neck. I begged for help. The operator instructed me on how to give the kiss of life – and promised an ambulance would soon be there. Vinney helped me lay Emma on the floor. He held her head as I tried desperately to breathe life into her. The 999 operator had stayed on the line. Vinney picked up the phone and began describing what was happening. Then he started passing on further instructions from the operator to me. I felt Emma's heart stop. I shouted at Vinney: 'Tell them her heart's stopped! Tell them her heart's stopped!' The operator told me via Vinney to try to restart her heart by pushing her chest down with the palm of my hand. I did as instructed, crying the whole time, pleading with her to wake up, but I knew my Emma had died.

Sobbing and shouting, I continued doing everything to get her breathing again, but she'd gone. The paramedics arrived swiftly. They set to work urgently, but Emma failed to respond. I slammed the door shut. I said no one could leave until they'd saved my Emmie. They fought for more than an hour to revive her, but it was too late. They pronounced her dead at '2024 hours'.

The next day a pathologist performed an autopsy. I can't bear to think of what he had to do to my beautiful Emma's body, but his work meant he could tell me why she'd died. He said a common flu virus had attacked her heart. Normally, this virus just travels round the bloodstream till it's zapped either by antibiotics or the body's own defences, but sometimes, rarely and unpredictably, it attacks the heart. The pathologist told me he'd only ever come across one other case. The victim then had also been a woman in her 20s. He said once the virus had started attacking Emma's heart nothing could have saved her. She could have been on antibiotics in the best hospital in the world, but she'd still have died.

One day short of five months since our marriage, and only ten days before Christmas, I buried my wife in her wedding dress. More than 100 people followed the horse-drawn carriage containing her coffin. At the cemetery in Codsall, my four best friends – Rachie, Gavin, Adolf and Hughie – together with my sons Adrian and Vinney, and my brother Michael, helped me carry Emma to her grave.

We made our way through the cemetery at a solemn snail's pace. Each step brought me closer to the moment when Emma's body would disappear forever. My sense of dread filled my feet with lead. The coffin, too, grew heavier every second. I felt a stab of pain as I saw ahead of me the mounds of freshly dug earth that would soon cover my beloved Emmie. Slowly, we reached our grim destination. One day it'll be my grave too, but, as I helped lower Emma into the ground, I wished that day had come and I could have joined her.

All day I had to tell myself to stay strong, not just for myself but also for my mother, my children and Emma's sister Siobhan. I knew, too, that Emma wouldn't have wanted me to go to pieces in public. All day, I stifled my tears.

Only when everyone had gone home that night did I allow myself to break down. I walked crying through Codsall's empty streets and made my way back to the cemetery. In the darkness, I found Emma's grave and lay down on the thick carpet of flowers that covered her final resting place. Alone again with my Emma, I let my tears fall until I cried myself to sleep. My uncle Paul found me there at four in the morning. He lifted me to my feet, put his arm round my shoulder and helped me walk back to my mother's.

The following day I knew I would be faced with another new start, another new beginning, but this time I wasn't sure it was one that I could make.

I was dreading Christmas Day. Emma's presents lay untouched under the tree in the front room; every glimpse of them was a reminder that she was never coming home. Then again every object and every scent in my home was a reminder of the terrible event that had taken place in the lounge.

It was hard to control my emotions – I kept breaking down – so I asked the children to go and stay with their mother. Vinney was reluctant to leave me alone at first, but when I explained that I wasn't in the mood for any 'Yo Ho Ho', he agreed. I don't remember much about Christmas Day, but on Boxing Day evening I felt I couldn't remain in the house for a moment longer and so I went outside to sit in my car. I can't say how long I was there because I was weeping uncontrollably. I know that at some stage somebody tapped on the driver's door window and directed a torch into my eyes.

'Have you been drinking, sir?' a police officer asked.

'Do yourself a favour and fuck off, mate,' I replied. 'My wife has just died and I am not in the mood for your games.'

In a statement made later that evening, the officer said, 'O'Mahoney had glazed eyes and slurred speech. He was crying, telling us to leave him alone, that his wife had recently died. He kept repeating this. He was drunk. As O'Mahoney had clearly been driving whilst under the influence, I decided it would be necessary to breathalyse him. Due to his demeanour, I decided it would be better to wait until other officers arrived.'

My vehicle was in a private parking bay; my eyes were glazed because I had been crying, and so I have never been able to understand why it was clear to this officer that I had been driving whilst under the influence of alcohol. I knew what was coming. Reinforcements were on their way, so the police were clearly expecting trouble. I wasn't in the mood to disappoint. I was asked to get out of my car, and when I complied I noticed that the officer was the same one who had arrested me for the wounding offences of which I'd quite rightly been acquitted. 'I want you to get into the back of the police car, O'Mahoney, until other officers arrive,' he said.

I complied. According to the officer's statement, 'After a few minutes of O'Mahoney being sat in the car, Sgt Gadd and PC Baines arrived from Stamford. Sgt Gadd asked O'Mahoney if he was going to cooperate. O'Mahoney stated that he would not and again talked of his dead wife and how we were in the wrong. He then rolled onto his back on the back seat and drove his legs up and against the nearside rear passenger window, which was closed. He kicked out with great force, smashing through the window before sitting up again. I ran around to the window and Sgt Gadd, PC Capp, PC Baines and myself reached in, trying to grab O'Mahoney's arms to prevent him assaulting us. Due to O'Mahoney's manner, I sprayed him with a short burst of CS spray, which went on his clothing. I saw that PC Capp and Sgt Gadd had also sprayed him. As we restrained his arms, he became more compliant and I said to O'Mahoney, "I'm arresting you on suspicion of causing criminal damage to this police vehicle and driving a motor vehicle whilst unfit through drink." There was no reply, as we struggled to restrain him. Eventually, we handcuffed him to the front with two sets of handcuffs linked and double locked.'

What I failed to understand was what exactly I was supposed to be complying with. I had been asked to get out of my car and sit in a police vehicle, which I had done. Then at least four officers were demanding that I comply with what? I was equally puzzled as to why they'd had to use CS spray to prevent me from assaulting them. I was in the rear of a police car, all of which are fitted with child locks. They were outside the vehicle, so how could I possibly assault them?

My version of events naturally differed greatly from that of the officers. In my statement, I explained about the death of my wife, burying her just days before Christmas and the state of mind I was in over the Christmas period. I described sitting outside my home in my car and the police asking me to sit in their car. When other officers arrived at the scene, I was, as the officer quite rightly stated, talking about my wife and explaining that the officers were in the wrong to think that I had been drinking.

I alleged that one of the officers said to me, 'Fuck you and fuck your nigger-loving wife.' My wife's sister is married to a Basildon-born and bred black guy, so I took this to be a reference to that fact. The officer I alleged had made this remark has always denied it. The police had searched my home during the wounding investigation, so they would have seen photographs of Emma and me at her sister's wedding and have seen that the groom was black. After hearing the unnecessary racist remark, I said in my statement, I lost my temper and kicked the window out of the police car.

Understandably, my version of events was not believed and I was charged with driving under the influence of alcohol, having no driving licence or insurance, and criminal damage. I laughed when they charged me: no licence or insurance? Both items were in my vehicle, which they had searched. Another trial loomed, but, in all honesty, I couldn't have cared less. But that didn't mean I wasn't going to fight it.

Shortly before Emma's death, we had paid a local man named Cottam approximately £1,700 in cash to fit doors, skirting boards and wooden floors in an extension at our home. Cottam, a former friend, had completed most of the work, but after the young lad who was working with him at my house committed suicide, nothing further was done. I didn't want to trouble Cottam at such a difficult time, and then when Emma died all thoughts of such a trivial matter left my head. Approximately four months later, I decided that it was time to start picking up the pieces: I needed to get back to work and get my life in order. I telephoned Cottam and he agreed that £500 or so worth of work was still outstanding. On several occasions, he arranged to come and complete the work, but each time he let me down. What I didn't know at the time was that Cottam was avoiding me because he had run off with the wife of a man who he believed was my friend. I was acquainted with this man, Foster, but I would never have described him as a friend. What's more, I couldn't have cared less what they got up to in their sordid lives; it wasn't my business. I was due to go to Paris for the weekend, so I rang Cottam to tell him that he could either complete the work that weekend or put the money he owed me through my letterbox. He wouldn't answer his phone, so rather foolishly I sent him a text message explaining that I wanted the work done or my money back. As I drove to the airport, Kirsty, the woman Cottam had run off with, rang me, shouting at me for threatening Cottam. Rather bizarrely, she seemed to think I had given Cottam the ultimatum out of loyalty to Foster.

'Don't even begin to believe that you're important to me, dear,' I replied. 'Just get your boyfriend to finish my work or return my money.'

I received at least another three phone calls from the woman, all of which were abusive.

I had wanted to go to Notre Dame Cathedral in Paris ever since Emma's death because it was where I had proposed to her. Paris was also the first place we had ever travelled abroad together – Emma's mother had been killed the morning after we returned. That dreadful day also happened to be Emma's 21st birthday. It was to be an emotional journey for me, for many reasons.

As soon as I saw Notre Dame, I was reduced to tears. Only two years previously, on Christmas Eve, I had stood in that same spot and asked Emma to marry me. In the background, a choir had been singing Christmas carols and the cathedral entrance had been glowing from the light of hundreds of candles. It had been an emotional moment then; and two years on, it was equally emotional.

The memories of that day came flooding back. Emma had cried then; it was my turn now. I lit a candle in Emma's memory, prayed for her and then bought a beautiful rosary, which I intend to take to our grave for her when I die. Leaving Notre Dame cathedral broke my heart; it felt as if I was leaving behind something magical Emma and I had shared.

I made my way to the airport. I had a few minutes to spare, so I decided to ring Cottam to see if he had completed the work. He kept asking me what I intended to do if he didn't return the money or complete the work, and it's fair to say in my emotional state I lost my temper. Unbeknown to me, whilst I had been in Paris, Kirsty had been bombarded with text messages from Foster, who seemed to be suggesting that I had something far more sinister in mind for Cottam than simply getting him to complete the work at my home.

> Foster: Cottam is a fucking low-life and a snake. He's not getting away with this, I'm sorry.
> Kirsty: What do you think will happen to Cottam?
> Foster I think he will disappear.
> Kirsty: Disappear? How? Is that what you want? Have you asked for this?
> Foster: That Bernie thing is about Cottam, not you. He hates him more than you could ever imagine. It's between them, I can't stop that, sorry.

Deeper and deeper, Foster dragged me into his sordid relationship wrangle. He had not even spoken to me before I left, but he was giving his ex-wife Kirsty the impression that he was in constant contact with me and that I was going to do something terrible to Cottam – not because he hadn't completed the work at my home but because he had run off with Kirsty. Understandably, though wholly misguided, Cottam and Kirsty went to the police to report their fears. I should have been more alert, I should have seen it coming, but I wasn't thinking straight at that time. I was still grieving. I hadn't been sleeping and had been heavily medicated.

After landing at Heathrow, I rang Cottam, but Kirsty answered. She kept asking what I intended to do to Cottam. When I said nothing, she hung up. This happened on three occasions. Little did I know it at the time but both she and Cottam were sitting in a police station and my calls were being monitored. As I wasn't making threats and saying other things that perhaps the police were hoping to hear, Cottam's phone was switched off. I drove home and went to bed.

At approximately quarter past three the following day, I put my coat on and opened my front door. Eight policemen, two with snarling Alsatians straining at their leads, stood on my garden path.

'What the fuck's going on?' I asked.

'Calm down, Bernie, calm down,' one of them began shouting.

'I don't need to calm down because I've not lost my temper,' I said. 'I'm on my way to a medical appointment. Please don't cause me any shit, fellas.'

The officer in charge asked if I could prove I had an appointment with a doctor. I went into my house and fetched the appointment card. 'We need to speak to you at the police station,' the officer said.

'Fair enough,' I replied, 'but why turn up mob-handed with dogs?'

'You know the score, Bernie,' the officer said. 'We don't want any problems with you like we had on Boxing Day. If we let you keep this appointment, will you come down the nick afterwards?'

'Of course, no problem. I've got nothing to hide. I'll be there,' I assured him.

After attending my appointment, I drove to Market Deeping police station to meet up with the officers, as agreed. I had guessed that they wanted to talk to me about Cottam, but I assumed that it wouldn't take long. When I went into the police station, the same officer who had arrested me for wounding and driving under the influence walked into the public foyer and said he would have to talk to me at Spalding police station, as the paperwork concerning this matter was there. Despite this officer's enthusiastic police work, not one of his efforts had yet resulted in me being convicted of any offence. Had I been a member of a minority group, living in an inner city, I might have formed the opinion that I was being harassed.

The officer said it would be better if I drove my own vehicle to Spalding, as that would save time and trouble waiting for the police to give me a lift home when their inquiries were complete. Spalding police station is about ten miles from Market Deeping and I didn't relish the thought of sharing the journey with this particular officer and his sidekick, so I agreed. On the journey to Spalding, the police car remained immediately behind me; I felt uncomfortable being followed, so I tried slowing down in the hope they would overtake me, but the officers remained in my rear-view mirror throughout the journey. When we arrived at the police station, I was asked to go into the custody area.

As soon as I entered, one of the officers said, 'O'Mahoney, I am arresting you on suspicion of making threats to kill.' He then informed me of my rights and asked me if I understood them. I sensed he was enjoying his moment, so I made no reply. The officer then explained that, as it was such a serious allegation, detectives rather than police constables were going to have to interview me. These detectives, I was informed, were already in the police station and wouldn't be long, but meanwhile I would have to be put in a cell for ten minutes or so. As I was escorted to the cell block, I noticed the time was 5.10 p.m.

17

ALL THAT I AM,
ALL THAT I EVER WAS

THE wall in my cell was a mural of misery. *Lord my God, for fuck's sake, help me* had somehow been carved into the beige wall a dozen times. Next to these rather disturbing pleas was a somewhat less spiritual sentiment: *Gaz Barron of Newborough fucks pigs!* I immediately decided to become a vegetarian. The only institutional inscription was stencilled in large black letters to the right of the door. I'm not sure if the police were trying to be witty, but it stated that if anybody marked the wall in any way they would be charged with criminal damage. One assumes 'any way' did not include stencilling it with black ink.

At 11.40 that night, my cell door was opened and I was taken to the interview room. The officer's ten-minute wait had somehow stretched to six hours and thirty minutes. Pathetic and sad are words that spring to mind. I wasn't going to react angrily, if that was their intention; instead I chose to not even mention the matter.

Two detectives entered the room and introduced themselves as DC Gurney and DS Gibbon. I didn't like Gurney from the moment I set eyes on his weasel-like features. It seemed to me he had been watching too many American cop shows. He tried and failed miserably to be witty and smart throughout the interview. I explained the whole story. That Cottam had laid a wooden floor at my home and I had paid him approximately £1,700 in cash. Two people were present when I had given him the money. As well as laying the floor, Cottam and Foster were supposed to have hung a few new doors and fitted skirting boards and architrave. Halfway through the job,

Cottam's labourer had committed suicide and he had run away with Foster's wife, Kirsty. The work at my home had been left unfinished. I wanted the money back for work that was yet to be completed, which I estimated came to approximately £500, or I wanted them to finish the job.

I admitted to the police that I had contacted Cottam by phone and text and had told him that I would be in Paris for the weekend and expected the money to be posted through my letterbox or the work done by the time I returned. I told them I had even left the front door unlocked so Cottam could have access. The day before I left for Paris, I said, Cottam had agreed he would pay me back the money, but he must have mentioned it to Kirsty, who objected and rang me.

At approximately 1.15 a.m., I was returned to my cell. It was freezing cold. There was no bedding and the light was left on. I was expected to sleep on a coarse, four-inch-thick mattress, but when I laid down on it, my face stuck to its plastic covering. I gave up any thoughts of lying down and sat instead, waiting for the morning.

It was daylight when an inspector came to the cell door and informed me that he was authorising my detention whilst a search of my home was being conducted.

'Is that your Range Rover in the car park outside?' he asked.

'It is, yes,' I replied.

'Well, we're going to have to search that also, at some stage,' he said.

I'd had niggling concerns about the length of time I'd been kept over what was a non-criminal case. I had never made threats to kill, so I wasn't concerned about that particular allegation. As far as I was concerned, Cottam owed me money, he had denied it and therefore it was a civil matter. The fact the police were going to search my home and car really started to bother me, though. Why would the police need to search my home and car in connection with a telephone call anyway?

I asked the inspector if I could use the phone to ring my children, as they would be concerned about my whereabouts. Despite having the right to make a call, the inspector told me he was refusing my request, as he thought it might interfere with an ongoing police operation. The inspector's answer confirmed to me that things were far more sinister than I had imagined.

I asked if I could see the duty solicitor, who I knew was in the police station because I had heard her talking to whoever was in the cell next door to me. About an hour after I had made my request, an officer came to my cell and said I could not see the solicitor, as she did not cover the Spalding area and therefore would not be paid if she saw me. I was getting extremely anxious now, as the police had no right to deny me access to a solicitor of my choice. I asked the officer to ring my solicitor, Mr Cauthery, and inform him that I was being held in custody. The officer said that he would.

I was not worried about the police searching my home, as I didn't have anything I shouldn't have had there; however, the Range Rover was a different matter. I remembered that I had left a combat knife with a 12-inch blade between the passenger and driver seat. I knew the police would not believe that I had been using it in the yard to cut ropes for the lorries. Cottam had apparently alleged that I had threatened to cut his throat and the combat knife would be the hard evidence the police needed to support his allegation.

It smacks of desperation now, but I prayed to Emma to help me; I pleaded with her to stop them from finding it. I knew in my heart that professional, competent police officers searching the interior of a car in broad daylight would not fail to find a 12-inch-long knife lying between two seats.

Twenty-four hours after I had been put in the cells, my solicitor arrived at the police station. I was taken from my cell to the interview room, where we discussed the allegation being made against me. Shortly afterwards, DC Gurney and another officer named DC Skeath arrived and said they were going to interview me again. I was convinced they had found the combat knife and were going to ask me what I had intended to do with it. The interview went over the same ground as the first one and I was convinced the police were saving their best until last, but thankfully they didn't mention the knife. It turned out they had failed to find it. Whoever searched my vehicle clearly needed glasses because they hadn't spotted a long shiny object in a small confined space.

When the interview was over, Mr Cauthery and I remained in the interview room to discuss what had been said. Mr Cauthery said that he thought I would be charged with making threats to kill but that I should be bailed and out of the police station within the hour. I was taken from the interview room and asked to stand in front of the desk sergeant, whose job it was to either charge, bail, remand or free me. The desk sergeant, Gurney and Skeath asked Mr Cauthery if they could be excused for a moment. They disappeared into a back room, leaving my solicitor and I to exchange puzzled looks. When the beaming trio re-appeared, the desk sergeant addressed me.

'Patrick Bernard O'Mahoney, between the 29th of April 2005 and the 1st of May 2005, at Bourne Lincolnshire, with a view to gain for yourself or another or with intent to cause loss to another, you made an unwarranted demand of payment of money and property from James Cottam with menaces. This is contrary to section 21 (1) of the theft act 1968. In other words, O'Mahoney, you have been charged with blackmail. Have you anything you wish to say?'

I looked at Mr Cauthery, who appeared to be as shocked as me. I laughed and my solicitor shook his head. Unfortunately, the joke was far from over.

I was also charged with making threats to kill. The desk sergeant told me that he had followed the case from the outset and knew all about me; given the nature of the case, he said, he was not going to grant me bail because he believed I would interfere with the witnesses. I was going to be kept in police custody and taken to Grantham Magistrates Court in the morning.

Now that I had been charged, I assumed the police investigation concerning me had reached a conclusion, so there would be no reason why I could not phone Vinney. When I asked to use the phone, I was told I could do so, but that I would have to return to the cells first for a few minutes, as they had paperwork to sort out.

Two hours later I pressed the bell in the cell and an officer came to the door. 'Can you fetch the duty inspector, please?' I asked. 'I wish to make a complaint. I have been in custody for two days, I have been charged and I have requested to make a telephone call, and that right has either been ignored or denied.'

The officer said he would fetch the inspector, but two minutes later an officer opened my cell door and told me I could make my call. When I spoke to Vinney, he told me that Foster was also in custody at the same police station. I asked Vinney what, if anything, the police had taken from our home. He laughed and said they had taken Emma's phone as evidence. Vinney had told the officers that it wasn't my phone, but they had refused to believe him and seized it. My phone had been next to Emma's, but the cover and battery had been removed so they had assumed it was broken; in fact, I had just taken it apart to clean it. Searching and gathering evidence were obviously not Lincolnshire Police's greatest skills.

The following morning the police allowed me to take a shower. It was my third day in custody and I'd not been offered the opportunity to wash, shave or change my clothing. I stank. As I was drying myself, an officer unlocked a cell adjacent to the shower and Foster walked out. He barely looked at me, so I knew he had said things about me during his interviews that he was now regretting.

Around 9 a.m., a Group 4 prison security van came to collect Foster and me. Two female guards led us out of the police station in handcuffs and then locked us in adjacent cubicles in the van. It was the first opportunity I'd had to speak to Foster, but he wasn't in the mood for talking: his eyes were streaming with tears. He certainly wasn't filling me with confidence.

The driver of the prison van got lost before we had even left Spalding town centre and we ended up down a dead-end street on an industrial estate. The driver's mate asked Foster and me if we knew the way to Grantham. I was going to send them in the opposite direction for a laugh, but Foster gave them directions to put them on the right road. When we finally arrived at Grantham Magistrates Court, we were taken into the cell block and put in separate cells. Foster was still reluctant to talk to me, so I knew he had blamed me for everything to save himself. Mr Cauthery was unable to attend the court to represent me, as he had made a prior arrangement to visit an inmate in prison, so in his place he had sent a Mr Milligan to act on my behalf. Before the hearing convened, I had a meeting with him. He told me that Foster 'had done me no favours'. Since he had cooperated with the police, they were not going to oppose his bail, but they were adamant that I should not be released, as they were convinced I would interfere with witnesses.

'I don't know what you have done to them,' he said, 'but they certainly don't like you.' Mr Milligan said that my best bet was to offer the court a bail address outside Lincolnshire. The court could then make an order as part of my bail conditions that I was not to contact any witnesses directly or via a third party and I should not enter Lincolnshire unless attending court. Vinney had already sorted out two alternative bail addresses – my brother Michael's in Wolverhampton and my friend Dawn's in Cambridgeshire. Dawn, at that time, was a prison officer in top-security HMP Whitemoor, so I thought the court might have allowed me to be bailed to her home address. Mr Milligan pointed out that I had never been convicted of any offence relating to interfering with witnesses, I owned my own home, I had always been employed and therefore there seemed no reason why my legal right to bail should be denied.

Foster and I were taken from the cells and into the court at approximately 11.30. We sat down behind a glass screen flanked by four prison officers. The prosecution said they had no objections to Foster being granted bail on the condition he did not contact any of the witnesses and resided at his parents' home, which was some distance from Market Deeping.

Before the court began to hear my application for bail, Foster was told that he was free to leave the dock. I looked round the court; DC Gurney and Kirsty's parents were sitting together. Immediately behind them sat Vinney and Foster's latest girlfriend, Melanie.

I looked at Vinney, who raised his thumb, indicating that he thought I would get bail; I shook my head. The way I had been treated thus far indicated I was never going to get bail. Even so, the prosecution's objections took everyone in court, including me, by surprise. I couldn't believe what I was hearing. I was described as a 'gangster with underworld connections'. Police intelligence, the prosecutor said, had learned that I had 'paid a witness £500' during my trial the previous year 'for smashing a glass in a man's neck in a pub in Market Deeping'. Apparently, travellers had put a contract on my head to have me hurt – or worse – but, according to police intelligence, I had heard about it and those responsible had suffered serious injuries. Police intelligence (I doubted there was such a thing, considering the abilities of those who had searched my car and home) deemed me to have 'serious criminal connections' and I had 'for a number of years, been involved in serious crime'.

I was looking around the courtroom at one stage to see if I could spot this mafioso-type man they were describing. If it had not been such a serious matter, I would have laughed. DC Gurney was visibly excited: this, obviously, was what police work was all about – catching real criminals, like those he saw on TV, rather than rounding up poachers and intoxicated tractor drivers, which is the norm in rural Lincolnshire.

Gurney produced a 1993 *GQ* magazine article from the Internet, which had been written about a man named Harry in Essex. He said it was proof of my history of demanding money with menaces. Nowhere in the article was my name mentioned. He had also said that scenes in the film *Essex Boys* showed that my associates and I threatened and intimidated people in order to get our own way. I honestly found it hard to believe that I was in a British court of law.

My conversations with Cottam and Kirsty, the true crux of the case, became secondary.

Farce was quickly descending into complete lunacy. Mr Milligan questioned if, likewise, an actor in the film *Lock, Stock and Two Smoking Barrels* who was arrested by Lincolnshire Police would be questioned about the 'crimes' he had committed on screen. Mr Milligan was trying to make the point that the scenes portrayed in *Essex Boys* couldn't possibly be attributed to anything I might have done, but his noble efforts were in vain.

The district judge said he would need time to consider whether or not I should be granted bail, and the court adjourned.

Ten minutes later I was brought back up from the cells. The judge said he accepted that I was not a member of the Krays' gang, nor any other, but the prosecution had produced pictures from a website that clearly showed I had attended the Court of Appeal in support of the Rettendon murderers. 'Mr O'Mahoney, despite his denials, is clearly connected with serious criminals. It is my view that if he were to be granted bail, he may interfere with witnesses and therefore bail is denied.'

As I walked down the steps to the cell block, the guards said they had never heard anything like it in their lives. 'That was more like a seventeenth-century witch trial,' one of them remarked. His colleague added, 'Fucking hell, mate, you aren't going to have us topped for locking you up, are you?' We all laughed, but I had no doubt the police were laughing louder.

Mr Milligan came down to the cells to see me; he too had been surprised by the 'off-the-wall' allegations the prosecution had produced as hard evidence. My next court appearance was going to be the following Thursday at Lincoln Crown Court. Mr Milligan explained that the prosecution would probably present 'a slightly more temperate case' and I would be allowed to make a fresh application for bail. If that application failed, he said, I would have to remain in prison until the trial, which might not take place until November. The only exception would be if there was a dramatic change in circumstances, such as new evidence indicating my innocence. If that happened, I could apply for bail to a judge in chambers – in other words, a hearing that does not take place in open court. I thanked Mr Milligan and was returned to the cell to await the prison van that would take me to Lincoln prison. Later that day, as the prison van pulled out of Grantham Magistrates car park, the driver played a Bon Jovi CD so loudly the vehicle vibrated. I'm no fan of Bon Jovi – far from it, in fact – but the music and the countryside flashing by the small darkened window of the cubicle I was in helped me to escape from the reality of the situation. The allegation that I had paid a witness £500 in the Turton wounding trial troubled me. The prosecution case had not even been heard in full when they withdrew the charge and offered no further evidence. The defence did not have to produce a single witness. How, then, was I supposed to have paid a witness or influenced the trial in any way? Surely, they were not suggesting that I had paid one of the prosecution's own witnesses? It was laughable.

I guessed that Foster's texts about me making Cottam disappear had stoked Cottam's fear and he had told the police not only about the texts and phone calls, but also every rumour and story he had ever heard about me. The more dirt he served up, the more the police could blacken my character in court and the less chance I would have of getting bail. It all made sense to me now. That was why they had searched my home and car; no doubt they were looking for gold bullion, bodies, drugs and guns!

The prison van slowed as we drove into Lincoln city centre. I could see people going about their everyday business. My right to go about my everyday business had been taken away from me by the police and the courts because I had asked for what was rightfully mine.

The main gate of the prison swung open and the prison van drove inside. I knew the free world I had inhabited was gone for the foreseeable future. Twenty years ago, I had been incarcerated in the very same jail. The regime and conditions had changed dramatically; sadly, I had not. Perhaps in my heart I had mellowed. I was certainly not as reckless or as violent as I had been. But unlike others of my age, I had failed to mature during the last two decades. My inability to settle down, accept responsibility and adapt my social life accordingly had all conspired to prolong my youth. Had I been born in a different age, I might well have walked happily along a well-worn path, securing a trade after school, marrying Mrs Ordinary, having 2.5 children, then enjoying being a grandfather before heading off to my eternal rest with Emma in St Nicholas's churchyard in Codsall. Trouble is, the intense fire burning in my delinquent heart hadn't even flickered, let alone been extinguished. My heart has always ruled my head, that's the way it is, that's the way it's always been and that's why I always ended up getting into trouble.

I was put on J Wing, where I was told all prisoners coming into the jail have to spend a few days while they are assessed for risk prior to allocation. My cell contained a bunk bed, a toilet, a washbasin and a colour television. It had been a stressful day, so I got into bed at about 8 p.m. and soon fell asleep. The following morning was spent being interviewed and checked by people from various agencies or departments within the prison. Did I have a drug problem? Did I have a drink problem? Did I think I would benefit from an anger management course? Was I religious? Was I suicidal? Did I self-harm? Could I read and write? Was I on medication? Had I ever had any form of mental illness? Did I want to work? What type of work did I want to do? Would I need help with accommodation when I was released? Did I have any form of disease? From seat to seat, department to department, I was shuffled; hardly any of the questions applied to me. Anything that did apply to me, they chose to ignore.

I applied to work in the library and, having written several books about my life experience, I thought I might have had a fair chance of success, but they sent me to work on a sewing machine in the tailor's shop instead. In the afternoon, I was moved to cell number 8 on the ground floor of C Wing. Once more I was housed on my own. This cell did not have a television and, as I had no writing or reading material, the hours dragged on like entire days. Around 8 p.m., just as the daylight was fading, I got into bed to sleep. As soon as I closed my eyes, the entire wing began to reverberate to the sound of pounding house music. It was a bit like lying on the dance floor of a nightclub in full swing and trying to get some sleep. As well as the music, people were calling out to one another through the cell windows or screaming at the top of their voices as if in pain. I had no idea what was going on; the only thing I knew for sure was I wouldn't be getting much, if any, sleep that night.

The following morning I asked one of the inmates on the wing what had been going on. 'Landing two, mate,' he replied. 'Everyone on that landing is on detox. We call it the cluckers and rattlers' landing, since they're all trying to come off heroin. Friday night is party night. They either get out of their heads on gear and make a row or they're going through cold turkey and they shout, cluck, rattle and smash up their cells or scream the place down.'

'Great,' I replied. 'Trust me to get a cell underneath the highway to fucking hell.'

As it was Saturday, there was no work in the prison, so we were locked in our cells for most of the day. At 10.30, we were allowed out for exercise. It isn't exercise really, but it gets you into the fresh air, something I had not enjoyed for five days. The exercise yard reminded me of a school playground surrounded by a high wire fence. I counted 60 other prisoners out on the yard. Twenty-five of us walked in a clockwise circle, whilst the other inmates, under the constant gaze of four security cameras, sat on the floor with their backs against the fence. All of us were dressed in either grey or maroon elasticated, prison-manufactured tracksuits. Nearly every conversation I overheard seemed to revolve around crimes committed or crimes that might be committed in the future.

I'm no better than any man in or out of jail, but I chose to keep my own company. I knew that if I got involved with some of the inmates it would end in tears and undoubtedly more trouble.

To occupy my mind and avoid eye contact, I counted my footsteps as I walked around the exercise yard. One hundred and twenty-six steps long, twenty-five steps wide. Monotony, fucking monotony. I knew I was going to find the next few months difficult, but, to make matters worse, if I was found guilty of blackmail, I had been warned that I was facing three to five years. As I'd not slept much the night before, I felt exhausted and went to bed at about seven o'clock. My mind was awash with thoughts and every time I nodded off I began to dream. Emma kept appearing, lying next to me, putting her finger to her lips so I didn't speak, then smiling. I smiled back at her and she put her arms out to embrace me. The dream was so real, I could feel her in my arms: the tighter I pulled her to me, the warmer and happier I felt. I'm not sure if the detox inmates were 'rattling' that night or if they were playing their music because I didn't wake till morning. To be honest, I felt so incredibly happy in that dream I wouldn't have cared if I had never woke up.

On Sunday afternoon my cell door was unlocked and an officer informed me that I had a visit. I knew Vinney would be the first to see me. To get to the visiting room, I had to walk through B Wing and A Wing, where I had been housed 20 years earlier. A Wing was now empty, following a riot in the prison in October 2002. Reminders of that night were everywhere. Doors hung from their frames, and fixtures and fittings were strewn all over the floor. It was as if nobody had been on the wing since the night of the riot.

As I entered the visiting room, Vinney stood up and waved at me. Two friends, McDonald and another named Geordie Sean, were with him. We all shook hands and sat down. McDonald and Sean said, 'You'll be out of here in a few days. Cottam and Kirsty want to drop the charges. They've been constantly ringing us. It's Foster they are upset with, not you.'

I told them that I wasn't interested in what Cottam or Kirsty had to say. 'They exaggerated their statements so I wouldn't get bail. As far as I'm concerned, they've made their bed. Let them lie in it until the trial.'

'Where's Foster?' I asked Vinney.

'He was sitting in the pub crying last night,' Vinney replied. 'Nobody's talking to him because they know he's had you imprisoned because of his childish behaviour.'

This news cheered me up. 'But where is he? I thought he would come and visit me.'

Sean and McDonald said that Foster wouldn't come because his bail conditions prevented him from doing so. 'That's total bollocks,' I said. 'Tell him I need to see him.'

I told Vinney, McDonald and Sean not to discuss me or the case with Cottam – 'In fact, avoid him at all costs. This time in here is helping me clear my head. My barrister can deal with Cottam at the trial.'

When the visit was over, I returned to the wing feeling happier about my situation. I knew Cottam would chop and change his story – he was just one of those people who didn't think before he opened his mouth. I had told Mr Cauthery and the police who were interviewing me that he would do that even before I was charged.

Over the next five months, I was ferried back and forth to court. The prosecution charged me with six additional offences of blackmail/ demanding money with menaces, but I refused to accept that I was guilty. Cottam wrote out a statement regretting the allegations that he had made and promptly left the country 'on holiday'. The prosecution must have realised they had little or no chance of securing a conviction because the next time I appeared in court I was offered a deal. Plead guilty to sending a message that might have caused distress and you're free to go. I wasn't happy about pleading guilty to anything, but I had to think of my children, who had been at home alone for five long months, so I agreed.

When I returned to Market Deeping, it reminded me of Paris: a pissy little river ran through the middle of it and I couldn't understand a word the natives were grunting. I had grown to hate the place and the small-town mentality of some of the inhabitants. But it was home for now and I was going to have to remain there for the foreseeable future.

In September 2005, I stood trial for criminal damage, driving whilst under the influence of alcohol and having no licence or insurance. I had kicked the window out of the police car after they insulted my wife, so I pleaded guilty to that offence. I pleaded not guilty to all of the other charges. At least five police officers gave evidence against me, but their evidence was inconsistent and I was quite rightly found not guilty of each charge. It was accepted that one of the officers had made an insulting comment about my wife, but none of the officers could remember what exactly had been said or who had said it.

My wife had been dead for ten months; I had endured two separate prosecutions and spent five months in jail. It was time for a new start – a new beginning.

* * *

Just one week after my trial, I went for a quiet drink alone in a pub near my home. My son Vinney had recently cheated death after being involved in a head-on collision with an articulated lorry. Vinney's car had been crushed beyond recognition, but thankfully he had only suffered cuts, bruises and whiplash injuries. His vehicle had been taken to a communal parking area near my home following the accident, as Vinney's insurance company wanted to examine it. As I walked home alone from the pub about nine o'clock, I noticed a group of Vinney's friends standing around the car.

'Hello, Bernie,' one of them said. 'I can't believe Vinney walked away from this.'

I stood talking to the lads for a few minutes, then said I had to go, as Vinney's mother Debra was at my house, visiting the children. As we were saying our goodbyes, I noticed two middle-aged men jumping over the car park wall.

'Fucking hell, it's those blokes,' one of the lads said.

'We're going to fucking do you!' the men shouted, as they advanced across the car park. I couldn't quite believe what I was seeing. The men were both in their late 30s and were brandishing 14-inch-long kebab knives.

'You don't need knives to take on kids. Put them down,' I said.

Both men turned on me simultaneously. 'Do you want some? Do you want some?' they shouted.

'Threaten me with a knife and you'll fucking die,' I replied, before striking one of them. The man I punched raised the kebab knife and plunged it into the back of my shoulder; it exited through my chest. Blood pumped out of the wound and I could feel it running down my chest and legs. I knew it was only a matter of time before I passed out, so I knew I would have to kill my attackers before they killed me. Fortunately, when the other man brandishing a knife saw what his friend had done, he dropped his weapon and ran. I grabbed the man who had stabbed me and began punching him with one hand, whilst head-butting him in the face. He fought frantically to pull the knife out of my body: each time he pulled at it, the blade tore the wound until it was nearly five inches wide at the entry point. I was producing so much adrenalin, I couldn't feel any pain. I bent forward, enabling the man to pull out the blade that had skewered my body. Fearing he would stab me again, I hit him as hard as I could and he fell to the ground. I genuinely believed that he was trying to get to his feet to stab me again, so I kicked him as hard as I could in the head in order to incapacitate him. I stopped when he appeared to be dead. I picked up the knife, gave it to one of Vinney's friends for safe-keeping and then walked back to my home, where I collapsed in the kitchen.

I have no idea what happened after that. I awoke in hospital the following day, having undergone emergency surgery during which I was given five pints of blood. At first, I was told the man had died, but later that day I learned he was in fact in Addenbrooke's hospital, a specialist hospital in Cambridge for brain and head injuries. I wasn't proud of what I had done, but I felt no remorse either – there are many forms of justice. A surgeon told me that it was a miracle I had survived and that the person responsible should be charged with attempted murder, as my wounds were undoubtedly life threatening.

Lincolnshire Police thought otherwise. Three days after the incident I discharged myself from hospital and went to visit my friend Martin in Devon. Whilst there, I received a telephone call from the police, who said they wanted to interview me.

'I'm sorry. That's not going to happen. I have had enough trouble over the last few months, I'm not going to make a complaint against the guy who stabbed me and I definitely won't give evidence against him, so forget it,' I said.

'I don't think you understand, Mr O'Mahoney. It's you we are going to arrest,' the officer replied.

I am tempted to say that I couldn't believe what I was hearing, but the fact is I did; I had been half-expecting it. Knowing that I was now facing a charge of attempted murder, or at least wounding, I began ringing people to get some background to the incident. I learned that a few hours before I had encountered the men, one of them, forty-year-old Crowson, had been drinking heavily in one of the village pubs. He had started on a 20-year-old youth, who had retaliated and got the better of him. Crowson, a man who believes he has a deserved reputation as a hard man, was ejected from the pub. Outside, he picked up a bottle in frustration and hurled it at a passing car, which was being driven by a 'mature' lady. Quite rightly upset, the lady informed her teenage sons about what had happened when she arrived home. Her sons had left the house, found Crowson and sorted him out. After being humiliated twice in a short period of time by 'kids', hard man Crowson went to his brother's flat and kicked the door. His brother's girlfriend answered, Crowson burst in, grabbed two 14-inch kebab-type knives and made to leave. When his brother tried to prevent him from doing so, Crowson grabbed him and threatened to kill him.

Crowson had then telephoned his friend – another 40-odd-year-old hard man – and told him what had happened. Crowson met his friend and given him one of the knives. They then set off to find the kids who had assaulted Crowson. Unfortunately, they were Vinney's friends and they happened to be talking to me when the dopey duo finally found them.

I contacted my solicitor and he arranged for me to hand myself in at a police station. I was immediately arrested, interviewed and, after giving my version of events, bailed to reappear pending further inquiries. Later that day, Chief Inspector Kieran English and Inspector Andy McManus held a press conference during which they told reporters: 'This was not a random attack and the public are not at risk. The incident occurred due to an escalation of a prior disorder. There will be an increased police presence in the town to reassure people. Patrol officers will regularly be visiting the local pubs to ensure that there is no violence or other problems. Officers responded and dealt with the incident appropriately and at no time were other members of the public at risk. We will not tolerate acts of violence or those who increase fear within local communities. Our inquiries continue into this incident and we would welcome any information from members of the public.'

I laughed when I heard what they had said. Was I expected to tolerate an act of extreme violence?

After leaving the police station, I went for a drink, but the landlord politely informed me that Lincolnshire Police had advised all licensees that I should not be served in any premises in the county. This was no temporary ban; the landlord informed me that it was for life. At that moment, I knew my time in Market Deeping was over. I had only remained because I couldn't bring myself to sell the home that Emma and I had purchased together, but she hadn't been dead 12 months and my life had been turned upside down. Emma would not have wanted that, so after the police cancelled my bail on 14 December 2005 and said there would be no further action, I decided to rent out my home and leave.

Karis had returned to her mother's home in Essex and Vinney had moved in with a friend in Yorkshire. I was alone, so it didn't really matter where I chose to settle. The only kind of place I could think of moving to was somewhere where nobody would know me and I could live out the rest of my days in peace. My mother had recently been diagnosed with Alzheimer's and, although in the early stages, I knew it would only be a matter of time before she needed me. I decided to purchase a house in Birmingham, which is only 14 miles from Codsall, where my mother still lived. Nobody knew me in Birmingham, yet I was only a 30-minute drive from the village where I had grown up. I felt that I would have the best of both worlds: solitude in Birmingham, but friends just a short distance away, if I needed company. I had little contact with anybody other than my mother and children, and I felt genuinely content.

2006 began as I had hoped. I visited my mother each day and threw myself into my work. In October, I began to feel unwell, but the doctor could not diagnose any particular illness. Then on 28 October, I suffered a mild stroke and began to pass blood. Aged 19, I'd had testicular cancer, which had resulted in my undergoing surgery, so the doctor suggested I have a colonoscopy to check for bowel cancer.

On 6 December, I attended Selly Oak hospital in Birmingham for the 30-minute procedure, which involves a long, flexible tube called a colonoscope, or scope, being inserted into the rectum. This is then slowly guided into the colon, where the scope inflates the large intestine with carbon dioxide gas to give the doctor a better view. A small camera mounted on the scope transmits a video image from inside the large intestine to a computer screen, allowing the doctor to carefully examine the intestinal lining. In my case, the doctor had difficulty moving the scope, as he said it had looped. Eventually, he gave up and I was told the procedure had failed. Shortly afterwards I was discharged from the hospital. Ten minutes later I was doubled over as a huge air bubble forced its way from my stomach into my chest; a second followed immediately afterwards. I didn't know it at the time but some of my stomach had been pushed into my chest and I had suffered a tension pneumothorax. This is when a defect in the diaphragm allows air to flow into the chest cavity. Each breath allows air in, but none is allowed out. As the pressure builds in the chest, vital organs are displaced or unable to function. The force of the air entering my chest had burst my left lung and moved my heart to the right.

I somehow managed to make my way home and rang Vinney. Due to the mounting pressure in my chest, I was finding it increasingly difficult to breath, so he suggested I phone an ambulance immediately. When I was rushed back into the hospital, Vinney was waiting. A priest was summoned and he gave me the last rites as my son sat at my bedside. The doctors told Vinney that all of my family should be notified, as it was unlikely I would live.

I underwent emergency surgery and for the next three days I fought for my life in intensive care. When I began to make a recovery, the doctors told me that I would have to undergo major surgery to remove the stomach parts that were lodged in my chest and repair the damage the pneumothorax had caused. The operation lasted six hours and I have not been physically fit since. My left lung does not function properly and I have other related medical conditions such as small-vessel disease in the brain, which was triggered by a loss of oxygen.

I am certainly not complaining about my lot: few people in the world have survived what I went through. My case was, in fact, so rare that it was published in the unusual cases section of the *British Medical Journal*. I am eternally grateful to all of the people who brought me back from the brink of death, and to those who've helped me along the long road to recovery.

Unable to carry out any type of physical employment, I have concentrated on writing books. Whilst researching one of these books, I travelled to Newcastle and there I met a beautiful girl 20 years my junior named Roshea Tierney. At the time she was at college, studying music, but in her teens and early 20s she had earned a living as a singer, having secured a recording contract.

Romance was the last thing on my mind when we initially met, but in time we both knew that we were meant to be. One year later we married at Alnwick Castle, Northumberland, where the Harry Potter movies were made. Then on 15 January 2009, my mother's birthday, Roshea gave birth to our son, Paddy. A few weeks earlier I had found my mother in her home in bed unable to move. She was complaining bitterly about a pain in her back, so I had summoned an ambulance. When we arrived at New Cross hospital in Wolverhampton, the doctors told me that it was nothing to worry about and I should go home. My mother was kept in and given a course of antibiotics, and over Christmas her condition appeared to improve.

I visited her regularly, but one evening was told that I couldn't enter the hospital, as visitors had been banned following the outbreak of a vomiting virus. More than 20 members of staff had already been taken ill with the highly infectious norovirus bug. I don't know what it was, but I instinctively knew that I had to get into the hospital somehow to see my mother. I walked around the perimeter of the building until I found a staff door open. Once inside, I made my way to my mother's ward and slipped unnoticed into her private room. My mother was awake and alert; she smiled when she saw me. I sat on her bed, held her hand and we talked about many things. Within an hour, she appeared tired, so I kissed her goodbye before leaving. The following morning I received a phone call from the hospital telling me that I should make my way there immediately. When I arrived, my brother Michael and his wife Carol were already at my mother's bedside. A doctor took me into a room and explained that my mother had a kidney infection and it was unlikely that she would survive another day. Michael, Carol and I sat with my mother until the early evening. They had to return home to care for their children, so I was left alone with my mother. A nurse came in to see me and asked if there was anything she could do. I told her that if my mother's condition deteriorated, I did not want the doctors to help her. 'Please give her painkillers, but do not prolong her misery,' I asked. The nurse nodded and left the room.

I held my mother in my arms and, despite her being barely

conscious, I spoke to her throughout the night. I wept as I apologised for all the wrong I had done in my life and all of the upset that I had undoubtedly caused her. I thank God that I was able to have that time alone with her. At 8.31 a.m. the next morning, my heroine lost her brave fight for life. I wiped blood from her mouth, brushed her hair and then went to inform the nurse that she had died. Her life had ended as mine had begun: her alone with me, and me alone with her.

My mother's passing has taught me a lot. I no longer mix with people other than my family and on a rare occasion an old friend. Everything I do, I do in the name of my wife and children because they are all that matters in this world to me. My story isn't over. Who knows how it will end? It could be today or in 20 years' time. Until that day arrives, I intend to live every day as if it's my last.

In the eyes of the law, I have done many wrong things, but I firmly believe that throughout my life the law has wronged me. It's pointless dwelling on the past and apportioning blame, so what I intend to do now is glance back, learn from my mistakes and try to become a better person.

Yes, it's another new start for Bernard O'Mahoney, another new beginning. But only those who know me will be able to judge if this time I have been successful.